SERIOUS

VOLUME 1

CREATED & WRITTEN BY: MAYAMADA

ILLUSTRATED BY: PINALI (A L JONES)

EDITED BY: LAO K & LARA-LEE GREEN

EMAIL US: HELLO@MAYAMADA.COM

CONNECT ONLINE: WWW.MAYAMADA.COM

PUBLISHED BY MAYAMADA
SERIOUS © 2016 MAYAMADA LTD
ALL RIGHTS RESERVED

ISBN: 978-0-9931121-3-3

LIKE BLAKE SERIOUS, WE ALL HAVE A VISION OF HOW WE'D LIKE LIFE TO BE. SERIOUS IS ABOUT HAVING DREAMS AND MAKING MOVES TO ACHIEVE THEM.

SERIOUS IS ONE OF THE SHOWS WITHIN THE FANTASY TELEVISION NETWORK WORLD OF MAYAMADA. THEY ARE NOT ANIMATED SHOWS
...YET.

MAYAMADA IS A CHARACTER BRAND INSPIRED BY ANIME AND MANGA, FOUNDED IN LONDON BY NIGEL TWUMASI AND LAO K.

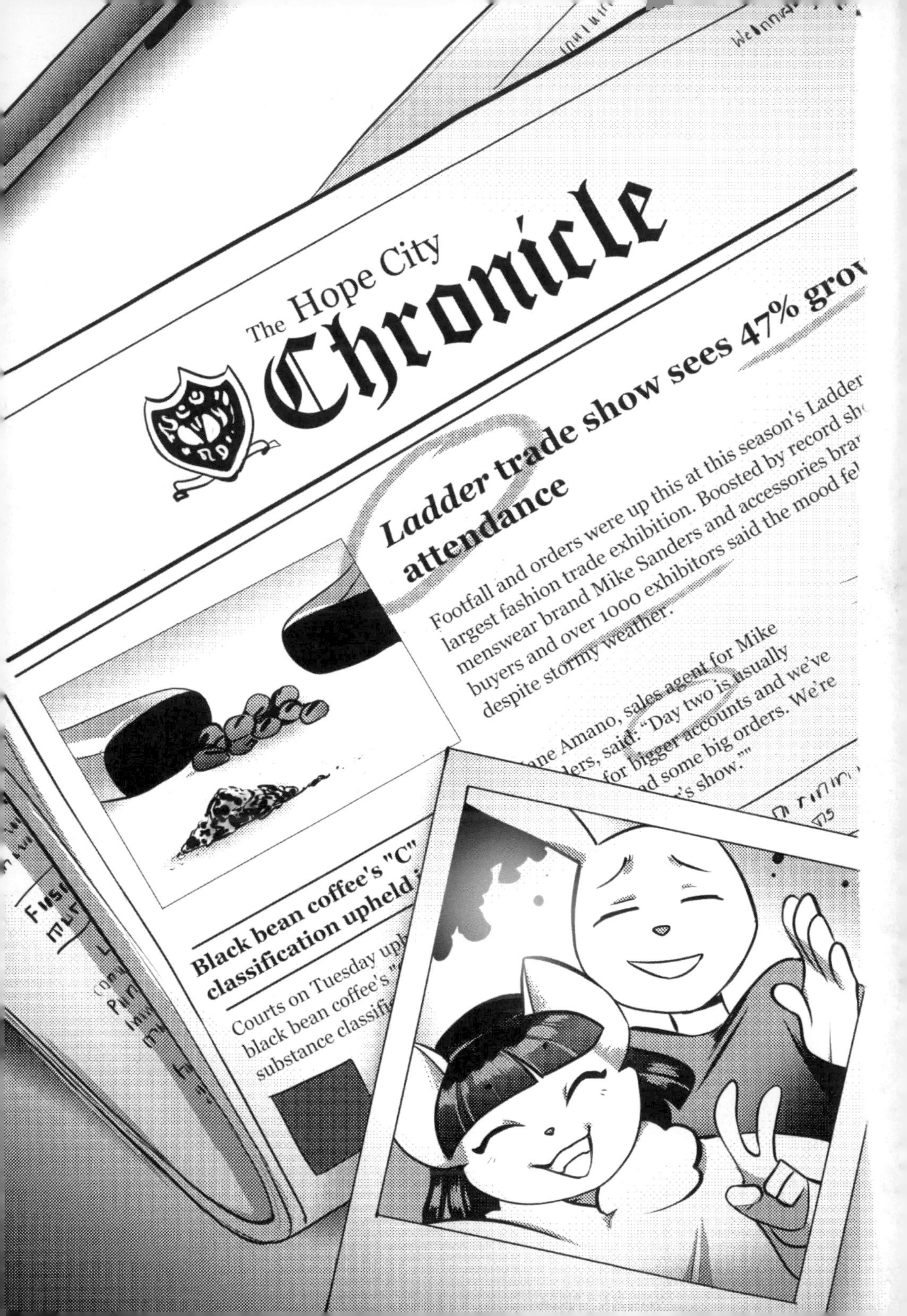

The Hope City Chronicle
Ladder trade show sees 47% grow
attendance
Footfall and orders were up this at this season's Ladder
largest fashion trade exhibition. Boosted by record sho
menswear brand Mike Sanders and accessories bra
buyers and over 1000 exhibitors said the mood fe
despite stormy weather.
ane Amano, sales agent for Mike
ders, said: "Day two is usually
for bigger accounts and we've
d some big orders. We're
's show.""
Black bean coffee's "C"
classification upheld
Courts on Tuesday up
black bean coffee's "
substance classifi

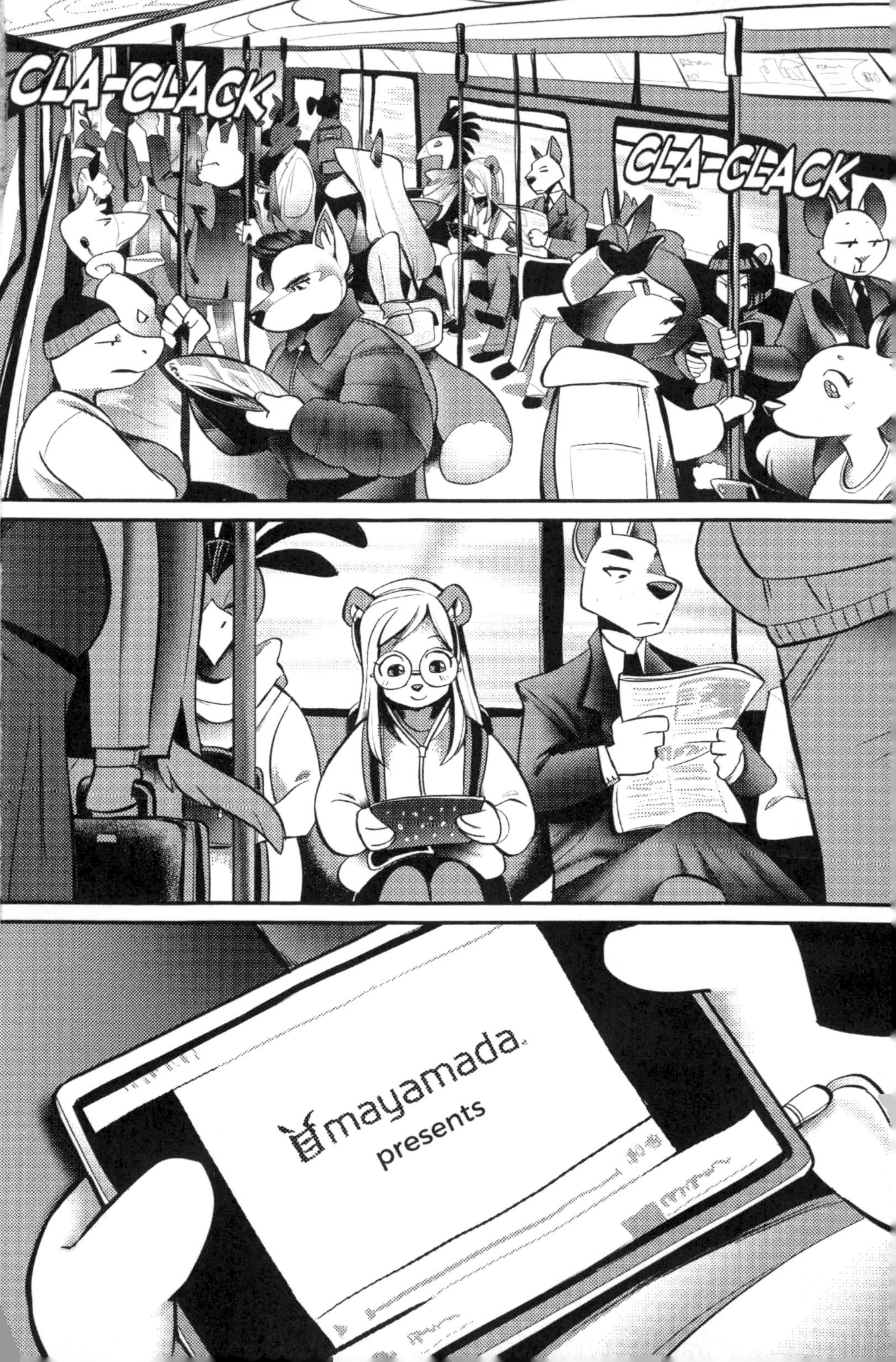
CLA-CLACK
CLA-CLACK
mayamada.
presents

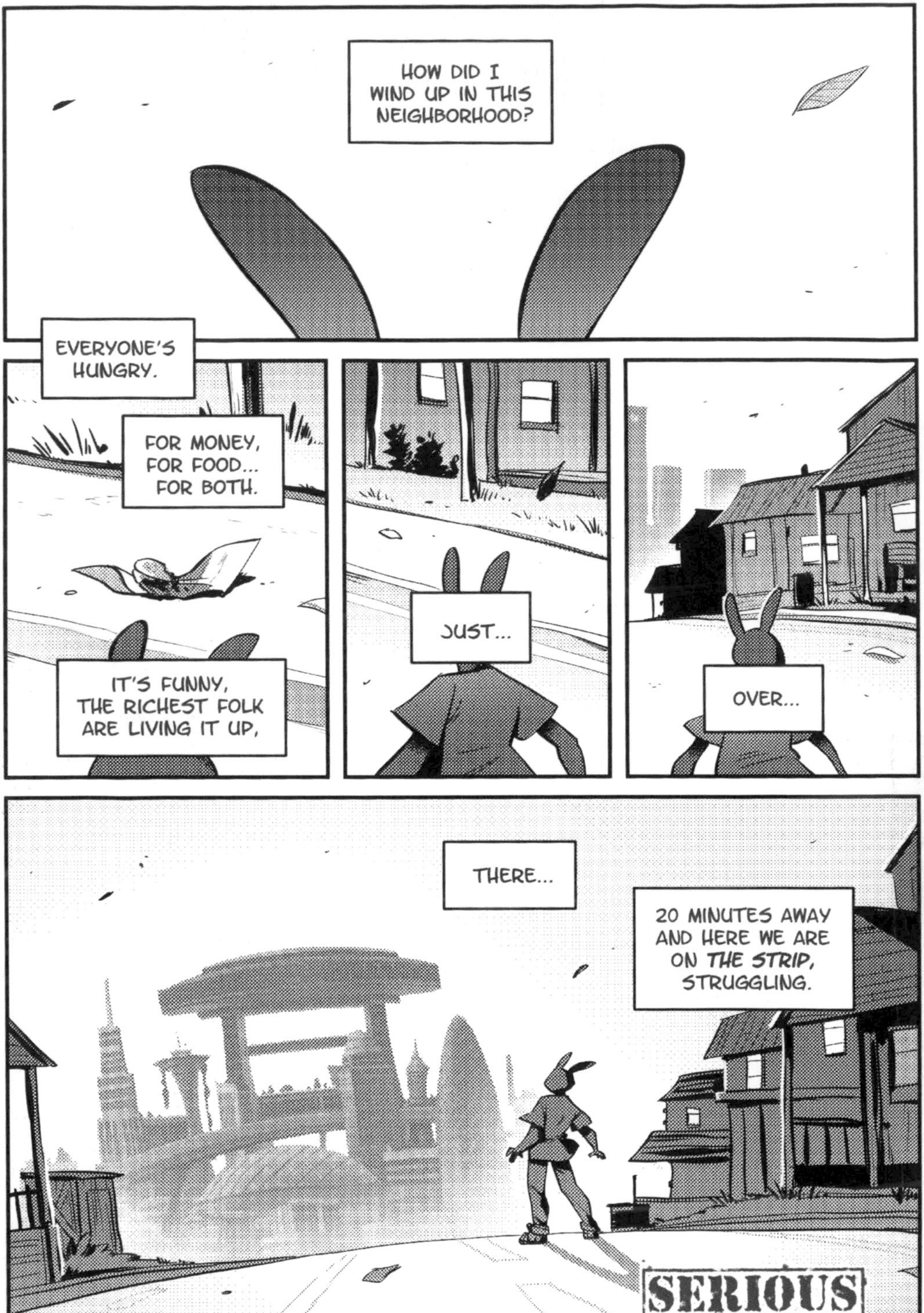
HOW DID I WIND UP IN THIS NEIGHBORHOOD?
EVERYONE'S HUNGRY.
FOR MONEY, FOR FOOD... FOR BOTH.
IT'S FUNNY, THE RICHEST FOLK ARE LIVING IT UP,
JUST...
OVER...
THERE...
20 MINUTES AWAY AND HERE WE ARE ON *THE STRIP,* STRUGGLING.
SERIOUS

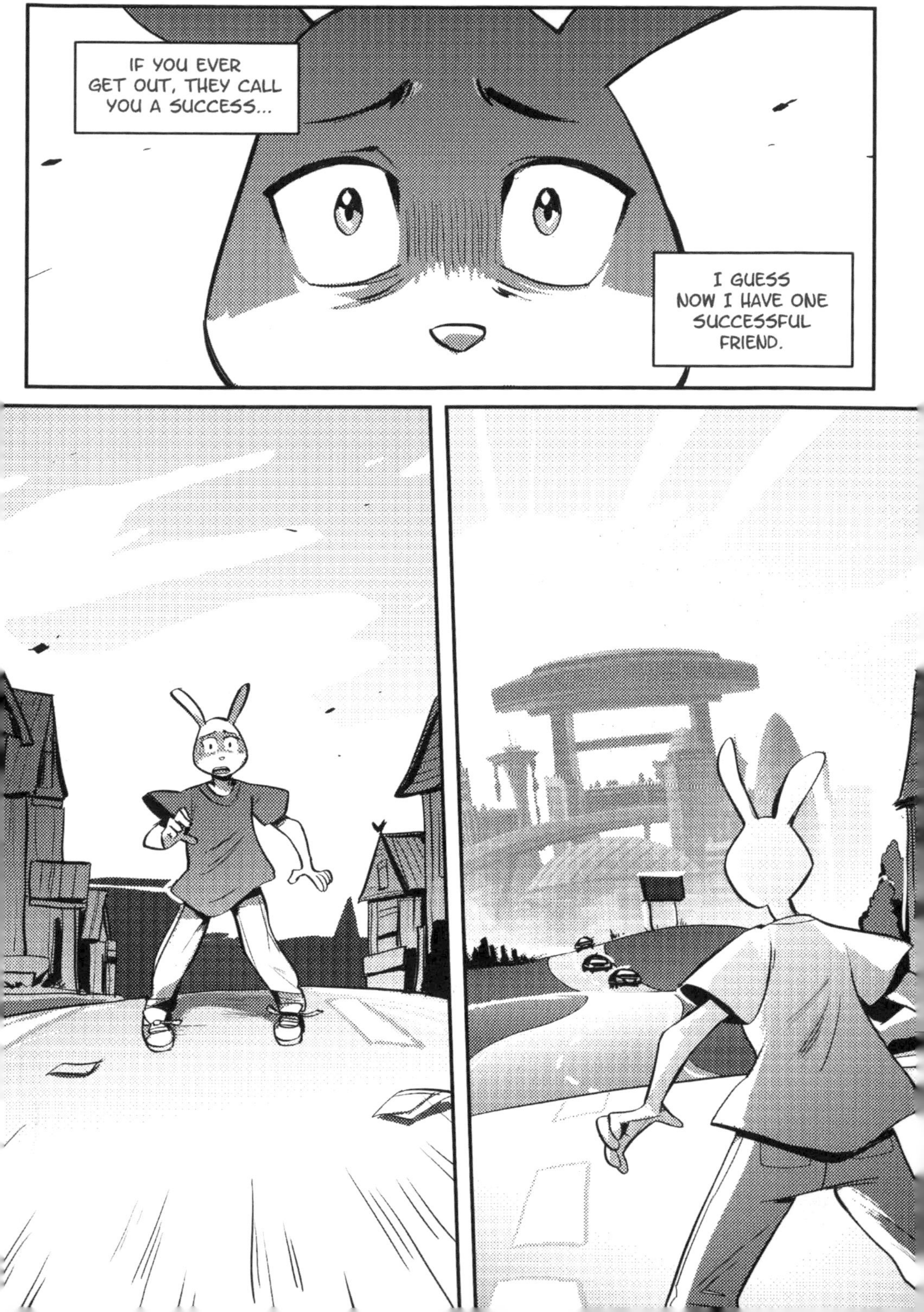
IF YOU EVER GET OUT, THEY CALL YOU A SUCCESS...
I GUESS NOW I HAVE ONE SUCCESSFUL FRIEND.

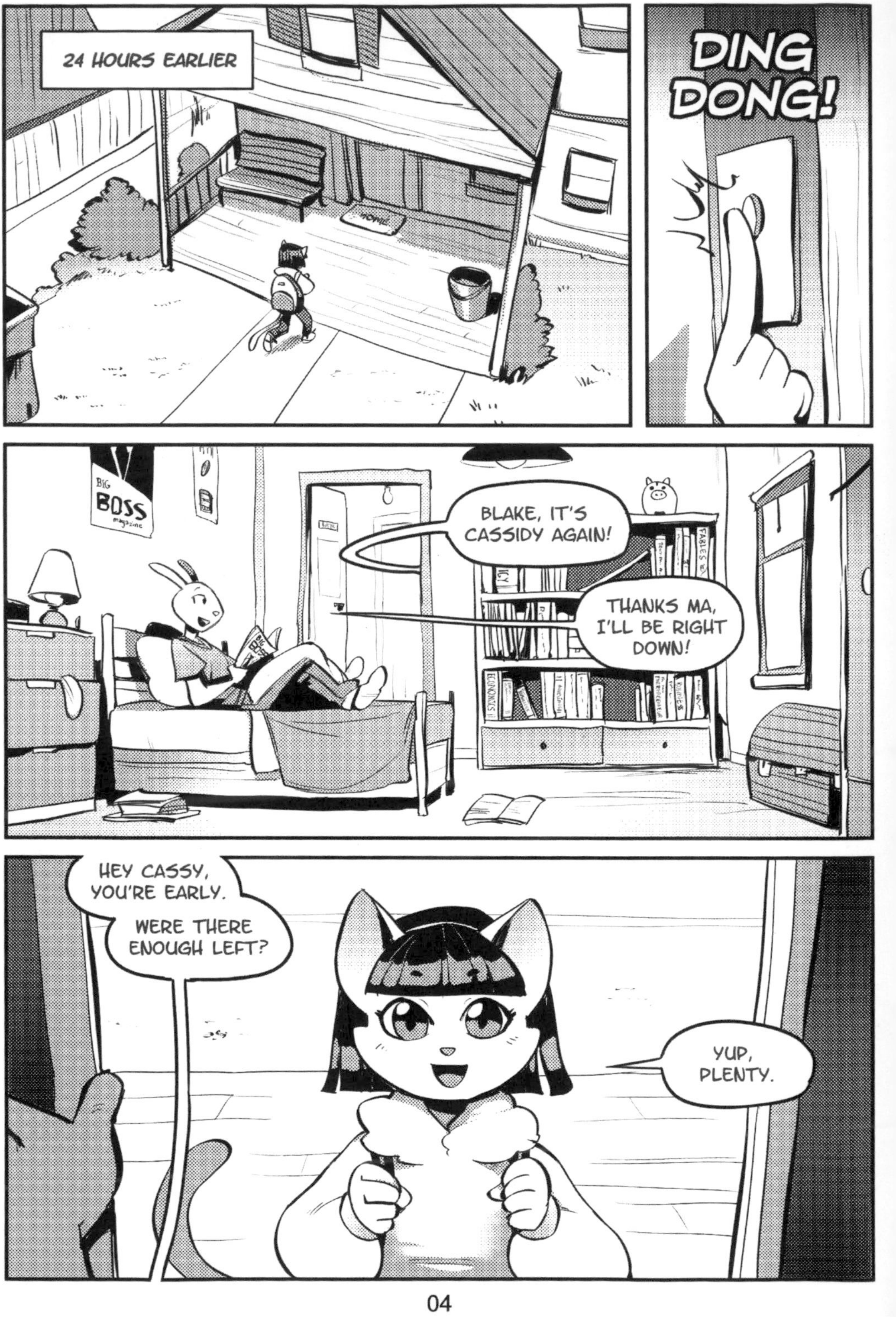
24 HOURS EARLIER
DING DONG!
BIG BOSS magazine
BLAKE, IT'S CASSIDY AGAIN!
THANKS MA, I'LL BE RIGHT DOWN!
HEY CASSY, YOU'RE EARLY.
WERE THERE ENOUGH LEFT?
YUP, PLENTY.

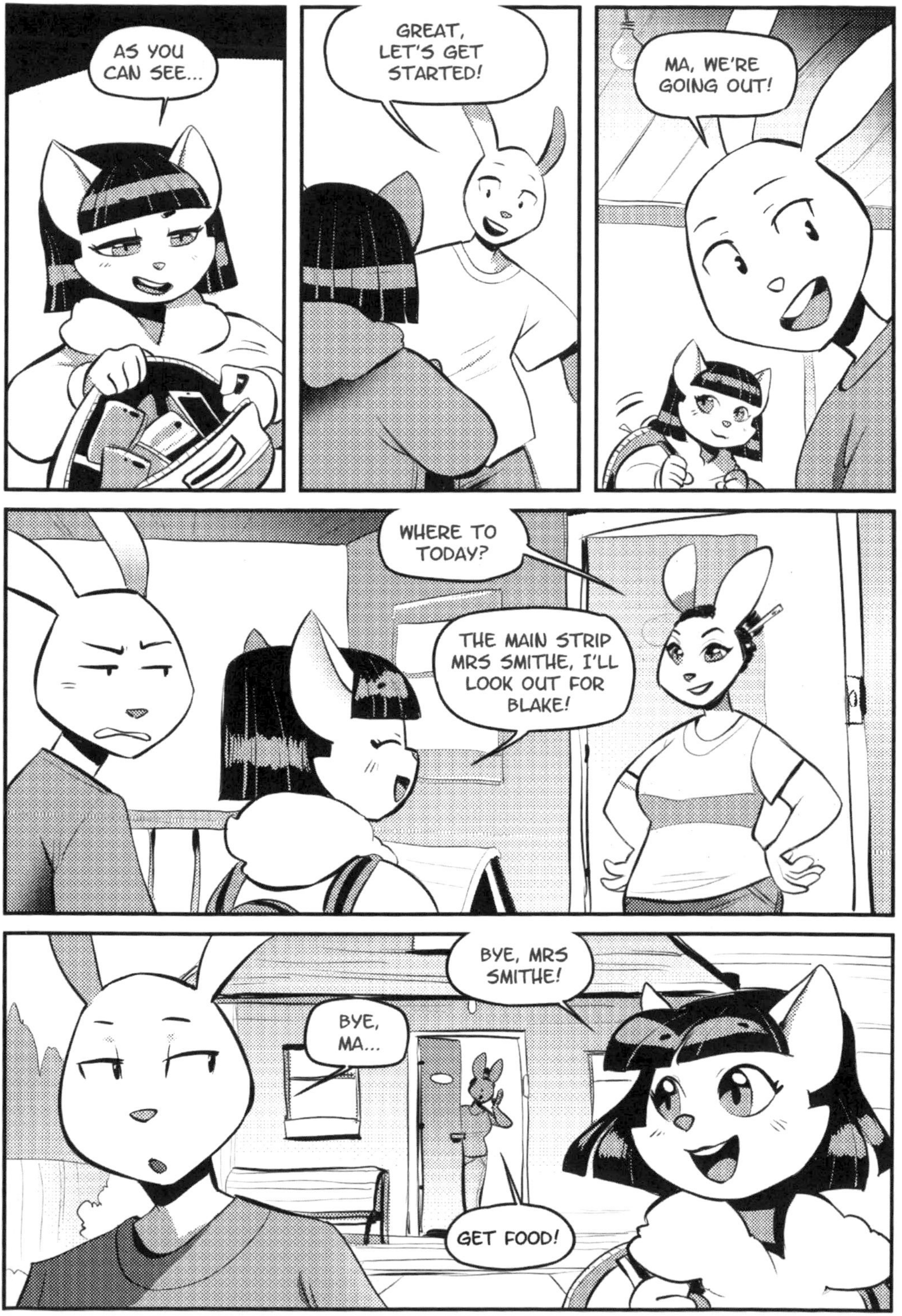
AS YOU CAN SEE...
GREAT, LET'S GET STARTED!
MA, WE'RE GOING OUT!
WHERE TO TODAY?
THE MAIN STRIP MRS SMITHE, I'LL LOOK OUT FOR BLAKE!
BYE, MRS SMITHE!
BYE, MA...
GET FOOD!

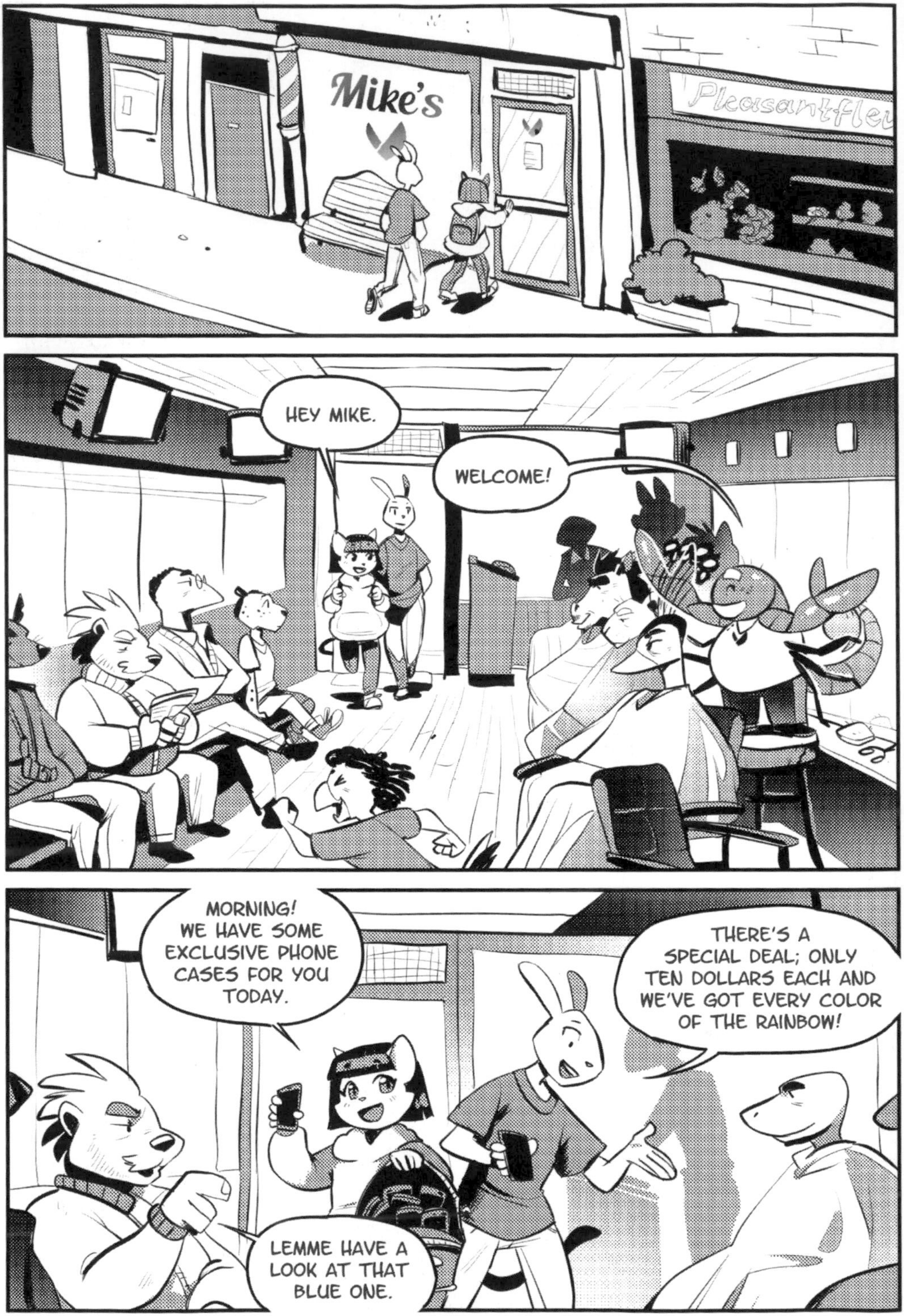
Mike's
HEY MIKE.
WELCOME!
MORNING! WE HAVE SOME EXCLUSIVE PHONE CASES FOR YOU TODAY.
THERE'S A SPECIAL DEAL; ONLY TEN DOLLARS EACH AND WE'VE GOT EVERY COLOR OF THE RAINBOW!
LEMME HAVE A LOOK AT THAT BLUE ONE.

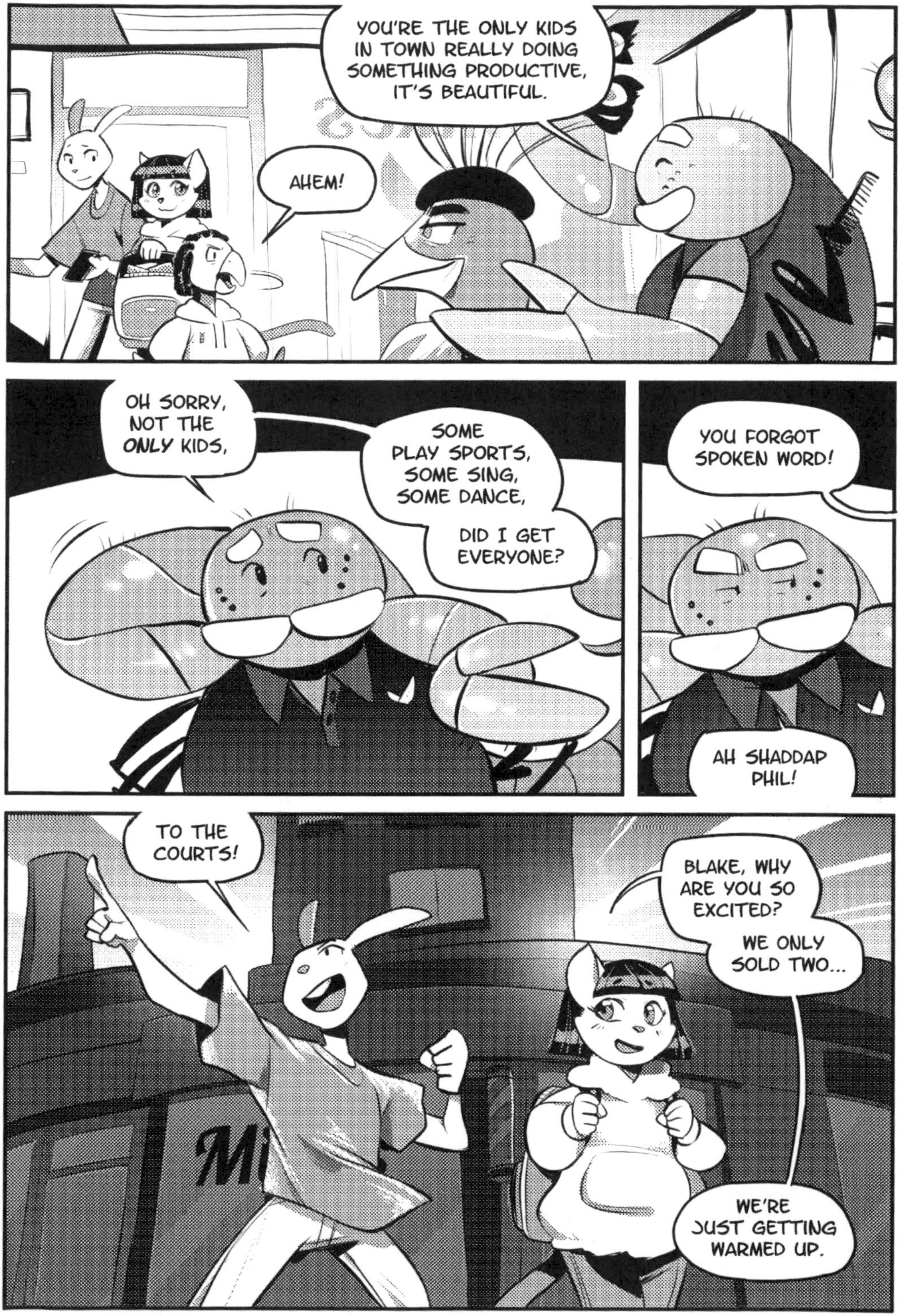
YOU'RE THE ONLY KIDS IN TOWN REALLY DOING SOMETHING PRODUCTIVE, IT'S BEAUTIFUL.
AHEM!
OH SORRY, NOT THE ONLY KIDS,
SOME PLAY SPORTS, SOME SING, SOME DANCE,
DID I GET EVERYONE?
YOU FORGOT SPOKEN WORD!
AH SHADDAP PHIL!
TO THE COURTS!
BLAKE, WHY ARE YOU SO EXCITED?
WE ONLY SOLD TWO...
WE'RE JUST GETTING WARMED UP.

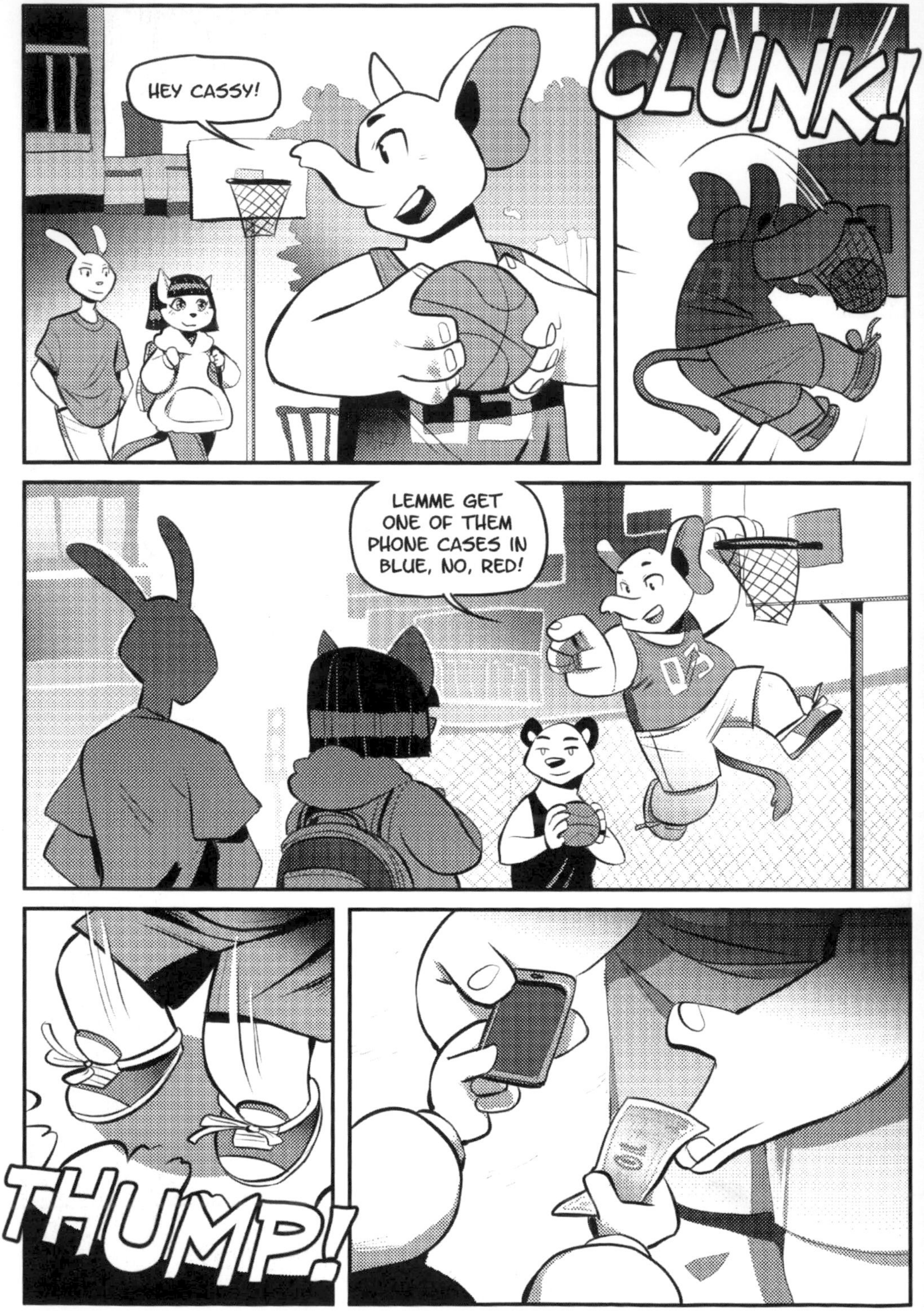
HEY CASSY!
CLUNK!
LEMME GET ONE OF THEM PHONE CASES IN BLUE, NO, RED!
THUMP!

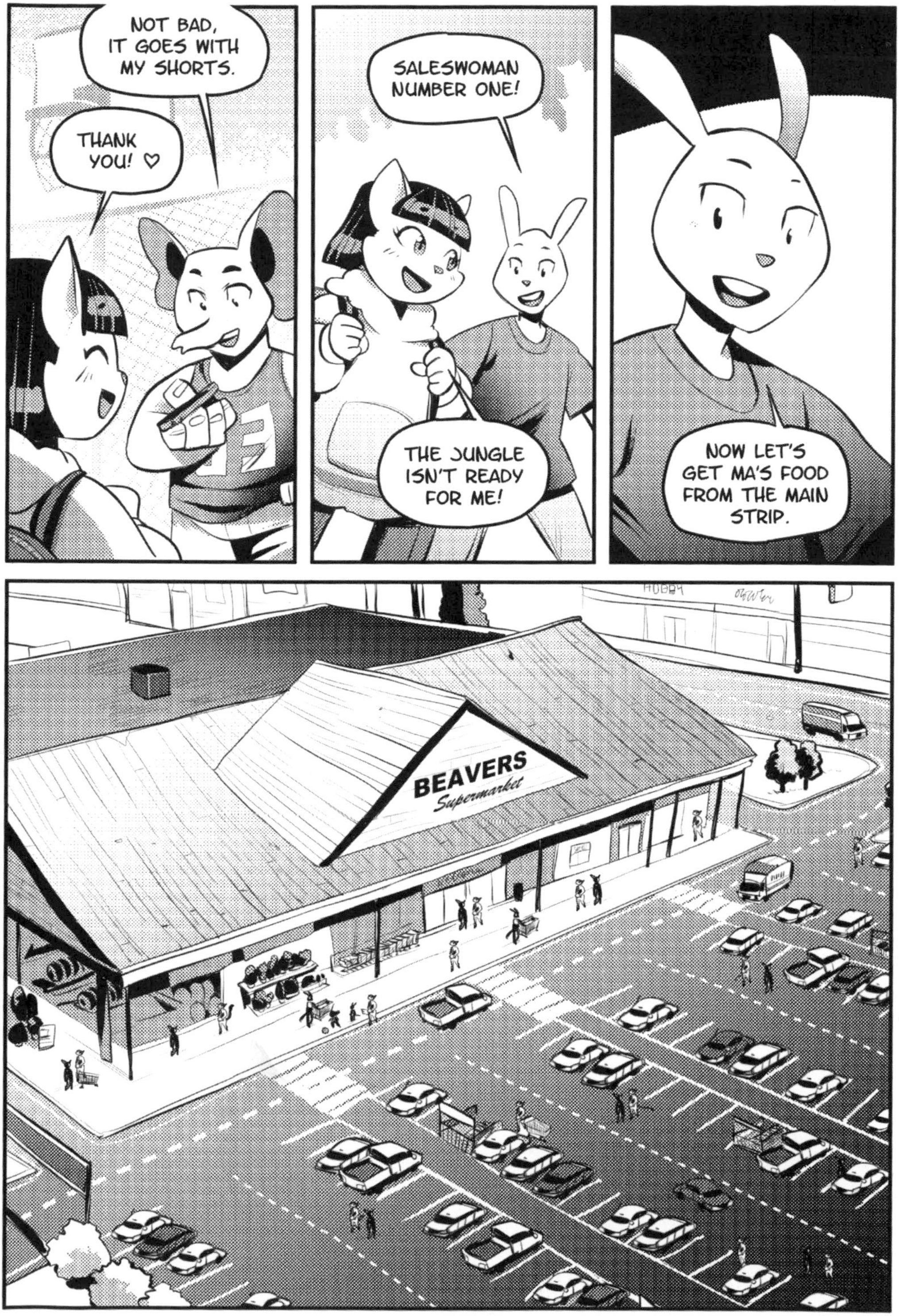
NOT BAD, IT GOES WITH MY SHORTS.
THANK YOU! ♡
SALESWOMAN NUMBER ONE!
THE JUNGLE ISN'T READY FOR ME!
NOW LET'S GET MA'S FOOD FROM THE MAIN STRIP.
BEAVERS Supermarket

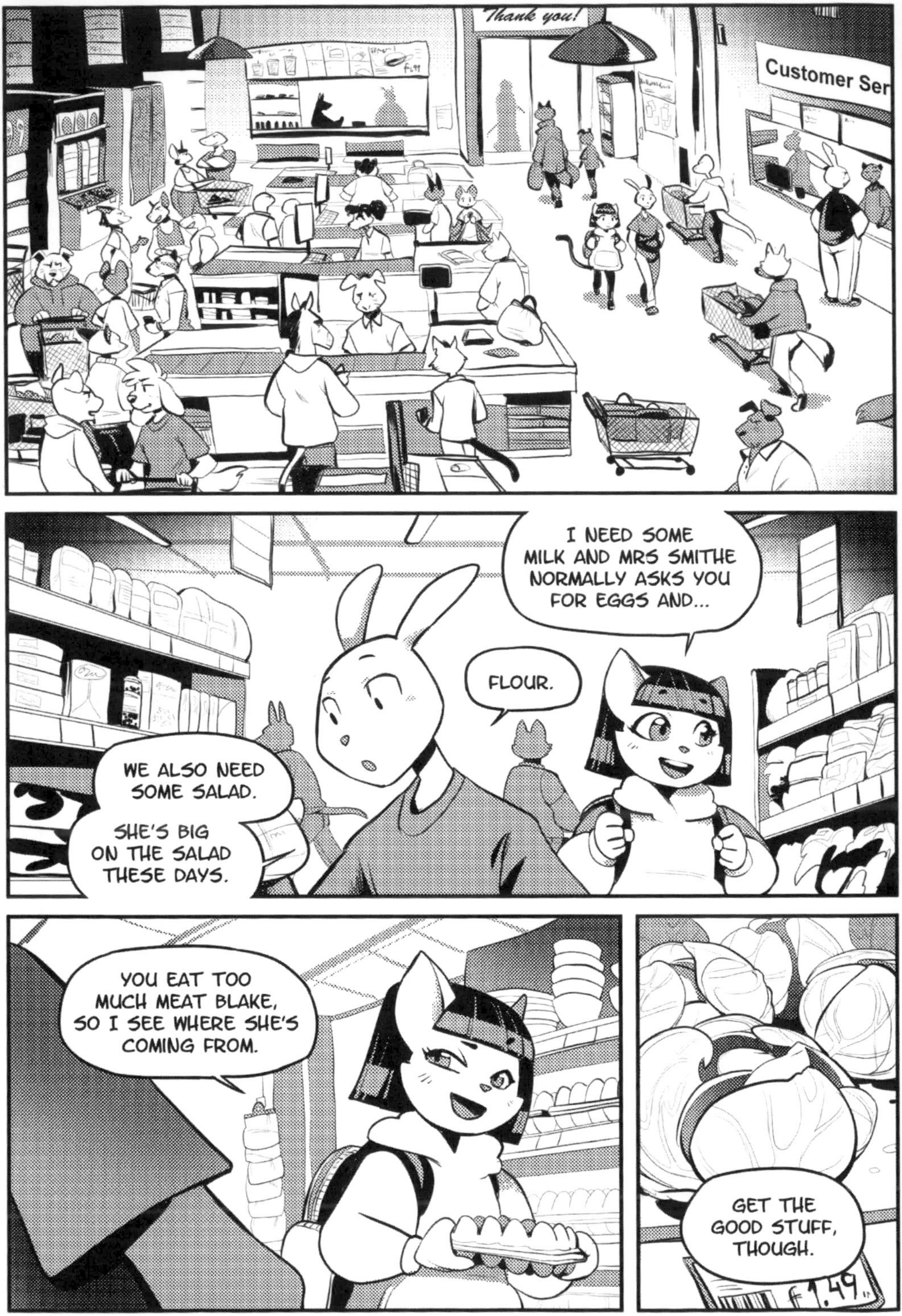
Thank you!
Customer Ser
I NEED SOME MILK AND MRS SMITHE NORMALLY ASKS YOU FOR EGGS AND...
FLOUR.
WE ALSO NEED SOME SALAD.
SHE'S BIG ON THE SALAD THESE DAYS.
YOU EAT TOO MUCH MEAT BLAKE, SO I SEE WHERE SHE'S COMING FROM.
GET THE GOOD STUFF, THOUGH.

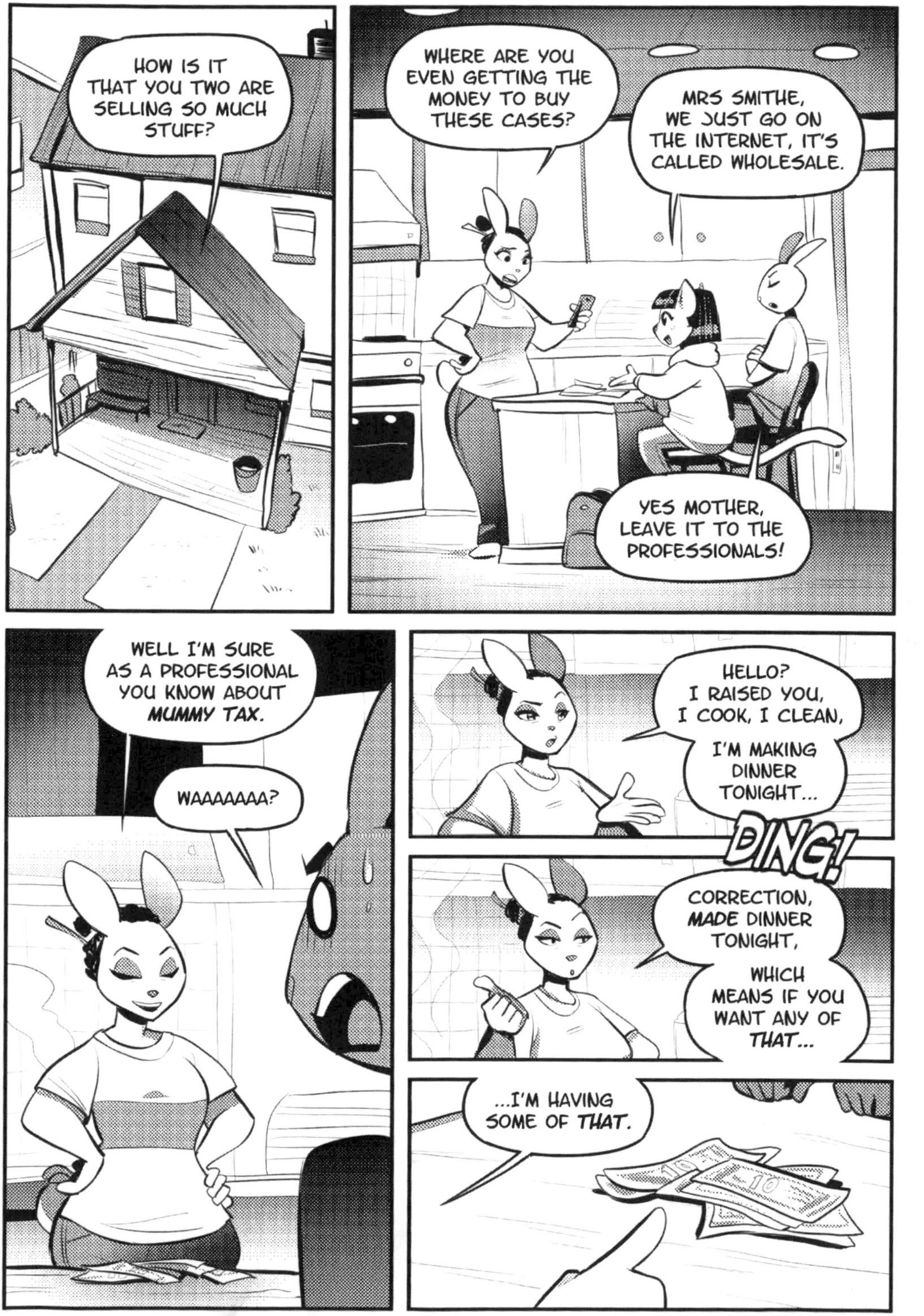
HOW IS IT THAT YOU TWO ARE SELLING SO MUCH STUFF?
WHERE ARE YOU EVEN GETTING THE MONEY TO BUY THESE CASES?
MRS SMITHE, WE JUST GO ON THE INTERNET, IT'S CALLED WHOLESALE.
YES MOTHER, LEAVE IT TO THE PROFESSIONALS!
WELL I'M SURE AS A PROFESSIONAL YOU KNOW ABOUT *MUMMY TAX*.
WAAAAAAA?
HELLO? I RAISED YOU, I COOK, I CLEAN,
I'M MAKING DINNER TONIGHT...
DING!
CORRECTION, *MADE* DINNER TONIGHT,
WHICH MEANS IF YOU WANT ANY OF *THAT*...
...I'M HAVING SOME OF *THAT*.

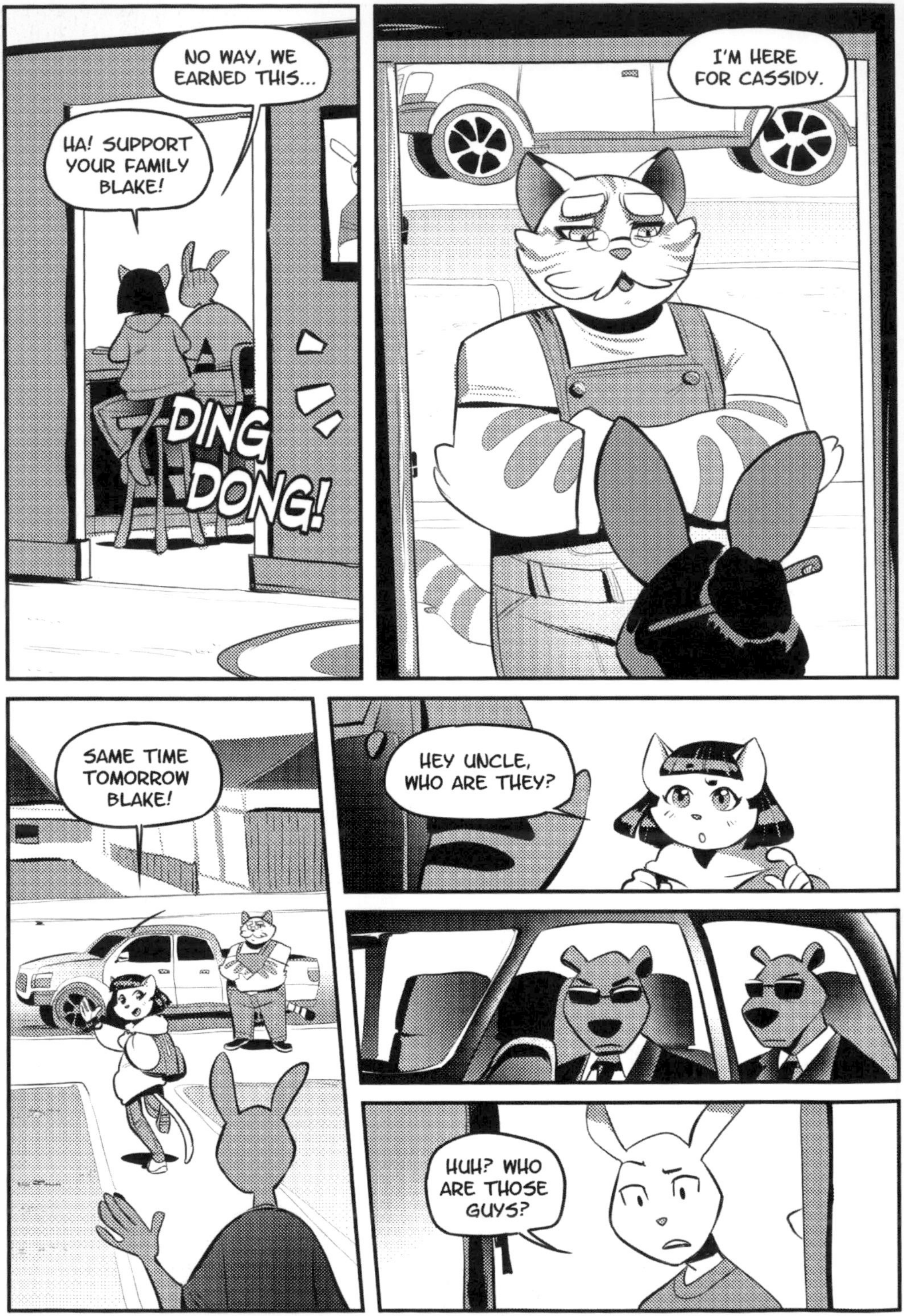

NO WAY, WE EARNED THIS...
HA! SUPPORT YOUR FAMILY BLAKE!
DING DONG!
I'M HERE FOR CASSIDY.
SAME TIME TOMORROW BLAKE!
HEY UNCLE, WHO ARE THEY?
HUH? WHO ARE THOSE GUYS?

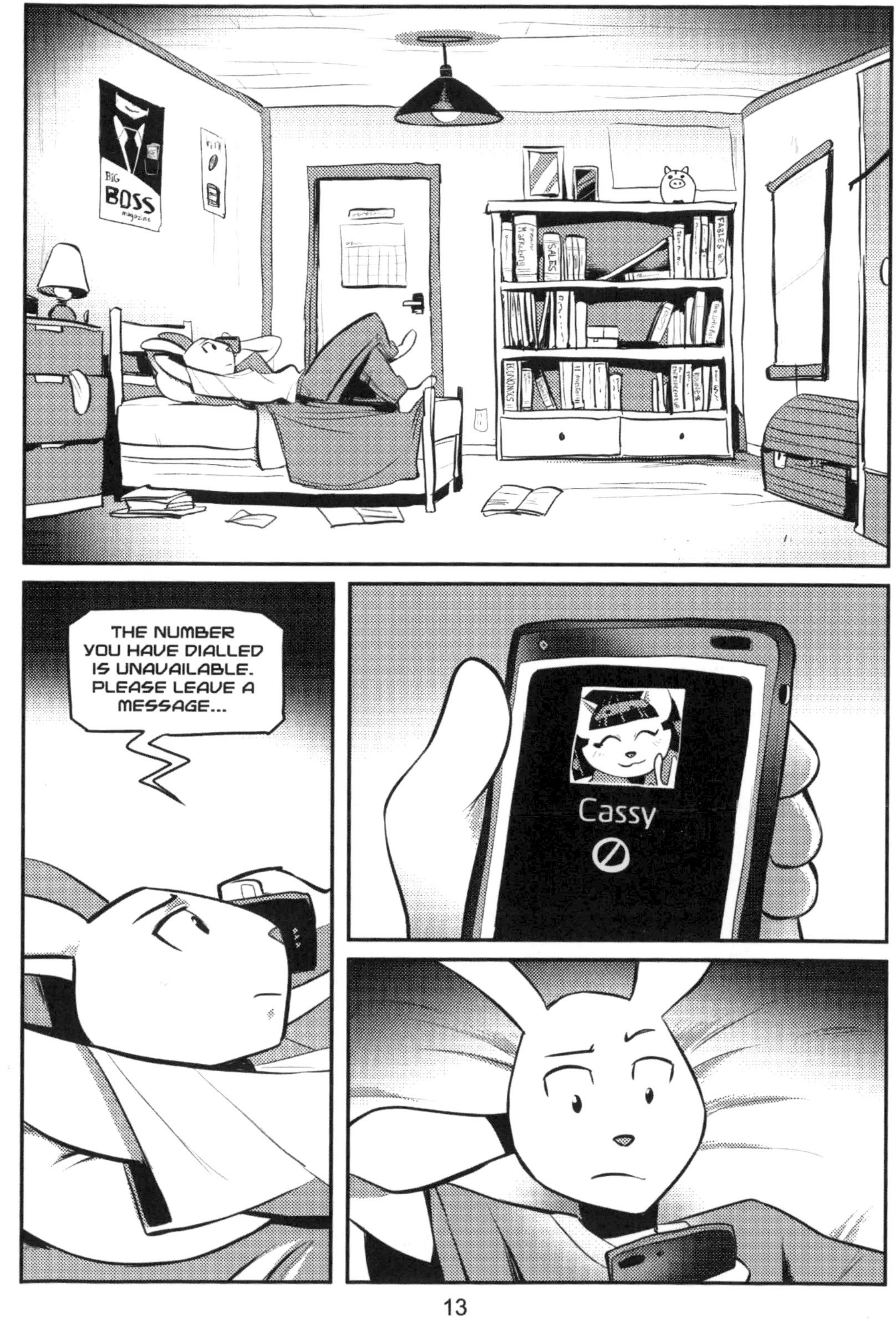
BIG BOSS
THE NUMBER YOU HAVE DIALLED IS UNAVAILABLE. PLEASE LEAVE A MESSAGE...
Cassy

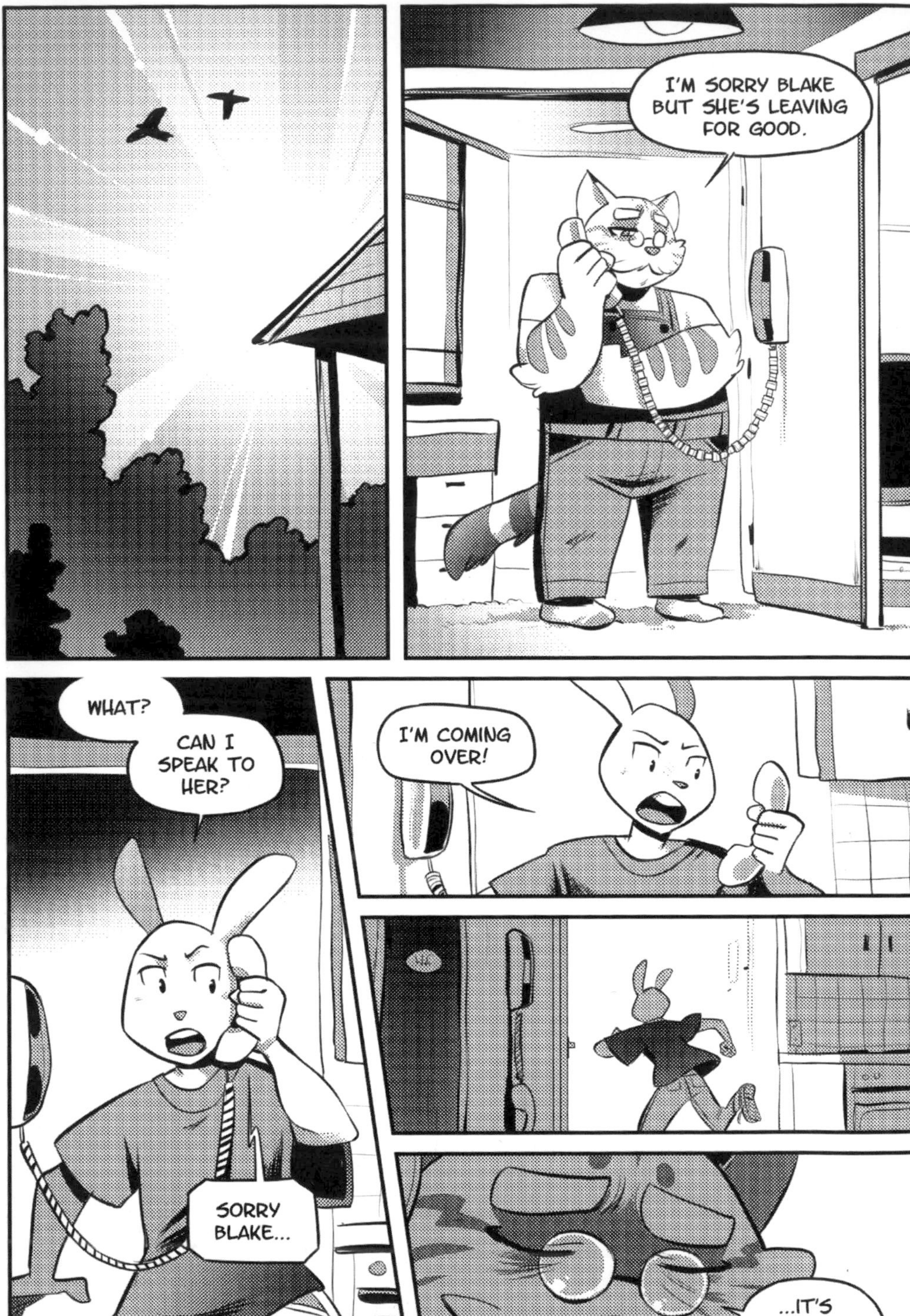
I'M SORRY BLAKE BUT SHE'S LEAVING FOR GOOD.
WHAT?
CAN I SPEAK TO HER?
SORRY BLAKE...
I'M COMING OVER!
...IT'S TOO LATE.

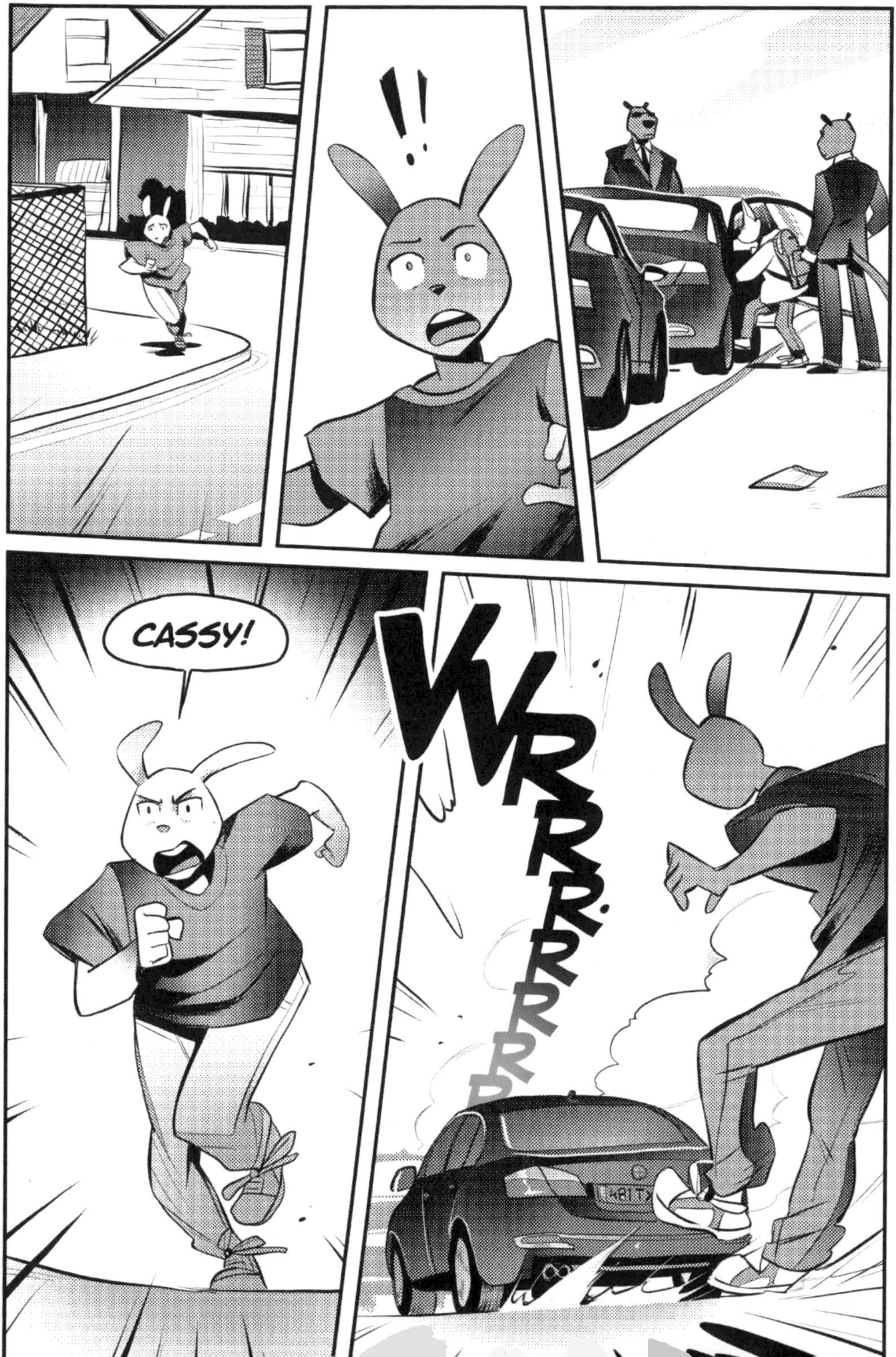
!!
CASSY!
VVRRRRRR

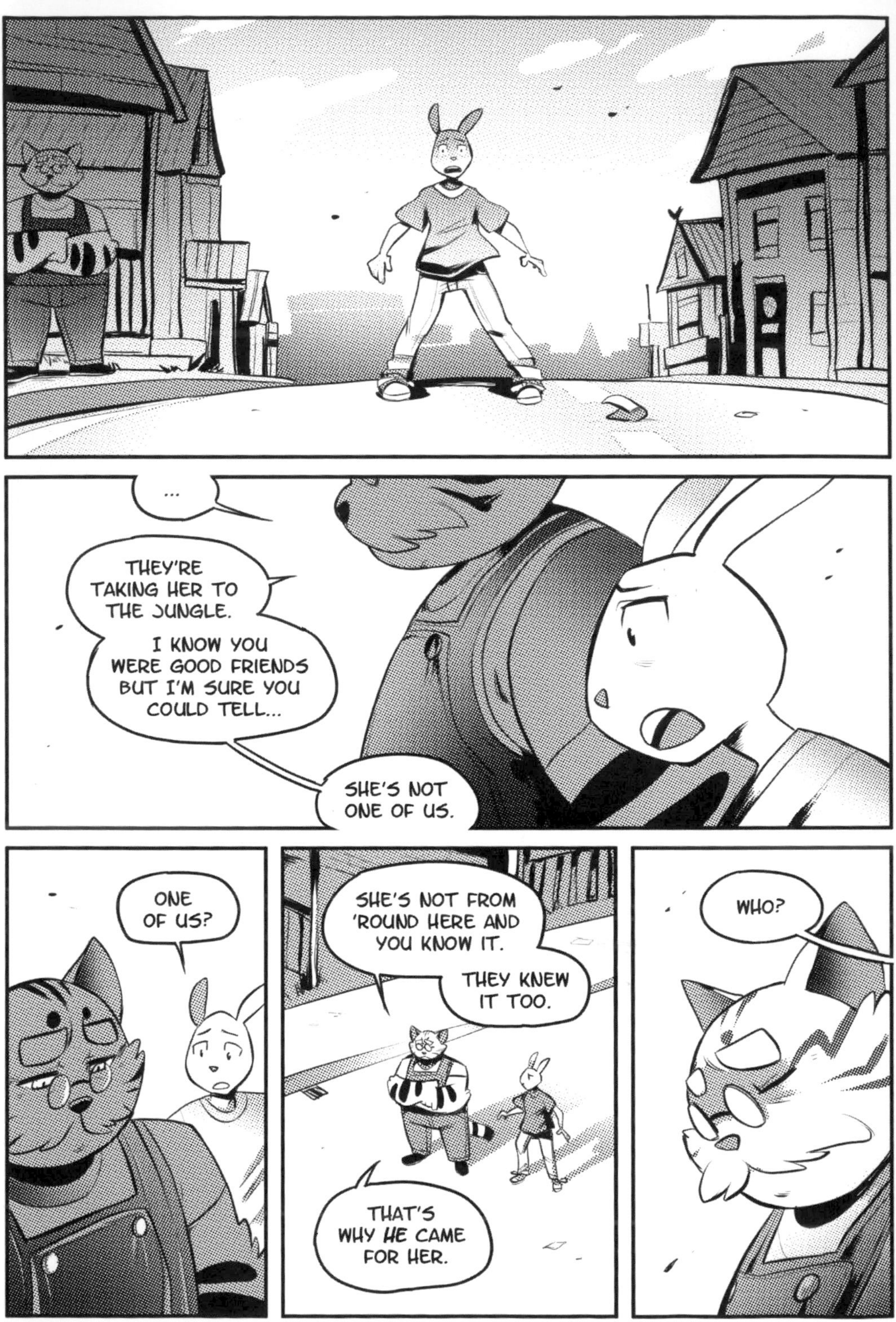
...
THEY'RE TAKING HER TO THE JUNGLE.
I KNOW YOU WERE GOOD FRIENDS BUT I'M SURE YOU COULD TELL...
SHE'S NOT ONE OF US.
ONE OF US?
SHE'S NOT FROM 'ROUND HERE AND YOU KNOW IT.
THEY KNEW IT TOO.
THAT'S WHY *HE* CAME FOR HER.
WHO?

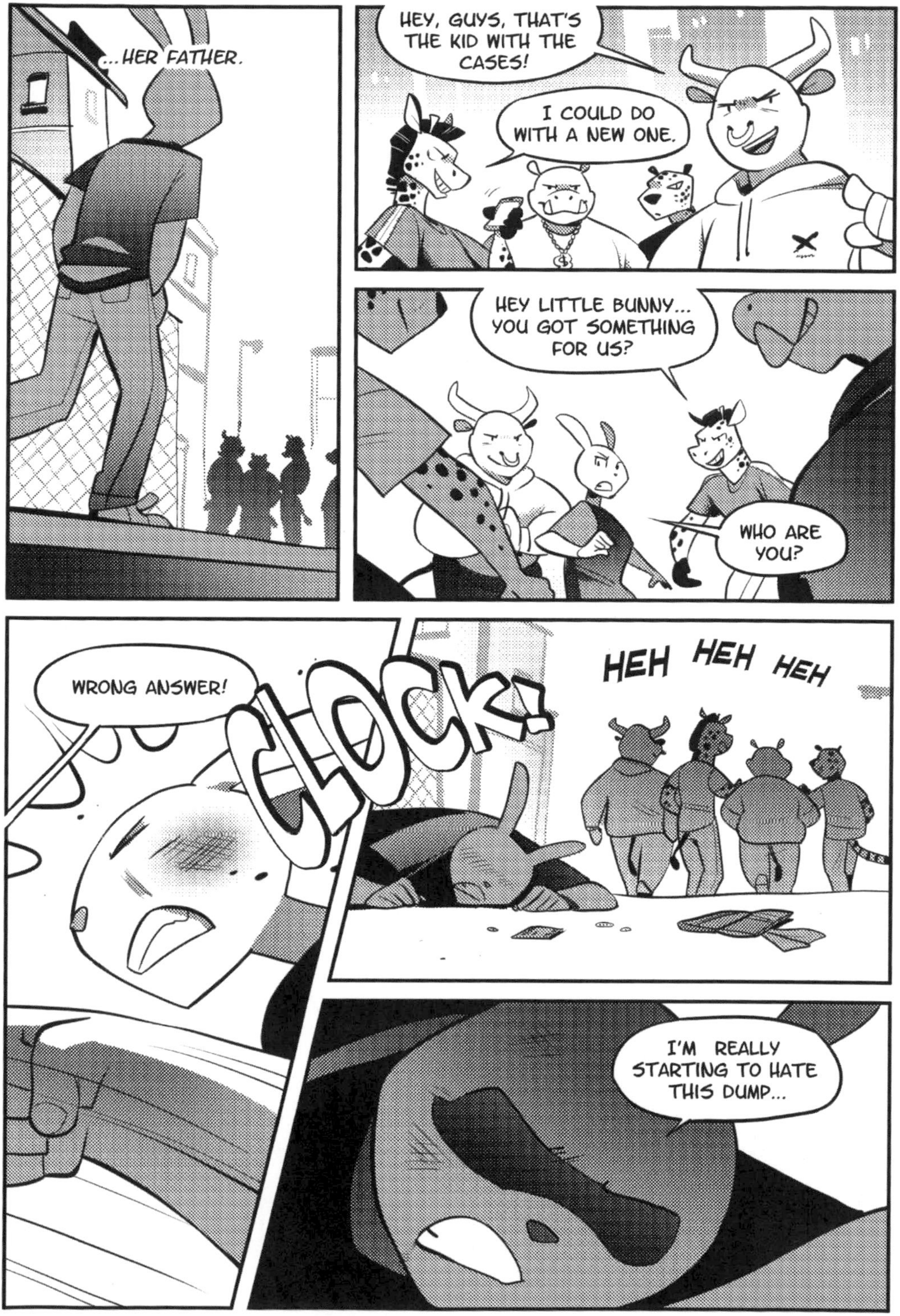
...HER FATHER.
HEY, GUYS, THAT'S THE KID WITH THE CASES!
I COULD DO WITH A NEW ONE.
HEY LITTLE BUNNY... YOU GOT SOMETHING FOR US?
WHO ARE YOU?
WRONG ANSWER!
CLOCK!
HEH HEH HEH
I'M REALLY STARTING TO HATE THIS DUMP...

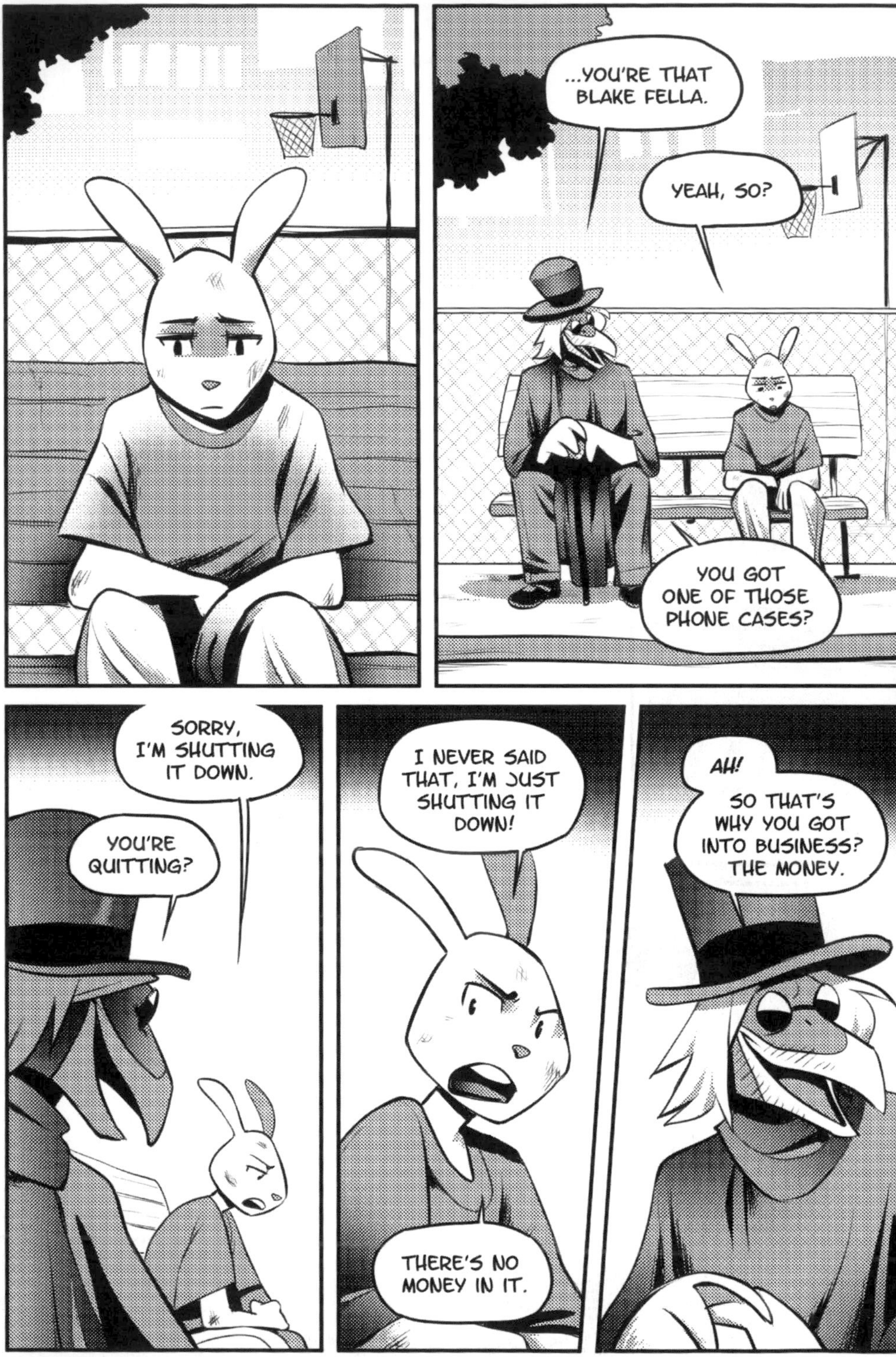
...YOU'RE THAT BLAKE FELLA.
YEAH, SO?
YOU GOT ONE OF THOSE PHONE CASES?
SORRY, I'M SHUTTING IT DOWN.
YOU'RE QUITTING?
I NEVER SAID THAT, I'M JUST SHUTTING IT DOWN!
THERE'S NO MONEY IN IT.
AH!
SO THAT'S WHY YOU GOT INTO BUSINESS? THE MONEY.

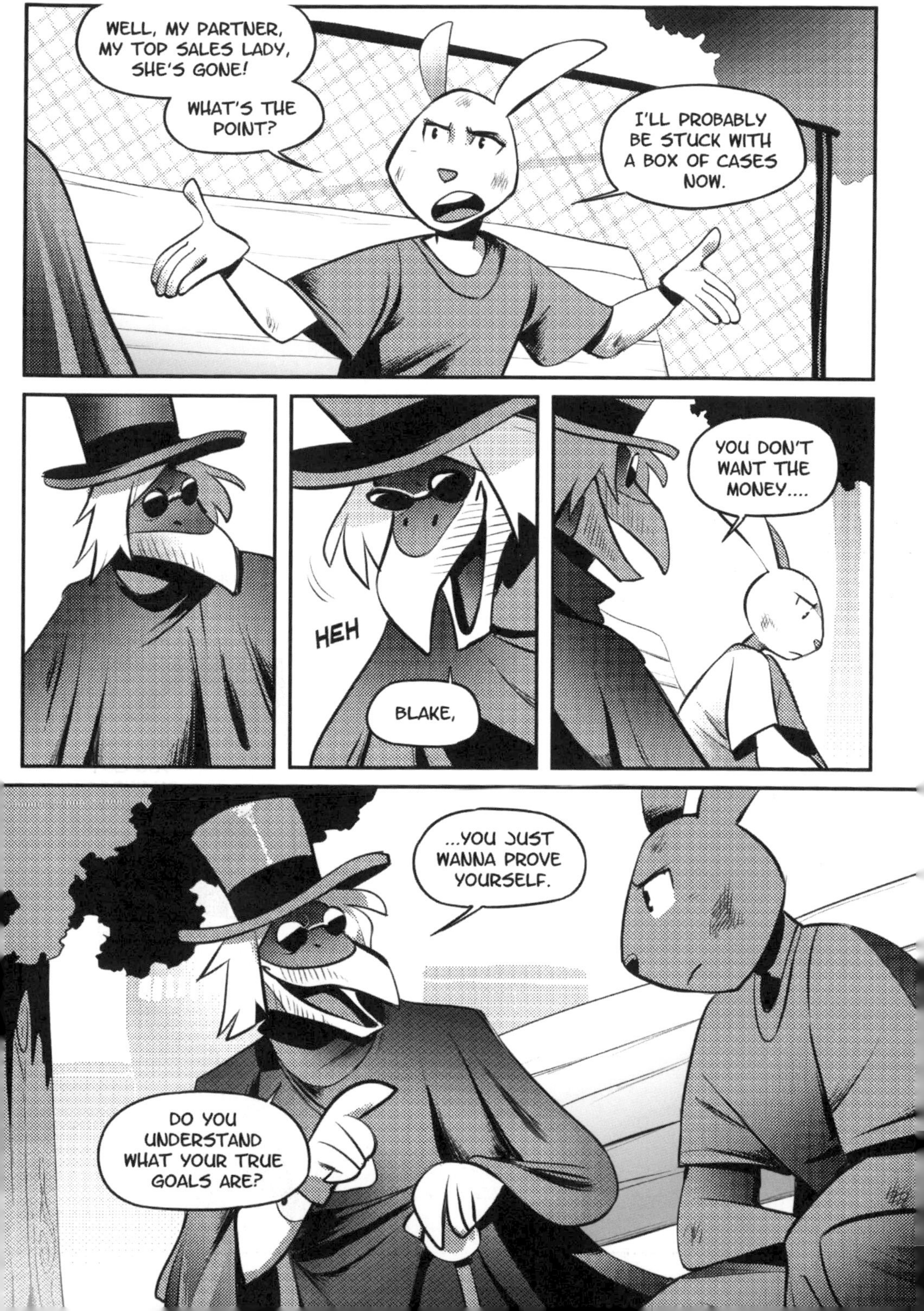
WELL, MY PARTNER, MY TOP SALES LADY, SHE'S GONE!
WHAT'S THE POINT?
I'LL PROBABLY BE STUCK WITH A BOX OF CASES NOW.
HEH
BLAKE,
YOU DON'T WANT THE MONEY....
...YOU JUST WANNA PROVE YOURSELF.
DO YOU UNDERSTAND WHAT YOUR TRUE GOALS ARE?

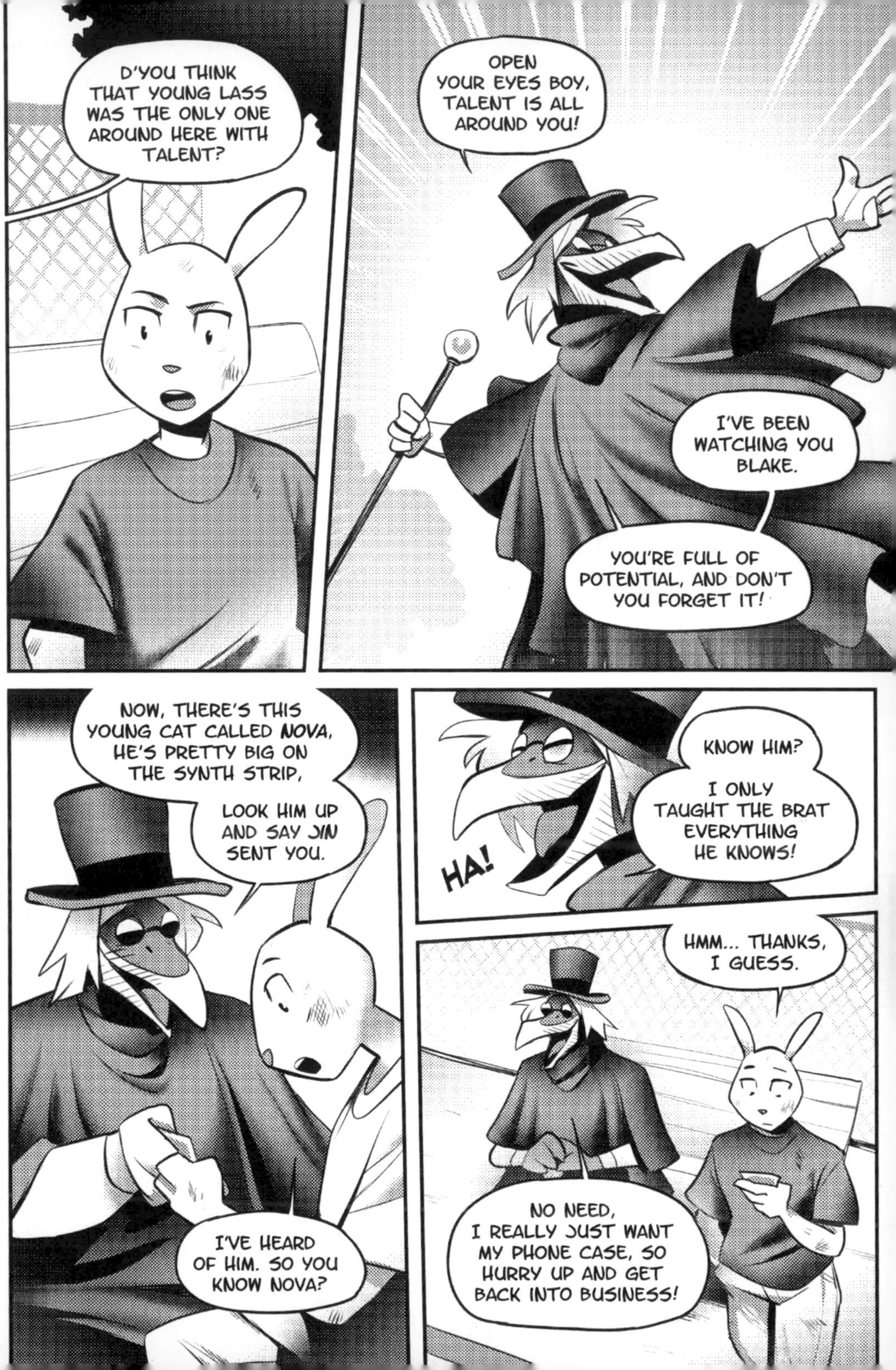
D'YOU THINK THAT YOUNG LASS WAS THE ONLY ONE AROUND HERE WITH TALENT?
OPEN YOUR EYES BOY, TALENT IS ALL AROUND YOU!
I'VE BEEN WATCHING YOU BLAKE.
YOU'RE FULL OF POTENTIAL, AND DON'T YOU FORGET IT!
NOW, THERE'S THIS YOUNG CAT CALLED NOVA, HE'S PRETTY BIG ON THE SYNTH STRIP,
LOOK HIM UP AND SAY JIN SENT YOU.
I'VE HEARD OF HIM. SO YOU KNOW NOVA?
HA!
KNOW HIM?
I ONLY TAUGHT THE BRAT EVERYTHING HE KNOWS!
HMM... THANKS, I GUESS.
NO NEED, I REALLY JUST WANT MY PHONE CASE, SO HURRY UP AND GET BACK INTO BUSINESS!

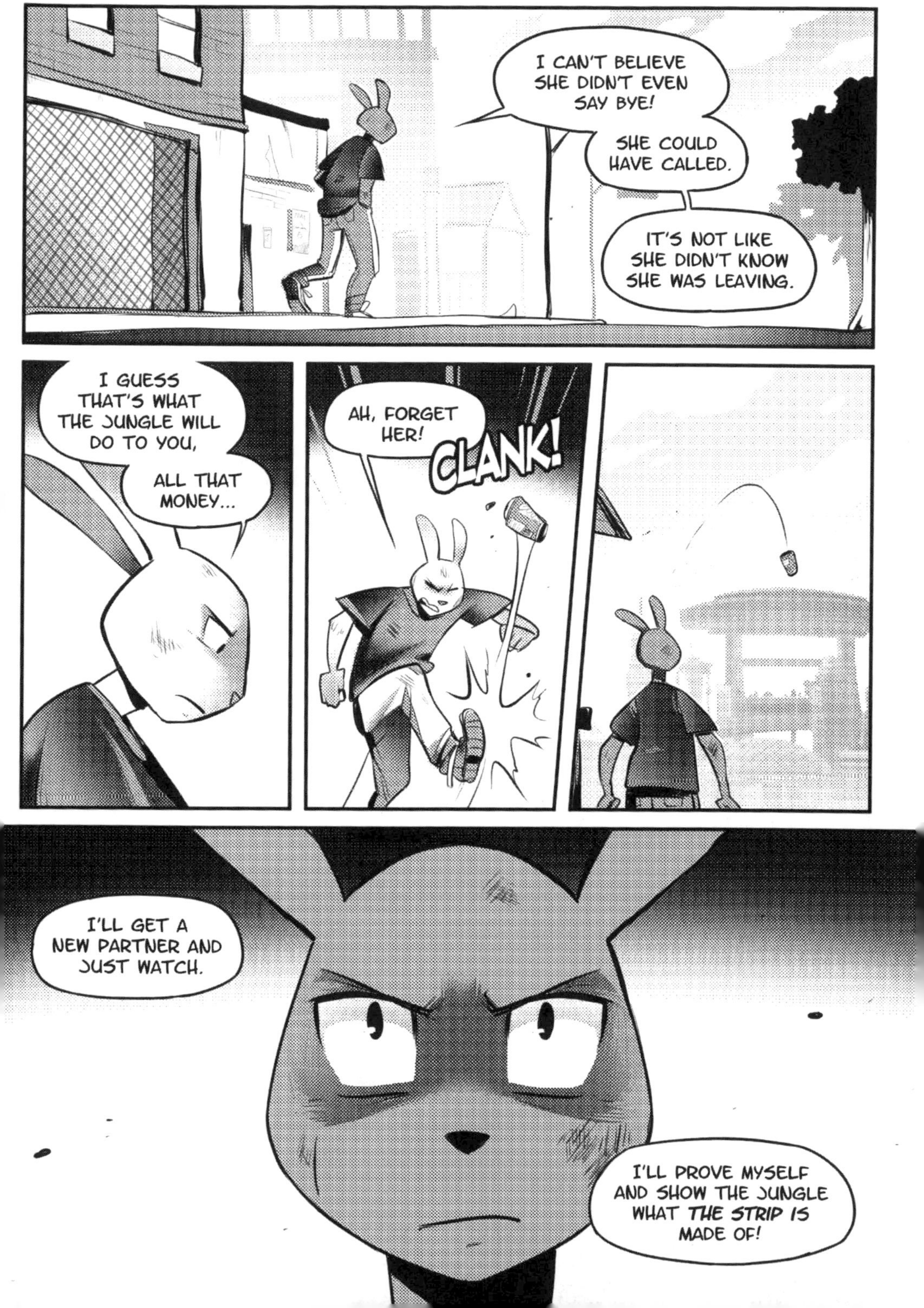
I CAN'T BELIEVE SHE DIDN'T EVEN SAY BYE!
SHE COULD HAVE CALLED.
IT'S NOT LIKE SHE DIDN'T KNOW SHE WAS LEAVING.
I GUESS THAT'S WHAT THE JUNGLE WILL DO TO YOU,
ALL THAT MONEY...
AH, FORGET HER!
CLANK!
I'LL GET A NEW PARTNER AND JUST WATCH.
I'LL PROVE MYSELF AND SHOW THE JUNGLE WHAT *THE STRIP* IS MADE OF!

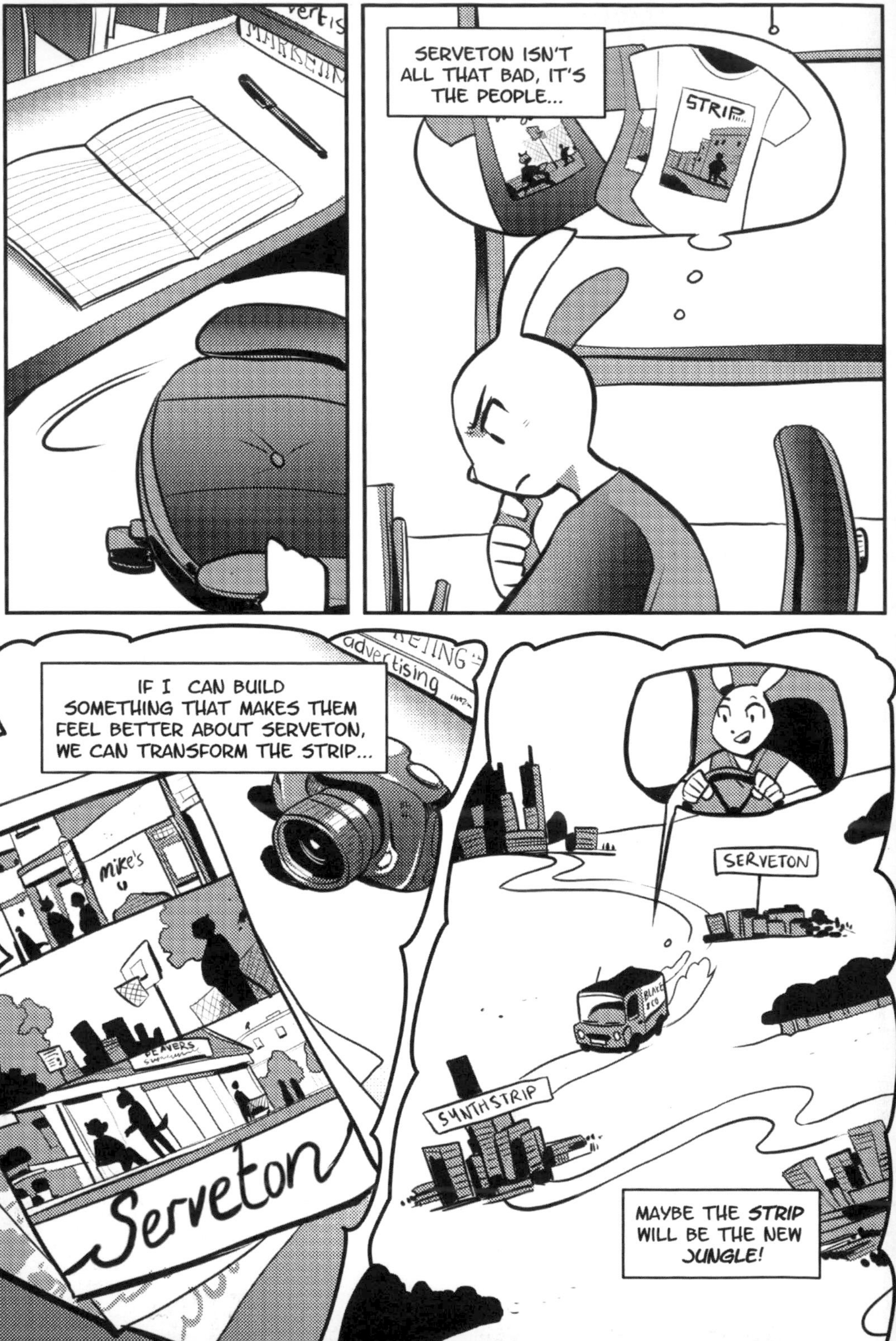
SERVETON ISN'T ALL THAT BAD, IT'S THE PEOPLE...
STRIP
IF I CAN BUILD SOMETHING THAT MAKES THEM FEEL BETTER ABOUT SERVETON, WE CAN TRANSFORM THE STRIP...
advertising
mike's
Serveton
SERVETON
SYNTHSTRIP
MAYBE THE STRIP WILL BE THE NEW JUNGLE!

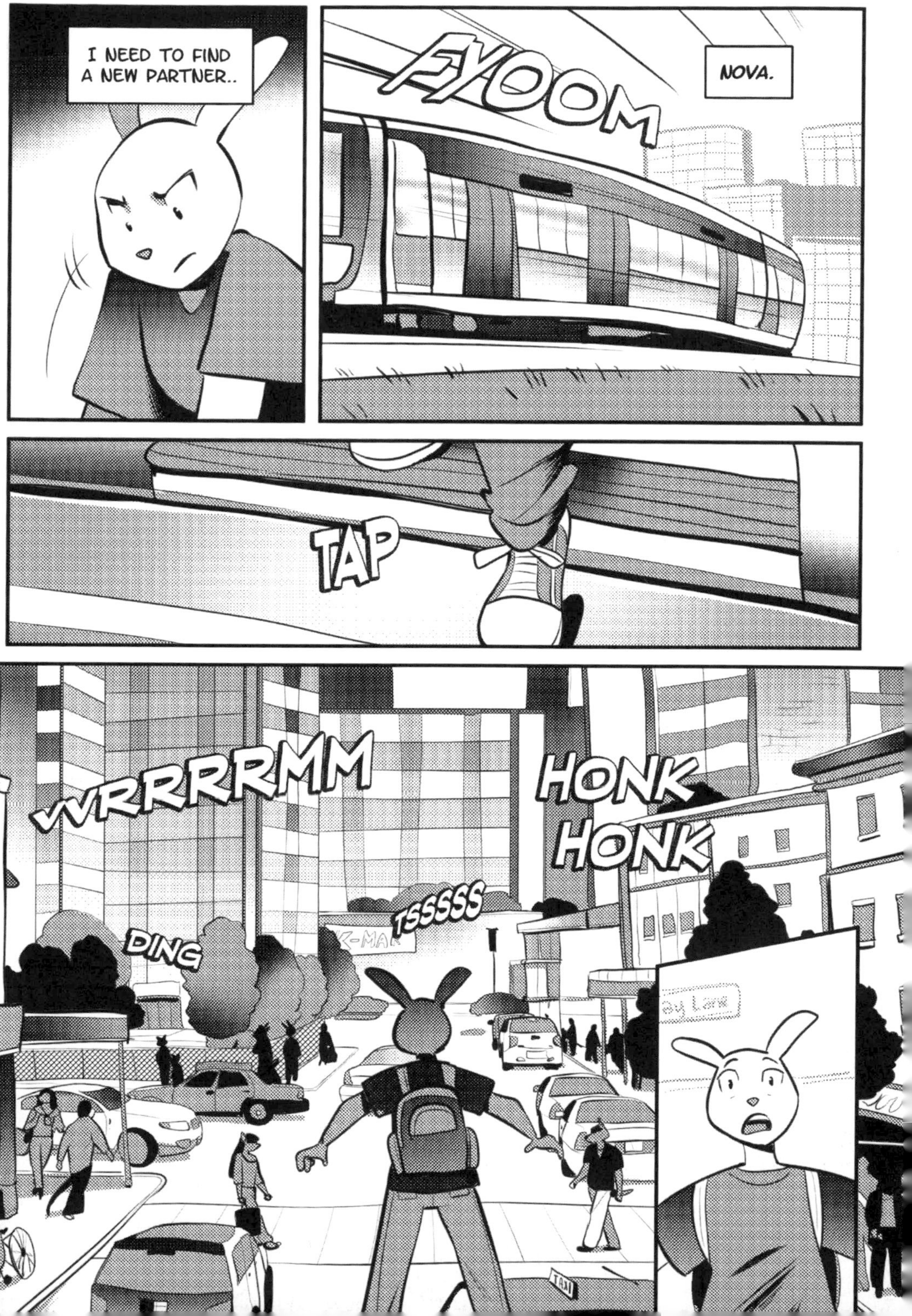

I NEED TO FIND A NEW PARTNER..
FYOOM
NOVA.
TAP
WRRRRMM
HONK
HONK
TSSSSS
DING
TAXI

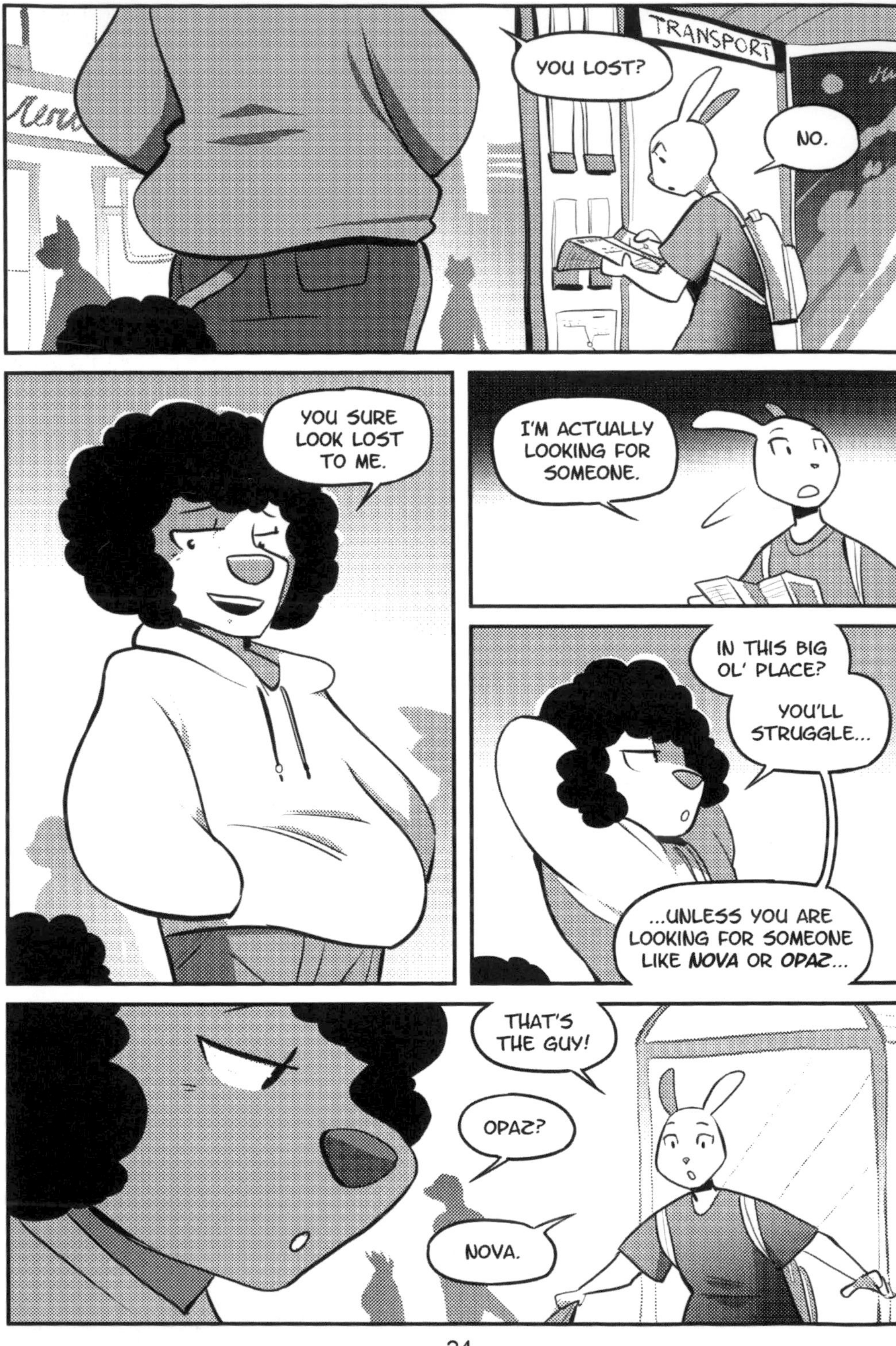

TRANSPORT
YOU LOST?
NO.
YOU SURE LOOK LOST TO ME.
I'M ACTUALLY LOOKING FOR SOMEONE.
IN THIS BIG OL' PLACE?
YOU'LL STRUGGLE...
...UNLESS YOU ARE LOOKING FOR SOMEONE LIKE **NOVA** OR **OPAZ**...
THAT'S THE GUY!
OPAZ?
NOVA.

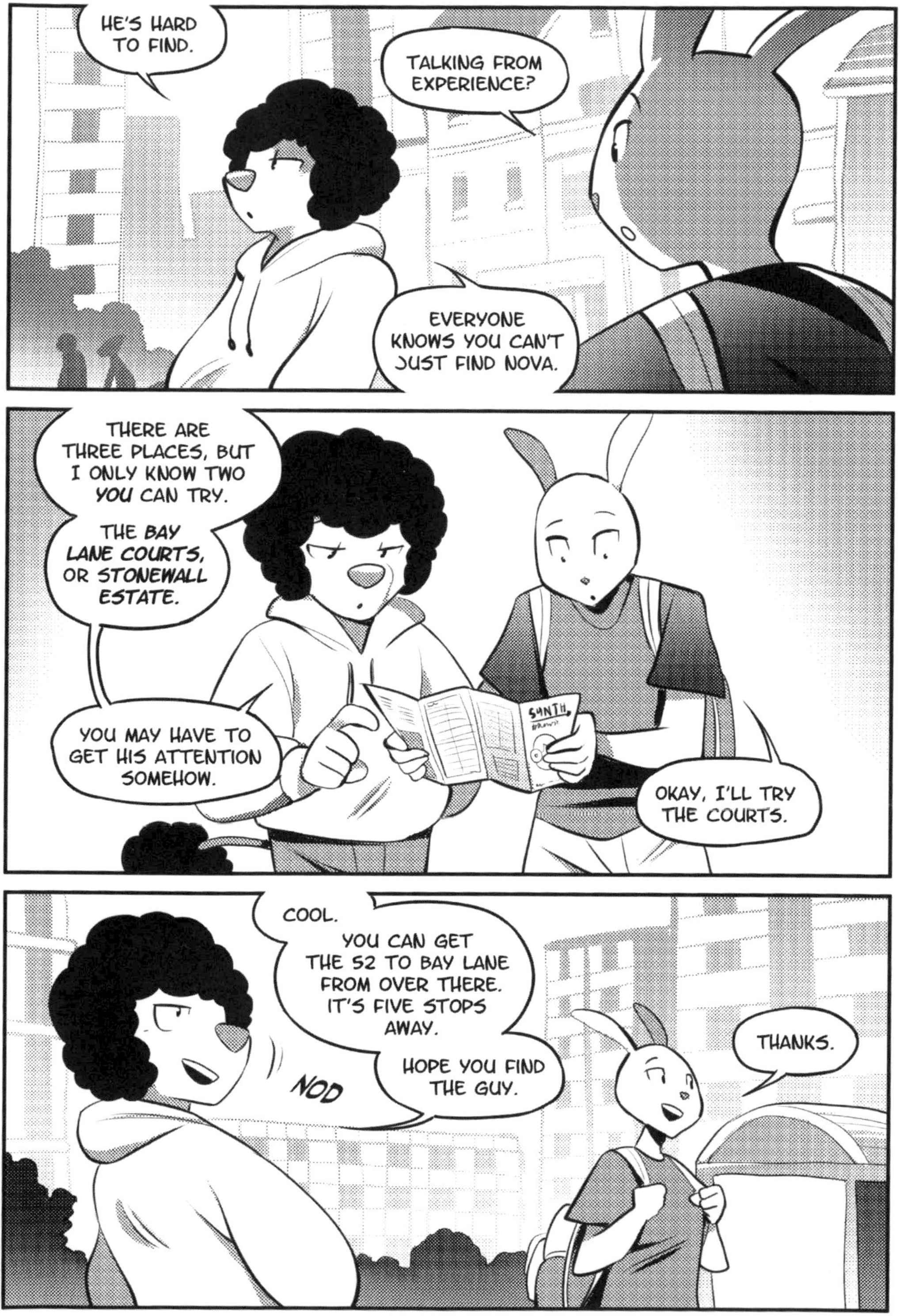
HE'S HARD TO FIND.
TALKING FROM EXPERIENCE?
EVERYONE KNOWS YOU CAN'T JUST FIND NOVA.
THERE ARE THREE PLACES, BUT I ONLY KNOW TWO *YOU* CAN TRY.
THE *BAY LANE COURTS*, OR *STONEWALL ESTATE*.
SYNTH
YOU MAY HAVE TO GET HIS ATTENTION SOMEHOW.
OKAY, I'LL TRY THE COURTS.
COOL.
YOU CAN GET THE 52 TO BAY LANE FROM OVER THERE. IT'S FIVE STOPS AWAY.
HOPE YOU FIND THE GUY.
NOD
THANKS.

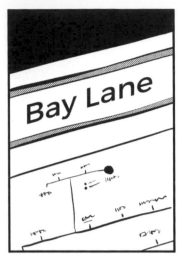

Bay Lane

RRRRRRRRRRRRR

I'M LOOKING FOR NOVA, ANYONE KNOW HIM?

EVERYONE KNOWS HIM...

YOU PLAY BALL?

NOD

WE'RE A MAN DOWN.

YOU WANNA KNOW WHERE NOVA IS, YOU GOTTA PLAY FOR THAT INFO.

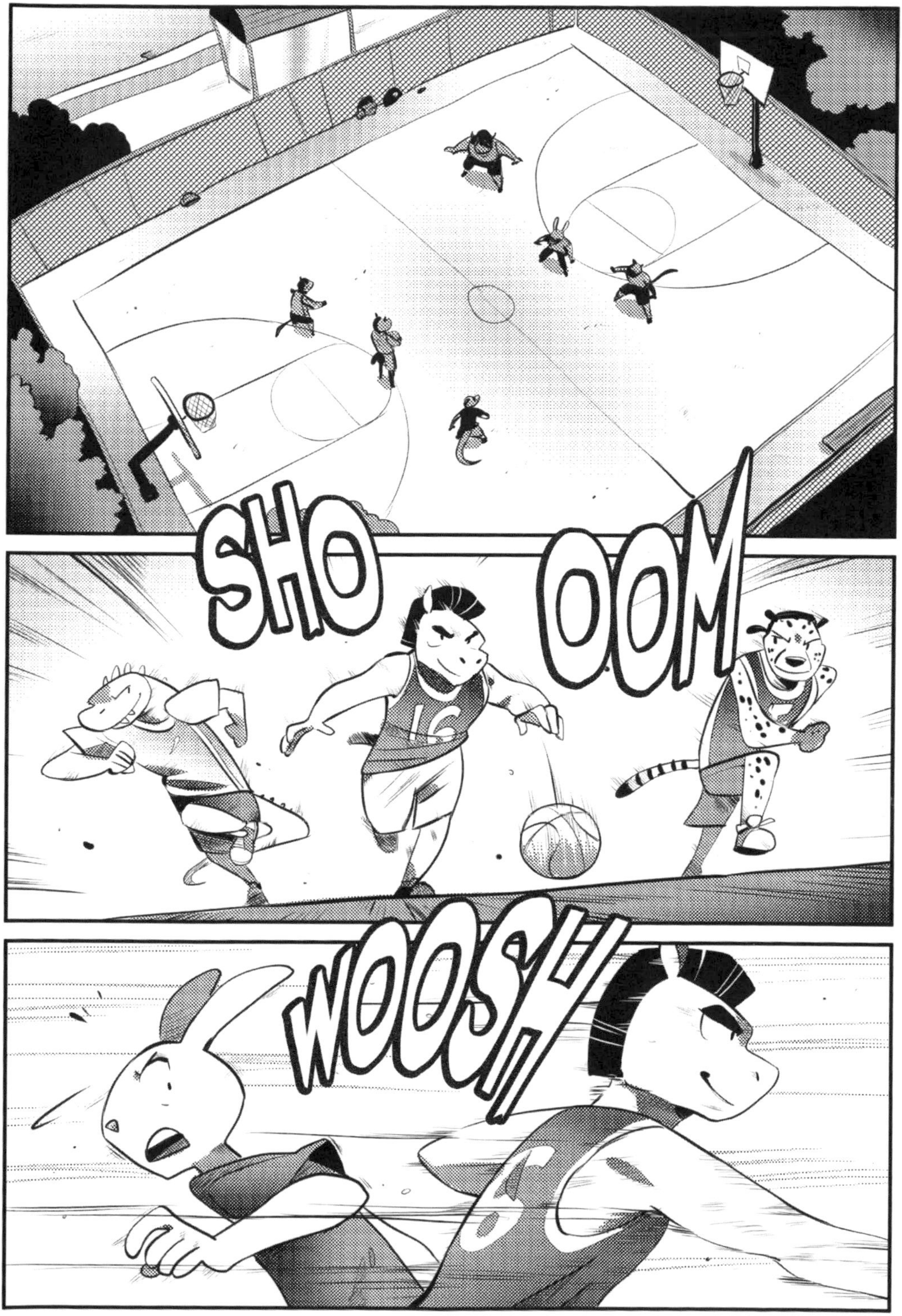
SHO OOM
WOOSH

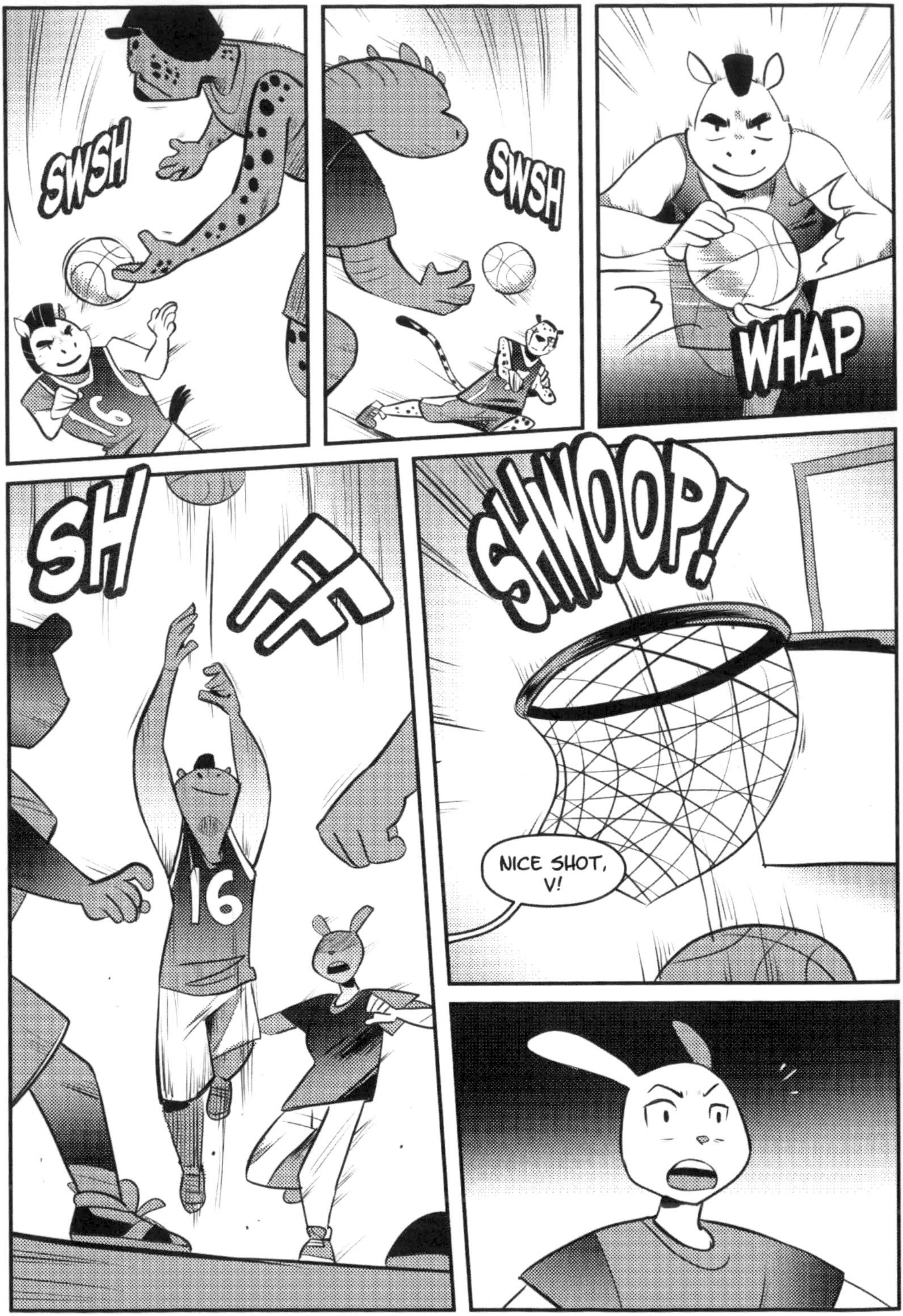
SWSH
SWSH
WHAP
SH
FF
SHWOOP!
NICE SHOT, V!

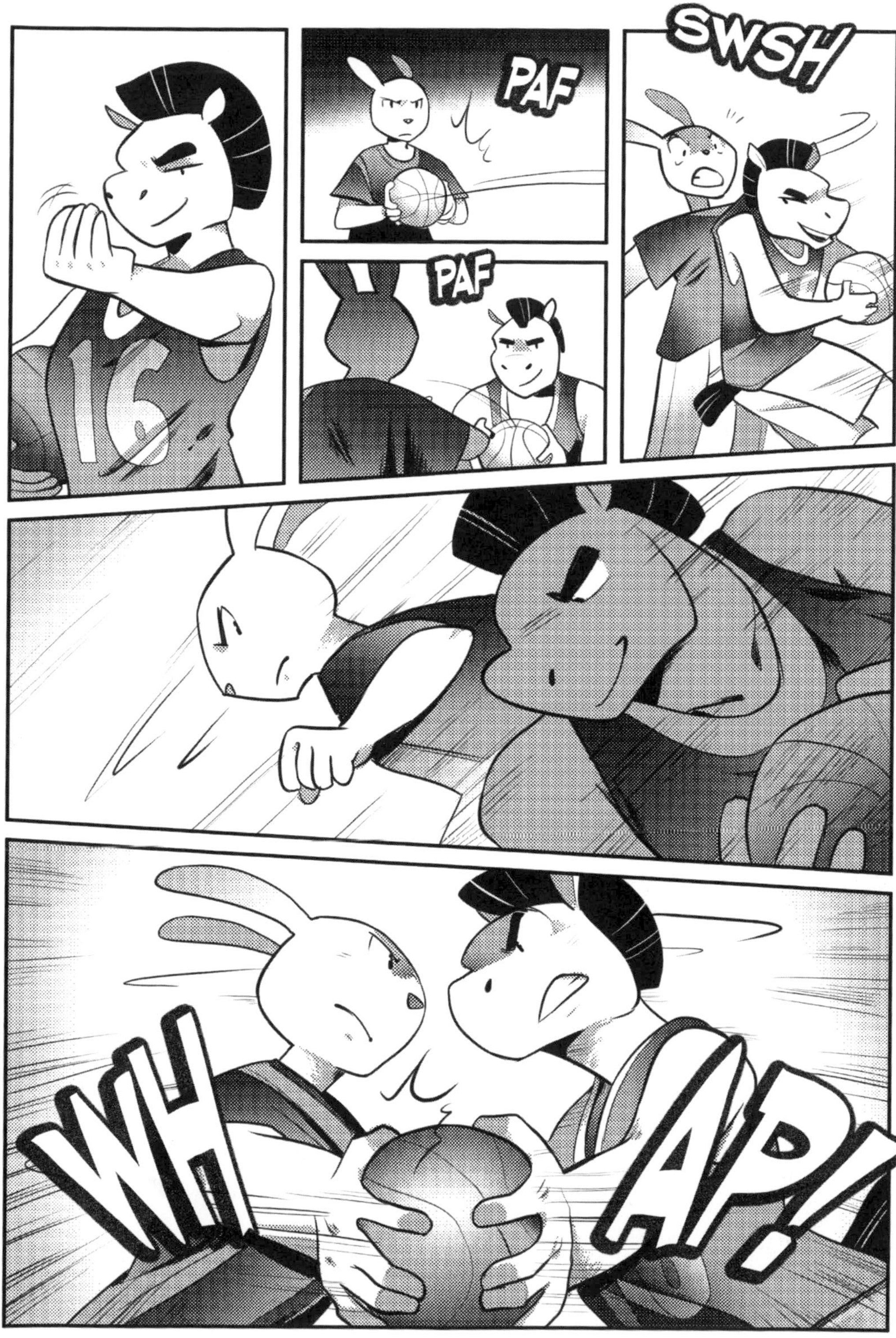
PAF
PAF
SWSH
WHAP!

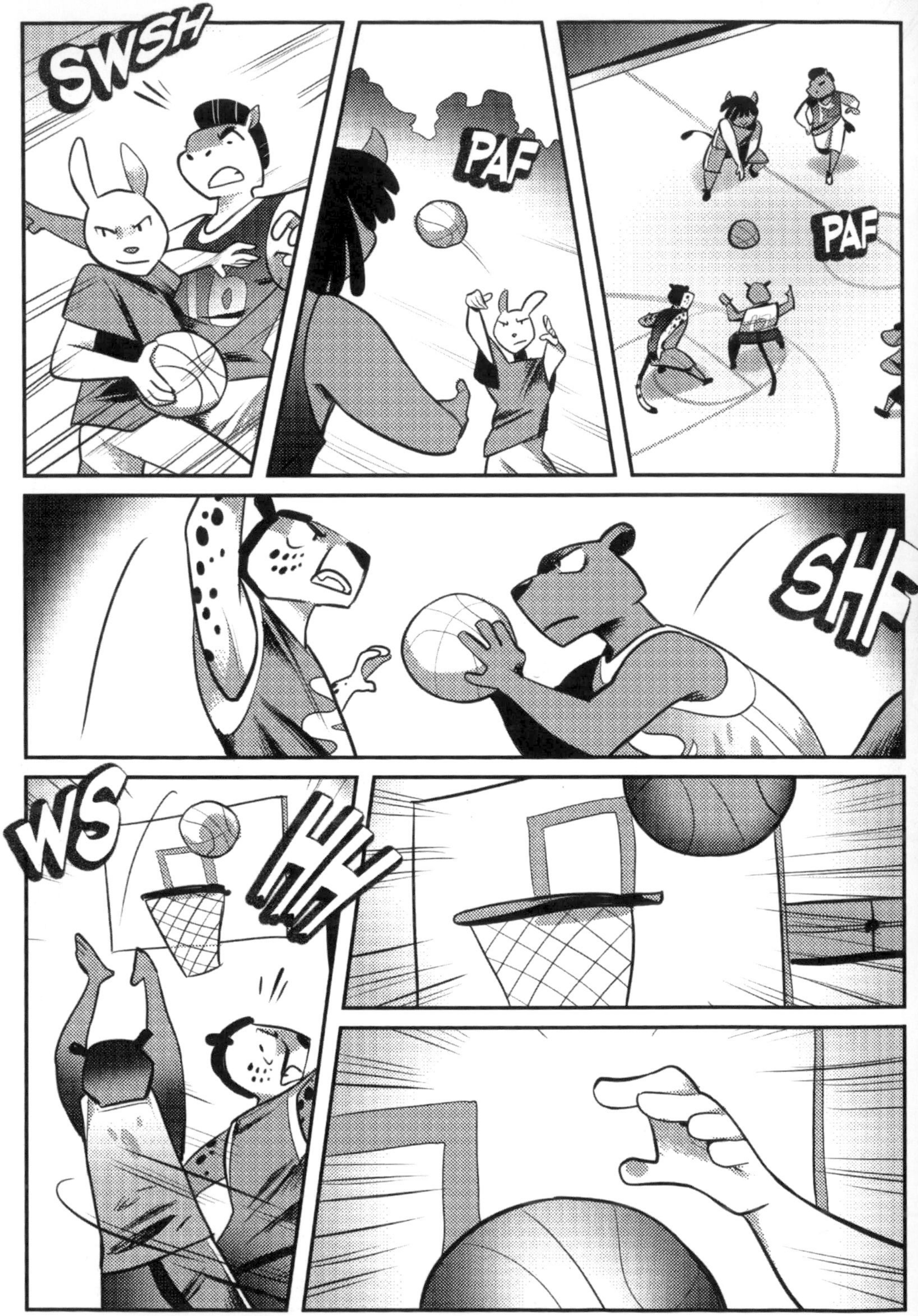
SWSH
PAF
PAF
SHF
WS
HH

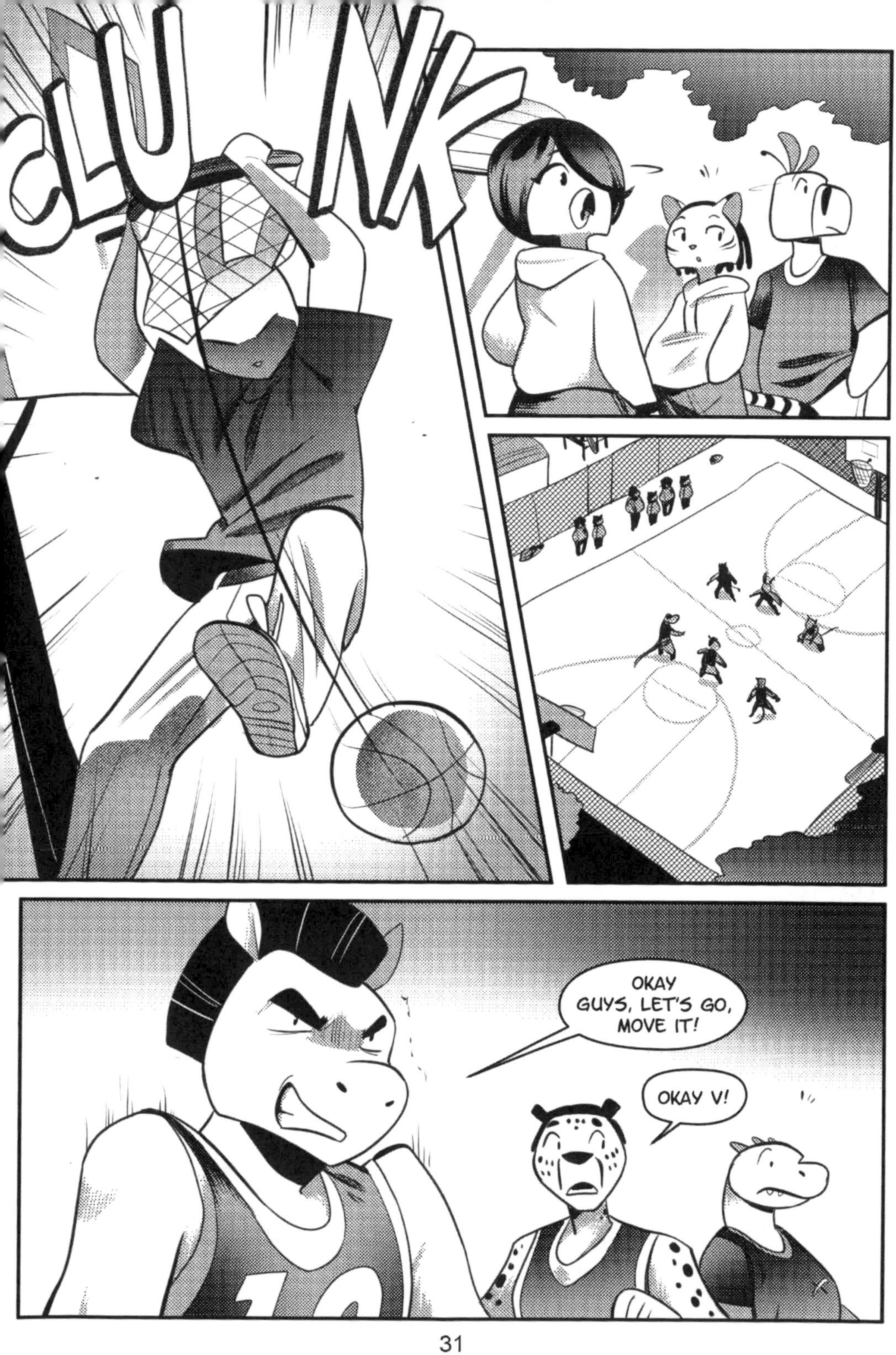
CLUNK
OKAY GUYS, LET'S GO, MOVE IT!
OKAY V!

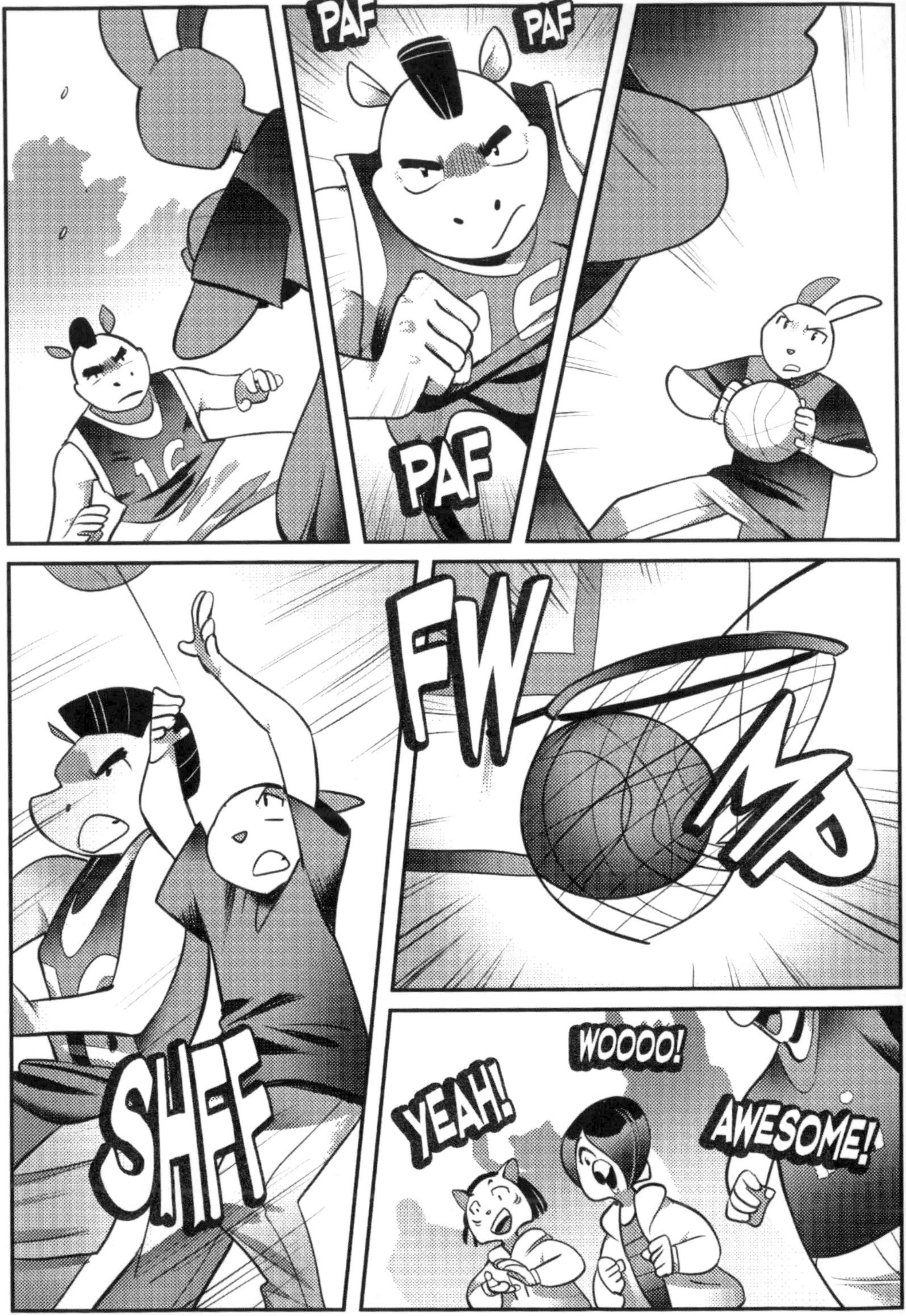
PAF
PAF
PAF
FW
MP
SHFF
YEAH!
WOOOO!
AWESOME!

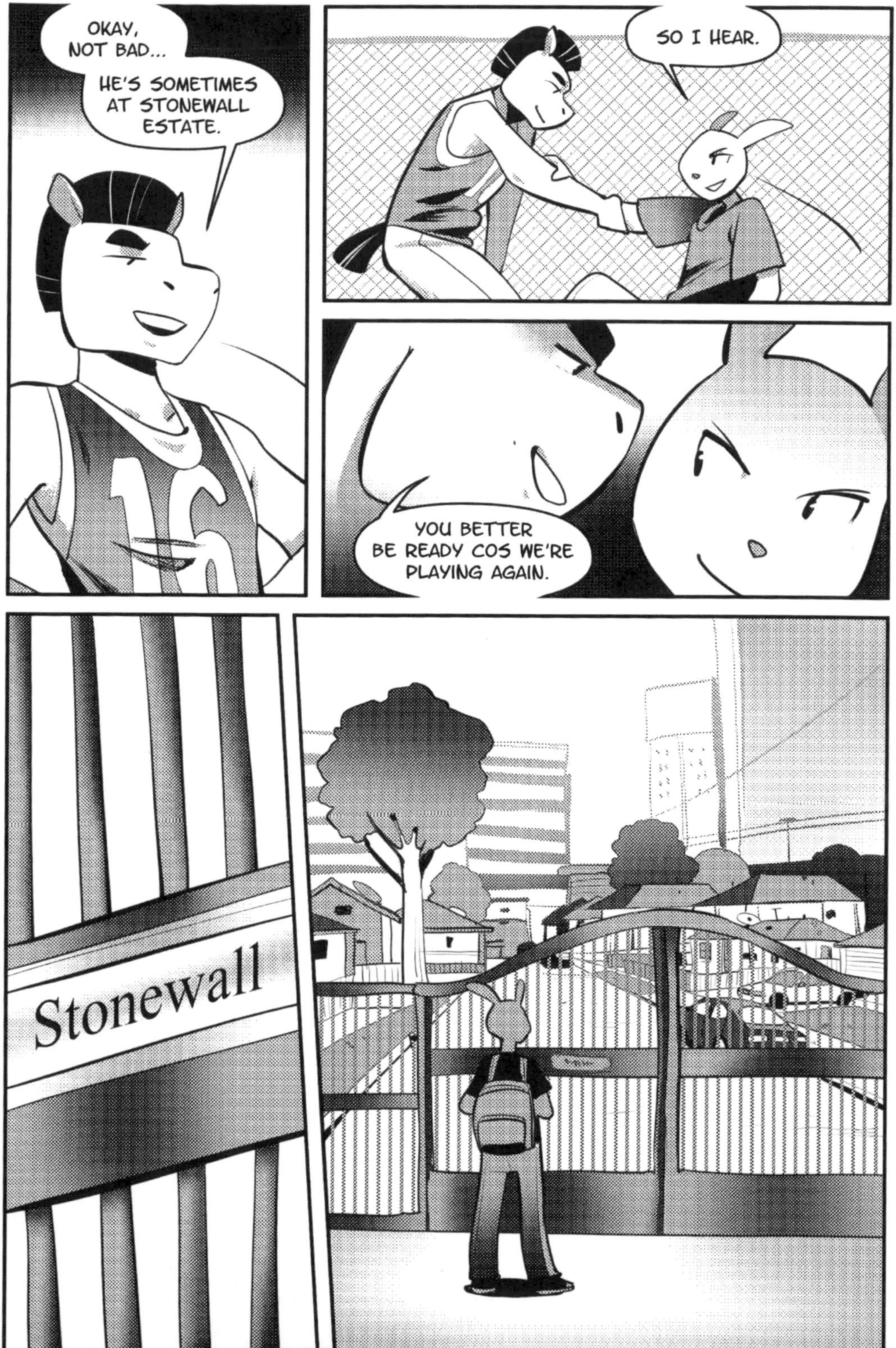
OKAY, NOT BAD...
HE'S SOMETIMES AT STONEWALL ESTATE.
SO I HEAR.
YOU BETTER BE READY COS WE'RE PLAYING AGAIN.
Stonewall

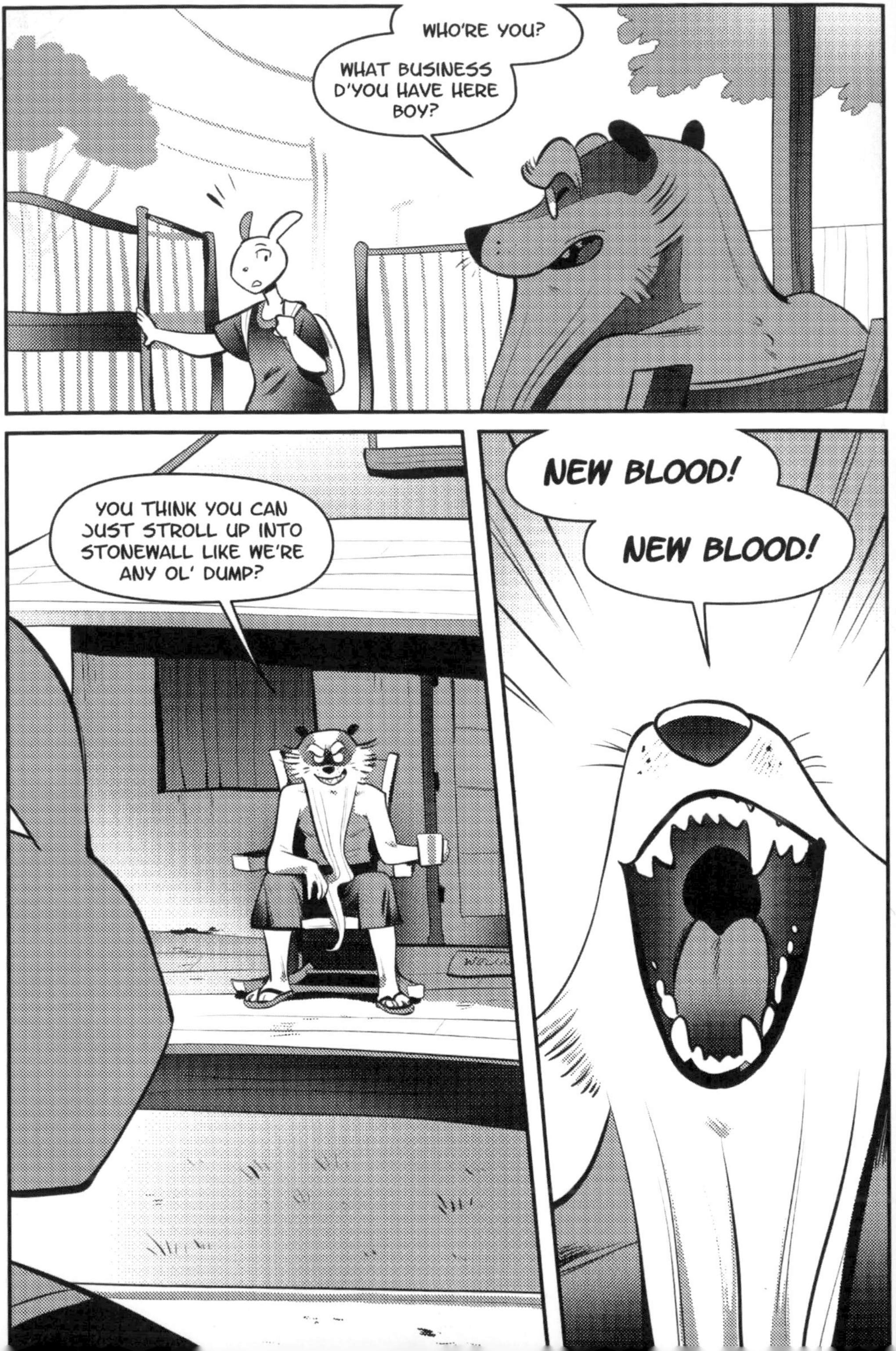
WHO'RE YOU?
WHAT BUSINESS D'YOU HAVE HERE BOY?
YOU THINK YOU CAN JUST STROLL UP INTO STONEWALL LIKE WE'RE ANY OL' DUMP?
NEW BLOOD!
NEW BLOOD!

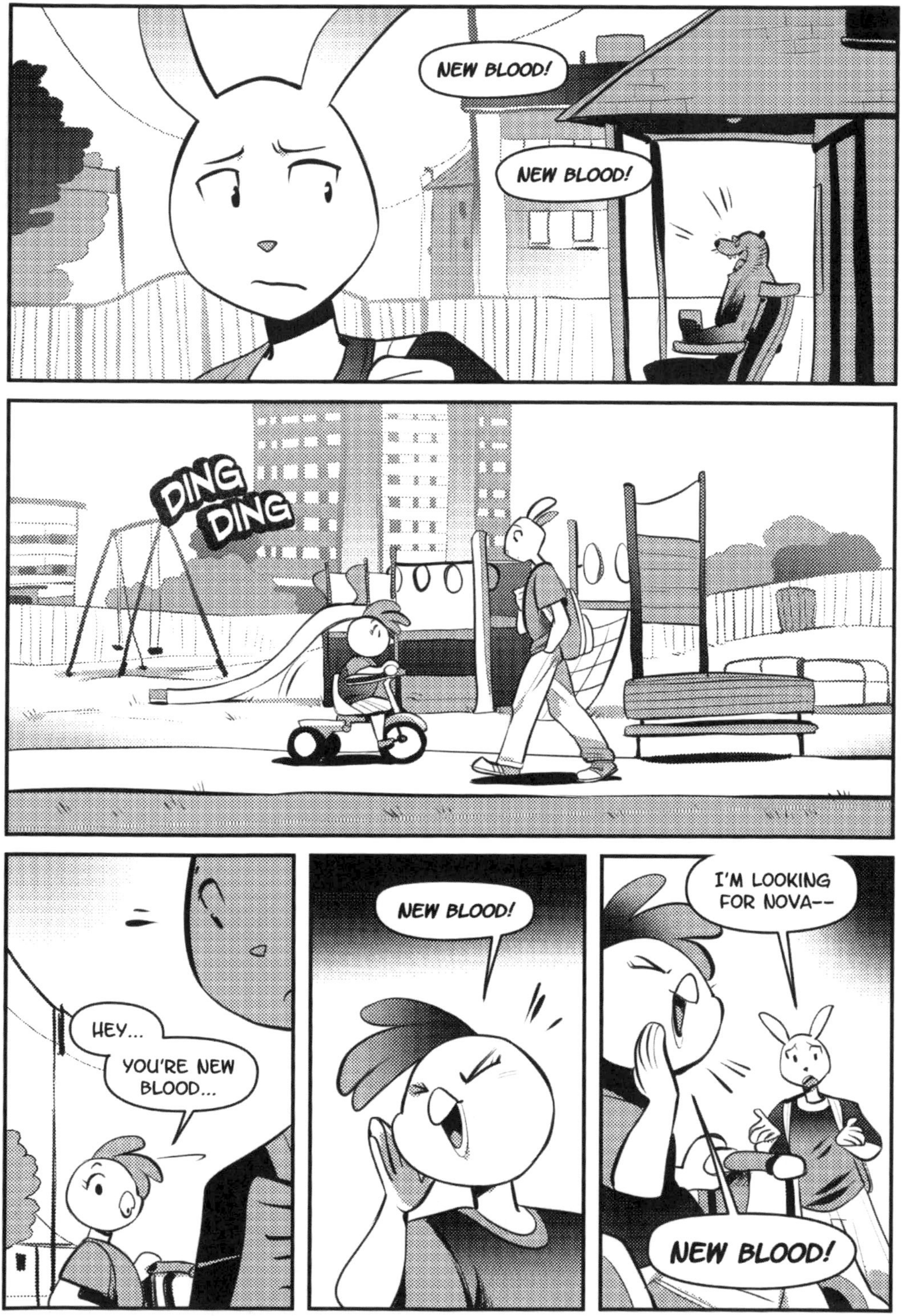
NEW BLOOD!
NEW BLOOD!
DING DING
HEY...
YOU'RE NEW BLOOD...
NEW BLOOD!
I'M LOOKING FOR NOVA--
NEW BLOOD!

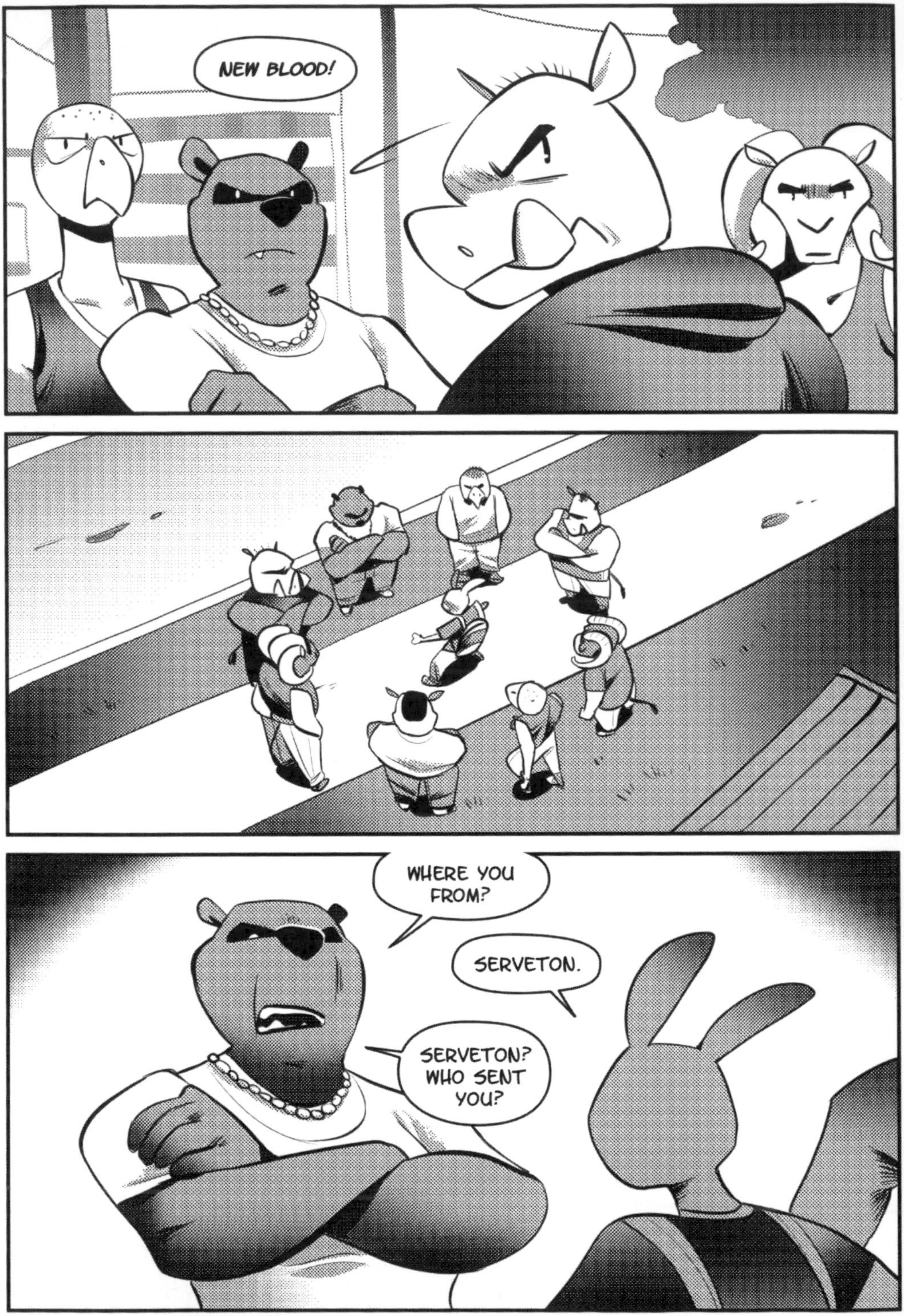
NEW BLOOD!
WHERE YOU FROM?
SERVETON.
SERVETON? WHO SENT YOU?

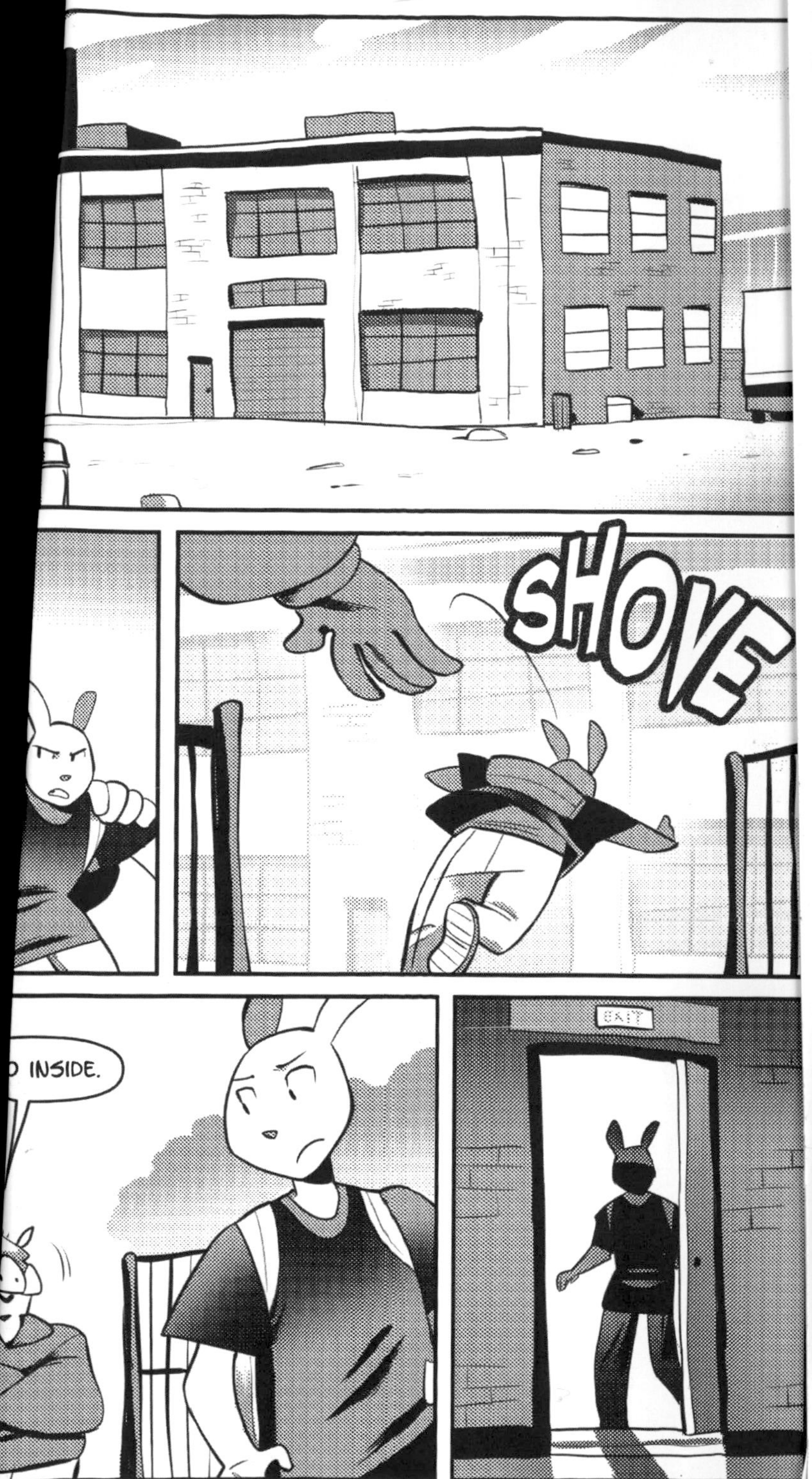
SHOVE
O INSIDE.

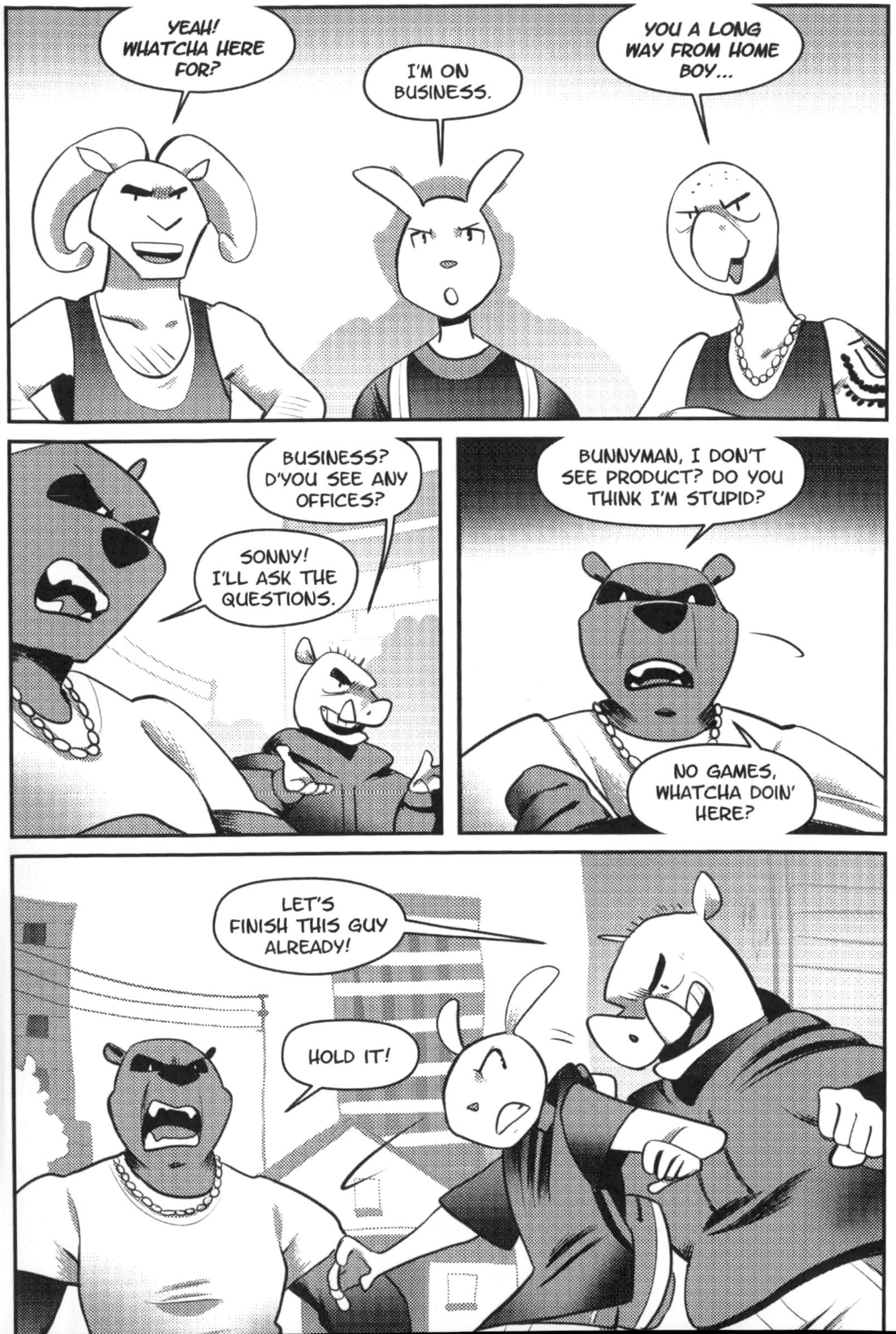
YEAH! WHATCHA HERE FOR?
I'M ON BUSINESS.
YOU A LONG WAY FROM HOME BOY...
BUSINESS? D'YOU SEE ANY OFFICES?
SONNY! I'LL ASK THE QUESTIONS.
BUNNYMAN, I DON'T SEE PRODUCT? DO YOU THINK I'M STUPID?
NO GAMES, WHATCHA DOIN' HERE?
LET'S FINISH THIS GUY ALREADY!
HOLD IT!

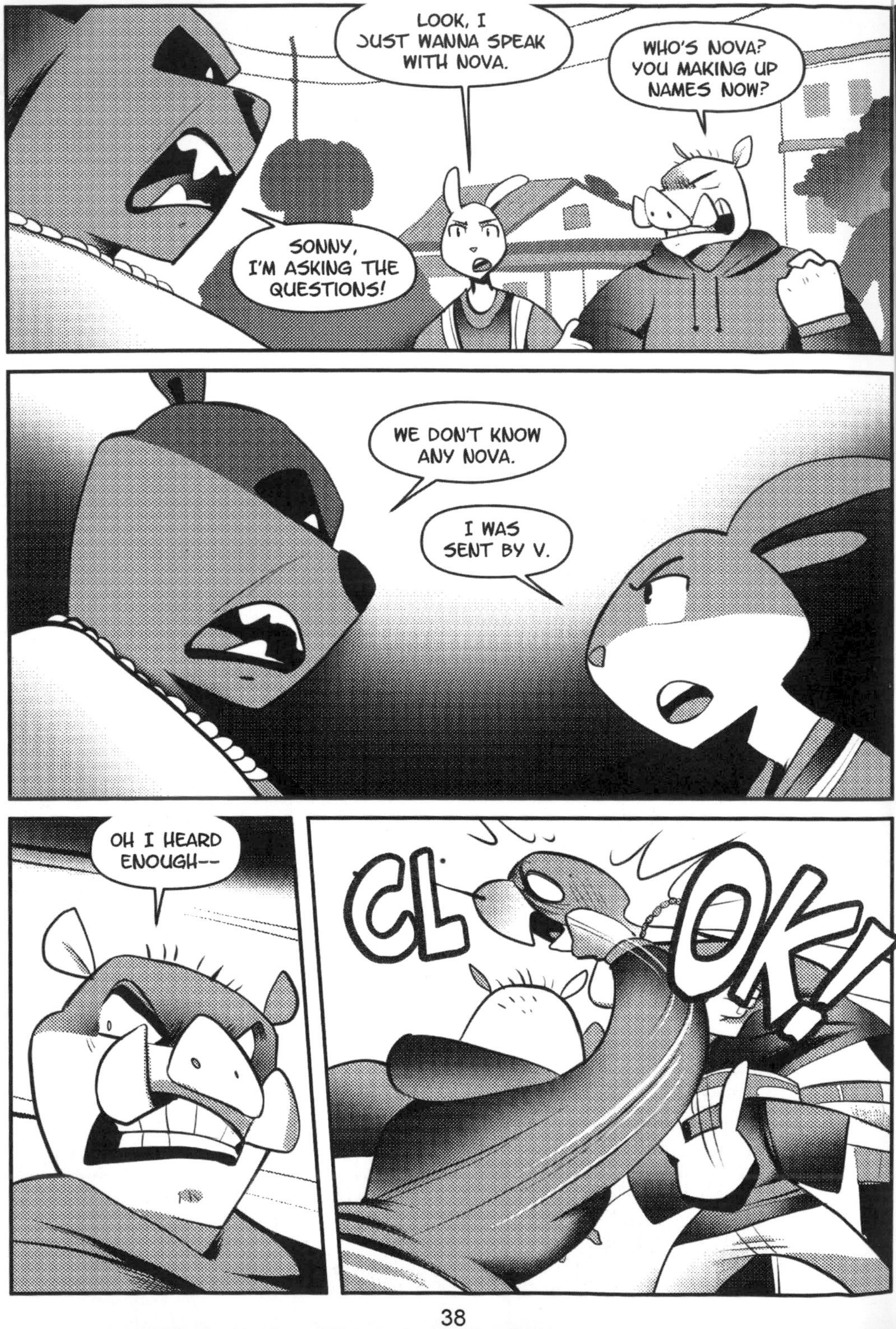
LOOK, I JUST WANNA SPEAK WITH NOVA.
WHO'S NOVA? YOU MAKING UP NAMES NOW?
SONNY, I'M ASKING THE QUESTIONS!
WE DON'T KNOW ANY NOVA.
I WAS SENT BY V.
OH I HEARD ENOUGH--
CLOK!

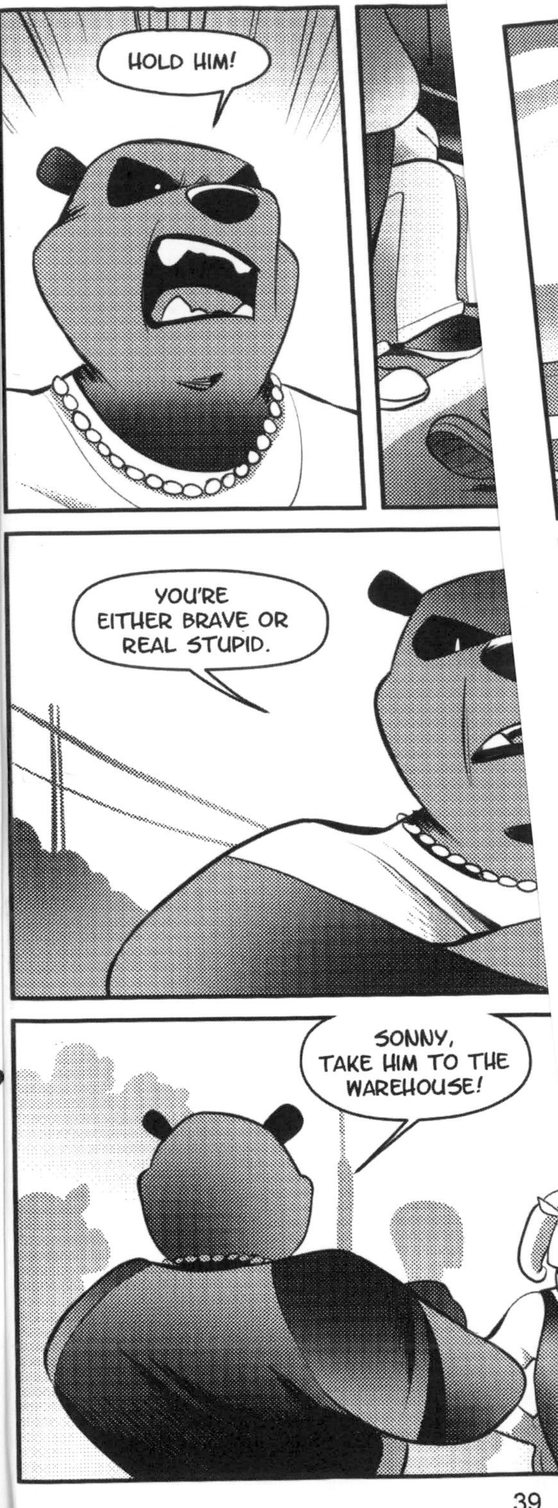
HOLD HIM!
YOU'RE EITHER BRAVE OR REAL STUPID.
SONNY, TAKE HIM TO THE WAREHOUSE!

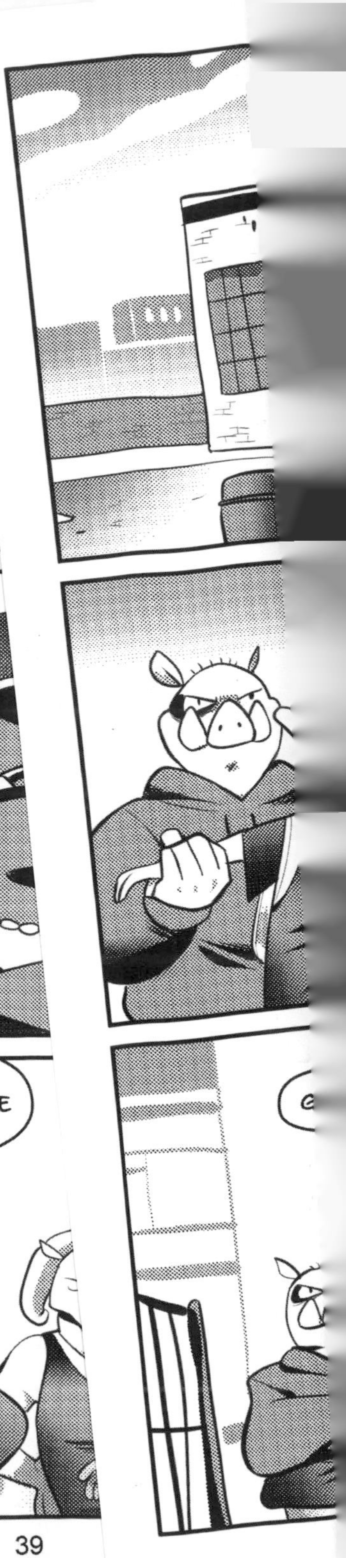

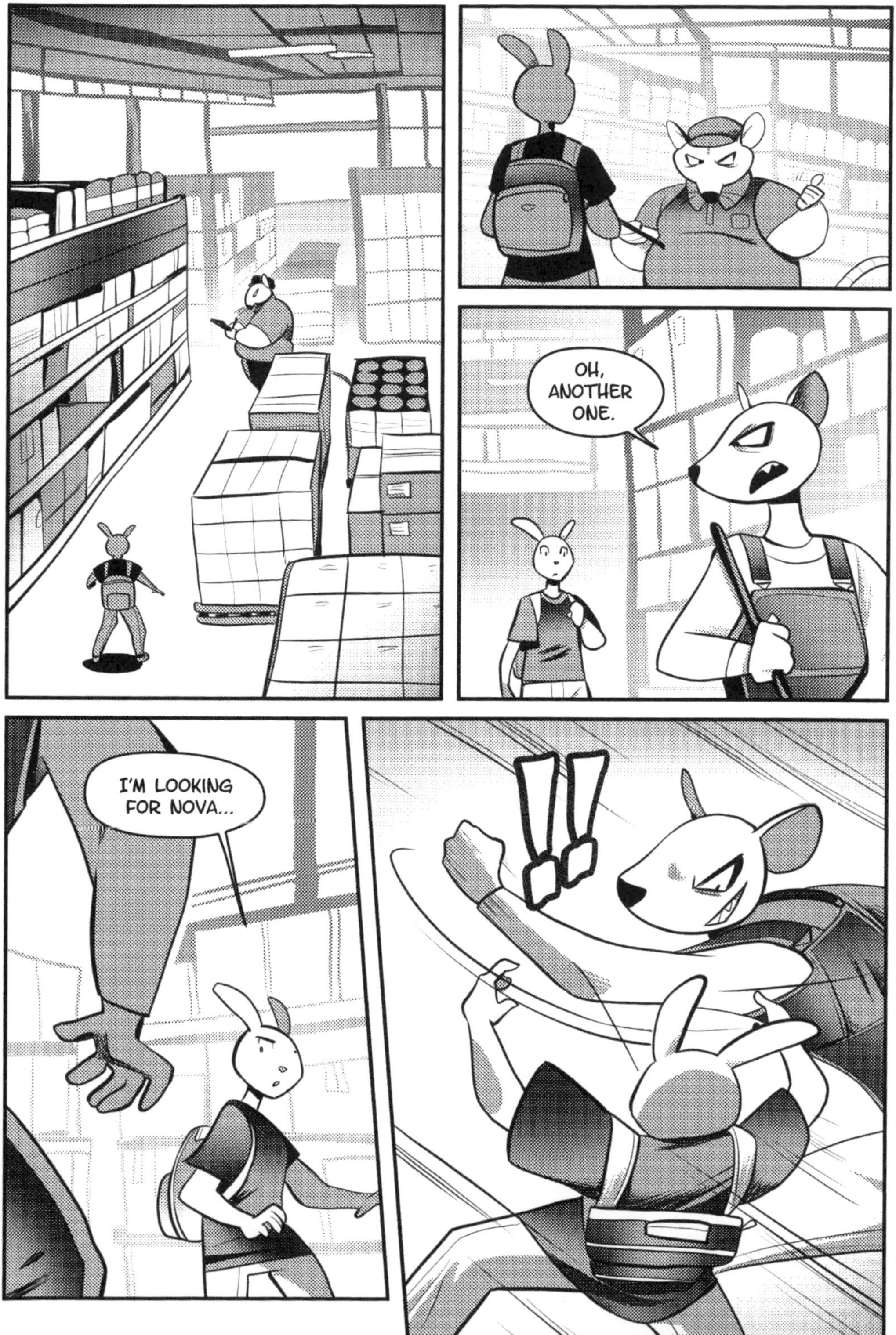
OH, ANOTHER ONE.
I'M LOOKING FOR NOVA...
!!

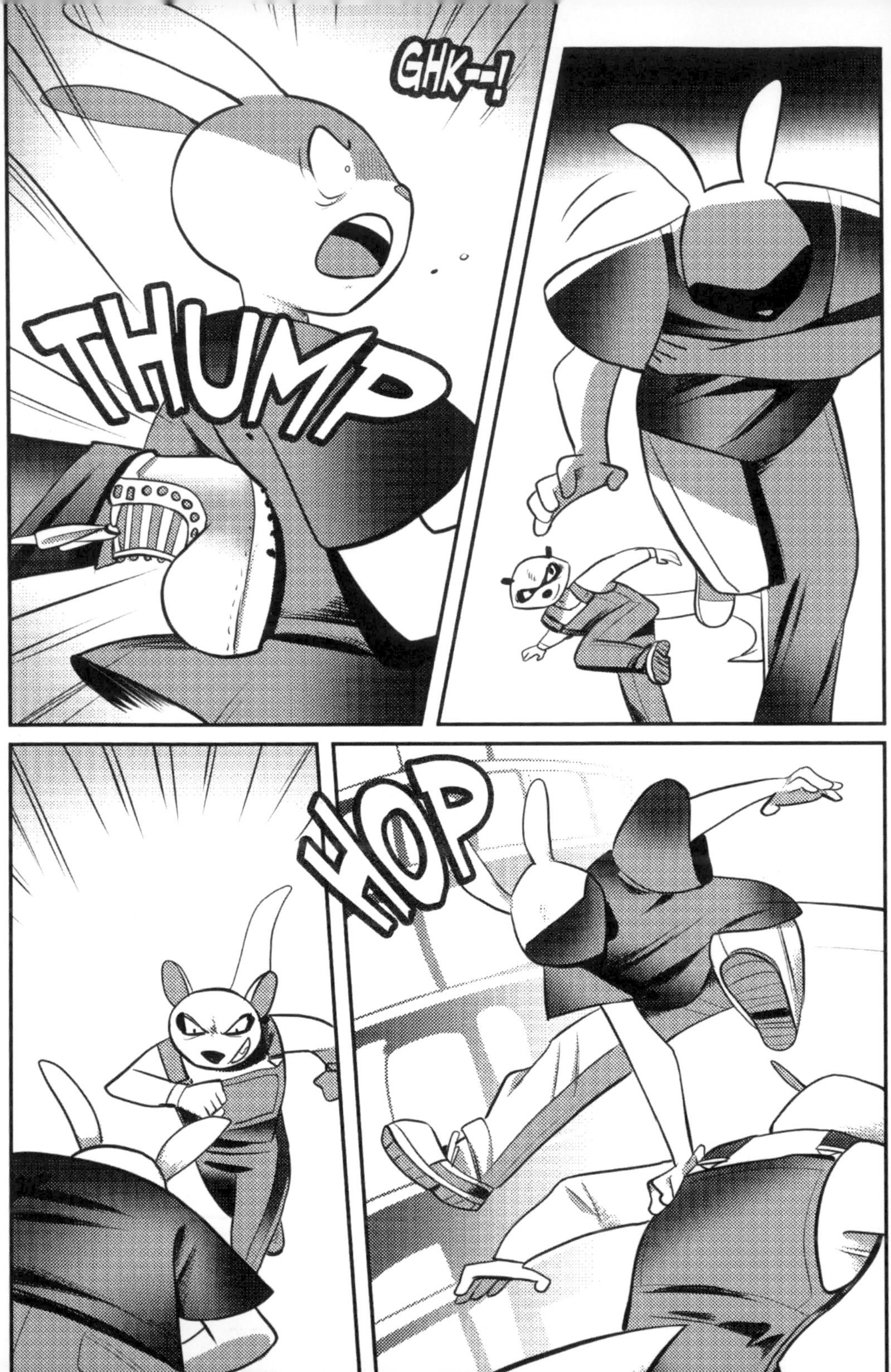
GHK--!
THUMP
HOP

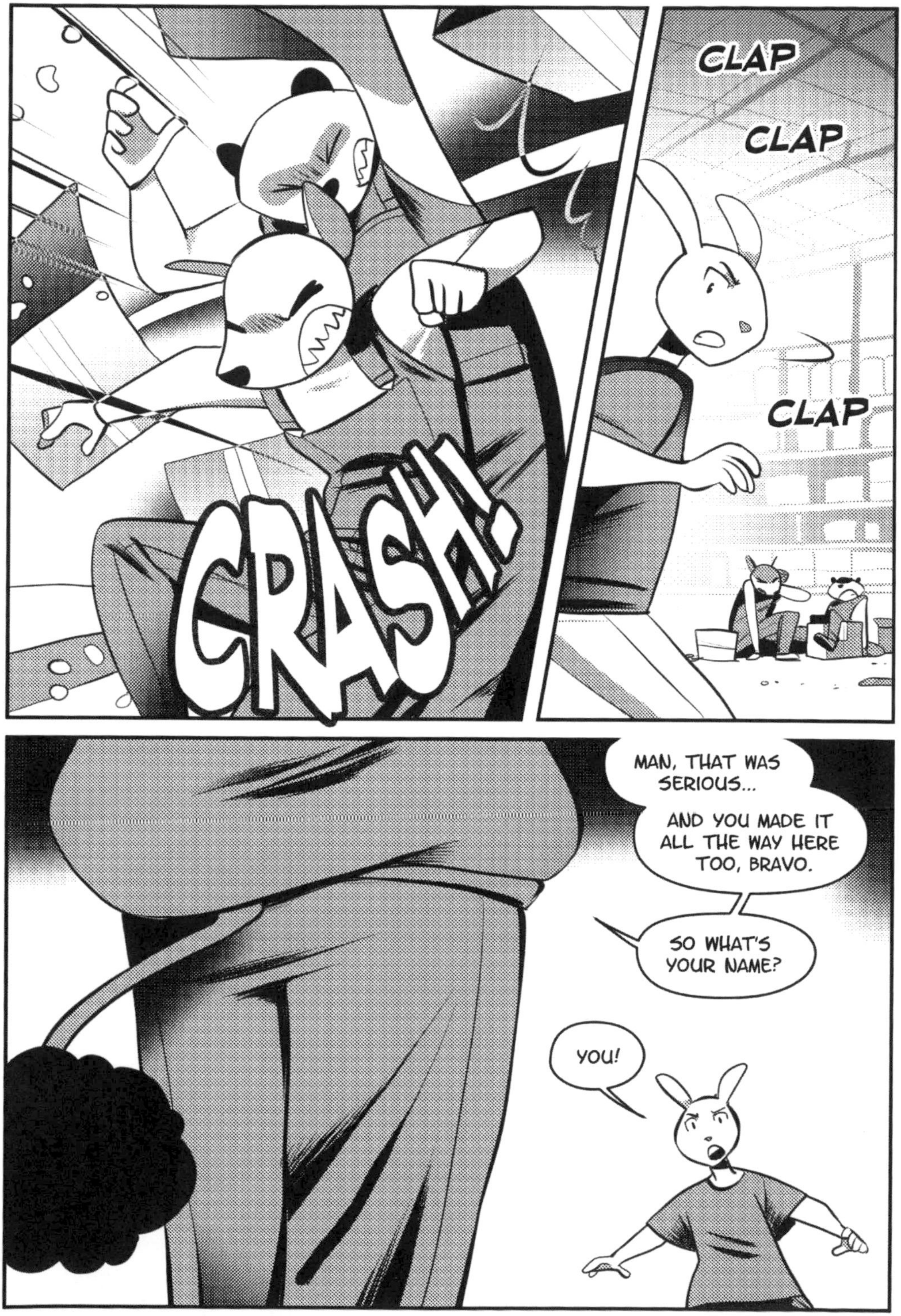
CRASH!
CLAP
CLAP
CLAP
MAN, THAT WAS SERIOUS...
AND YOU MADE IT ALL THE WAY HERE TOO, BRAVO.
SO WHAT'S YOUR NAME?
YOU!

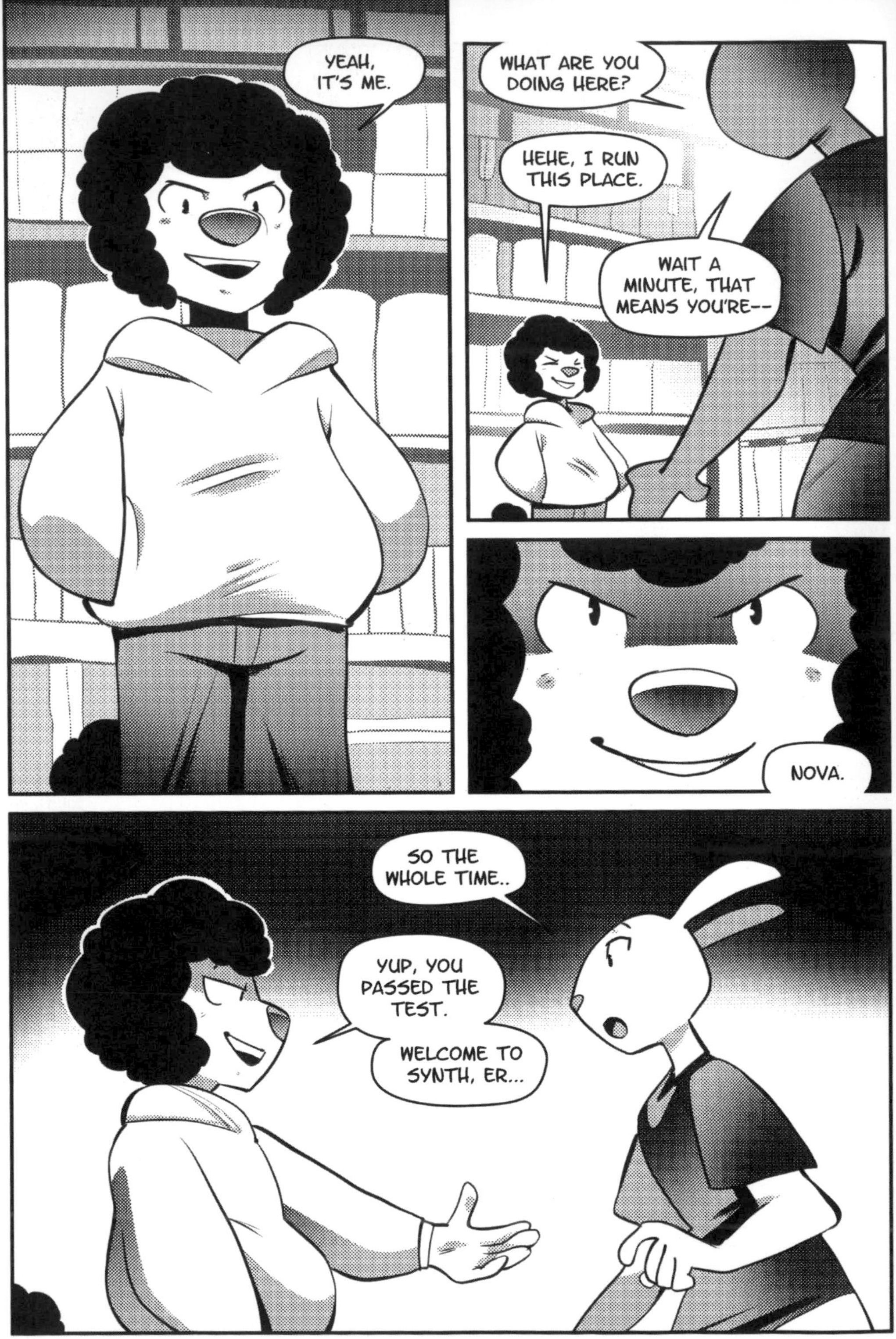
YEAH, IT'S ME.
WHAT ARE YOU DOING HERE?
HEHE, I RUN THIS PLACE.
WAIT A MINUTE, THAT MEANS YOU'RE--
NOVA.
SO THE WHOLE TIME..
YUP, YOU PASSED THE TEST.
WELCOME TO SYNTH, ER...

BLAKE, BLAKE SMITHE.

YOU'RE SERIOUS...

WE'RE GONNA CALL YOU *BLAKE SERIOUS.*

YEAH, KINDA CATCHY...

SO YOU WERE TESTING ME?

OLD MAN JIN SAID YOU WERE COMING.

SO?

C'MON, YOU GOTTA TEST PEOPLE RIGHT?

I WAS ALMOST KILLED!

PLEASE! THIS AIN'T CRIMSON.

CAN YOU COME TO SERVETON?

YEAH I GUESS.

HOW 'BOUT TOMORROW?

I NEED TO SEE THAT OLD CODGER ANYWAY.

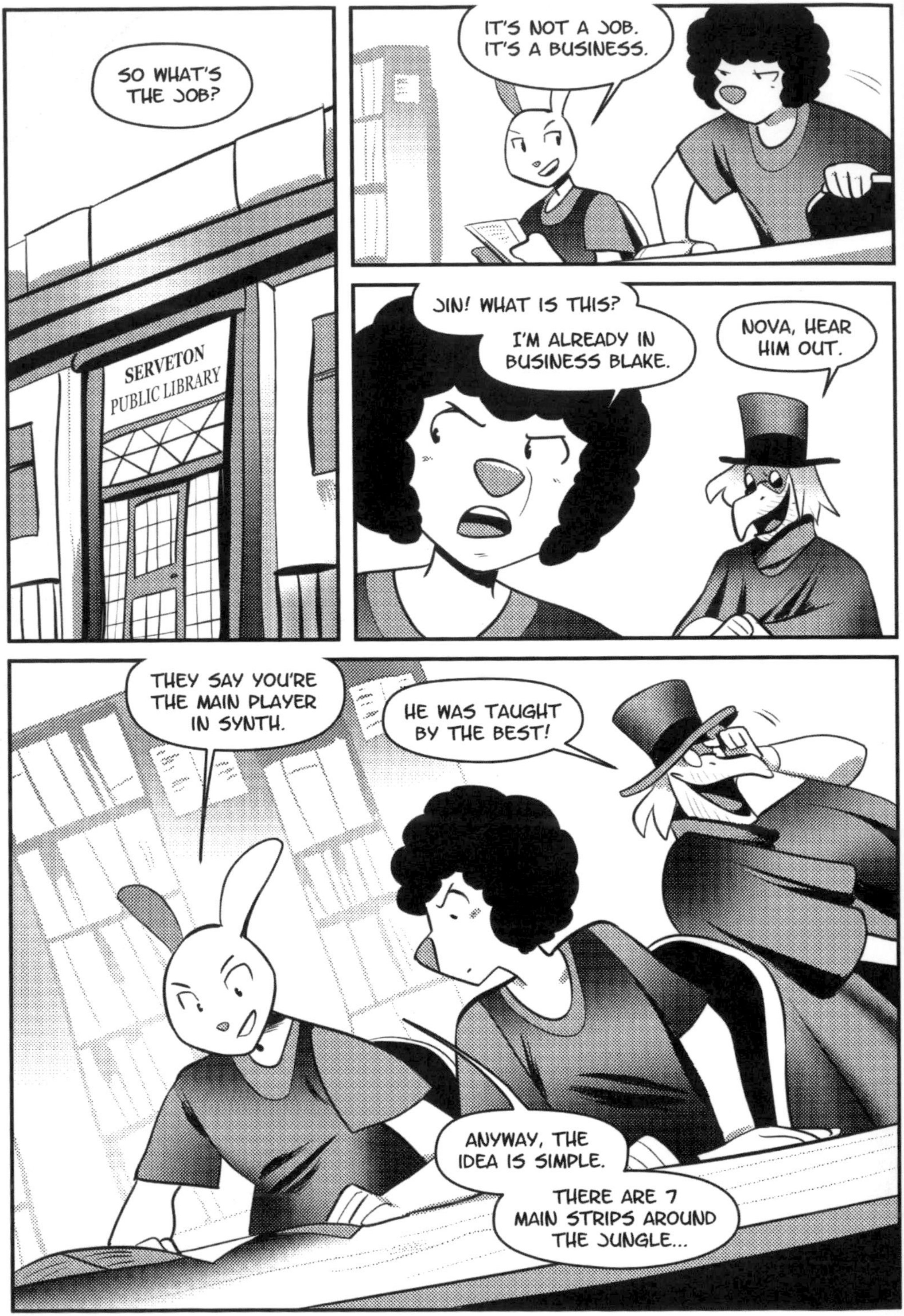
SO WHAT'S THE JOB?
SERVETON PUBLIC LIBRARY
IT'S NOT A JOB. IT'S A BUSINESS.
JIN! WHAT IS THIS?
I'M ALREADY IN BUSINESS BLAKE.
NOVA, HEAR HIM OUT.
THEY SAY YOU'RE THE MAIN PLAYER IN SYNTH.
HE WAS TAUGHT BY THE BEST!
ANYWAY, THE IDEA IS SIMPLE.
THERE ARE 7 MAIN STRIPS AROUND THE JUNGLE...

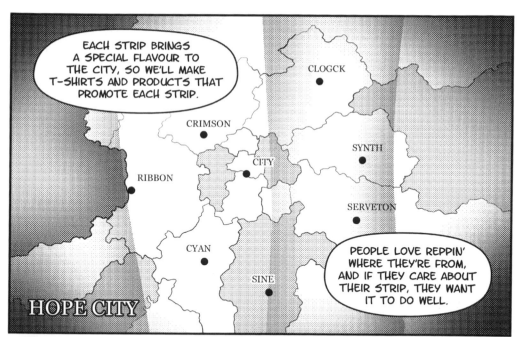

EACH STRIP BRINGS A SPECIAL FLAVOUR TO THE CITY, SO WE'LL MAKE T-SHIRTS AND PRODUCTS THAT PROMOTE EACH STRIP.

CLOGCK

CRIMSON

SYNTH

CITY

RIBBON

SERVETON

CYAN

SINE

HOPE CITY

PEOPLE LOVE REPPIN' WHERE THEY'RE FROM, AND IF THEY CARE ABOUT THEIR STRIP, THEY WANT IT TO DO WELL.

A MOVEMENT.

THIS COULD BLOW UP OVER HOPE CITY...

LIKE A *SUPER NOVA!*

HAHA, AH JIN...

YOU OL' DOG, SO THAT'S YOUR PLAN.

SO YOU'RE IN?

IT HAS POTENTIAL...

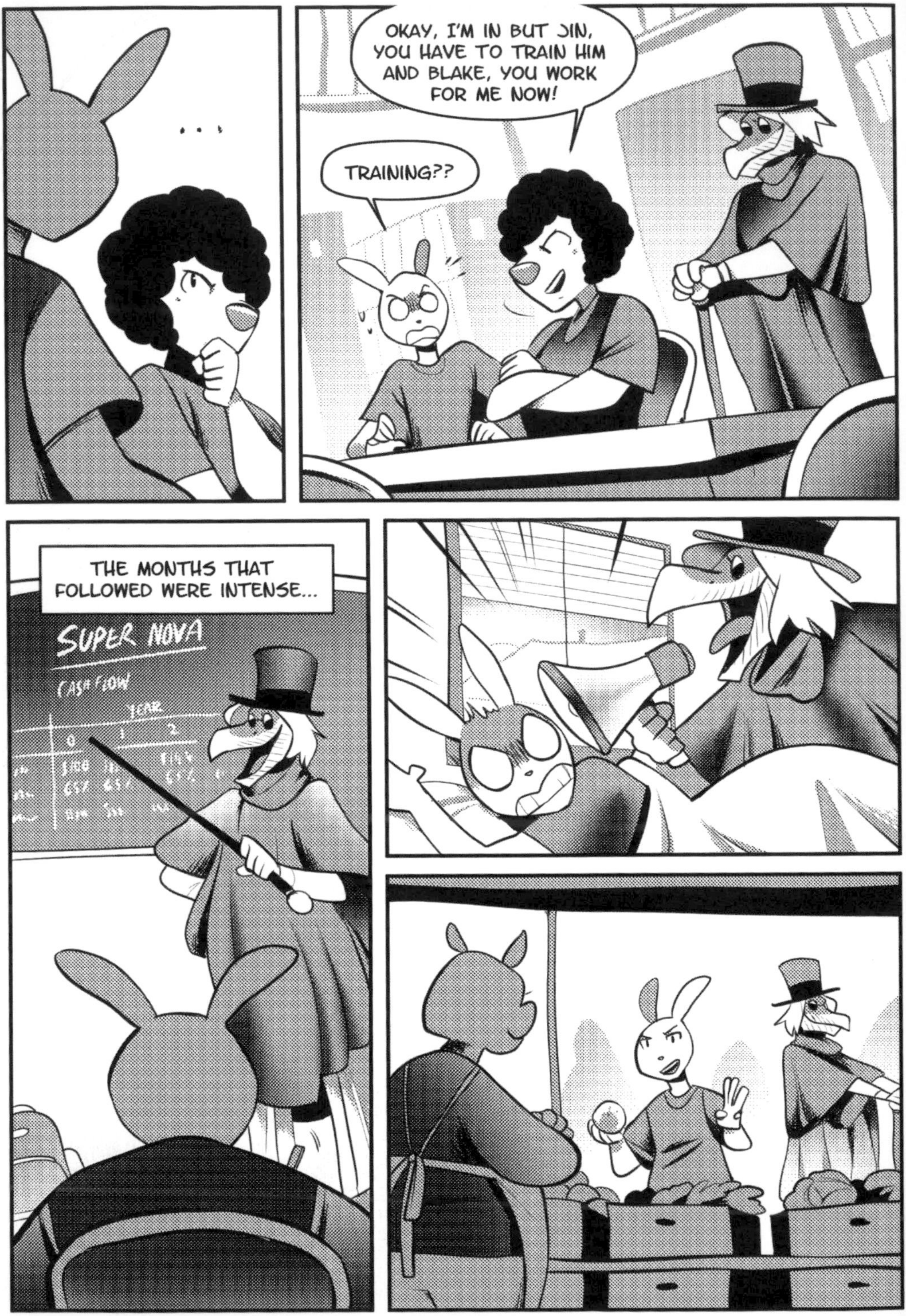
...
OKAY, I'M IN BUT JIN, YOU HAVE TO TRAIN HIM AND BLAKE, YOU WORK FOR ME NOW!
TRAINING??
THE MONTHS THAT FOLLOWED WERE INTENSE...
SUPER NOVA
CASH FLOW
YEAR

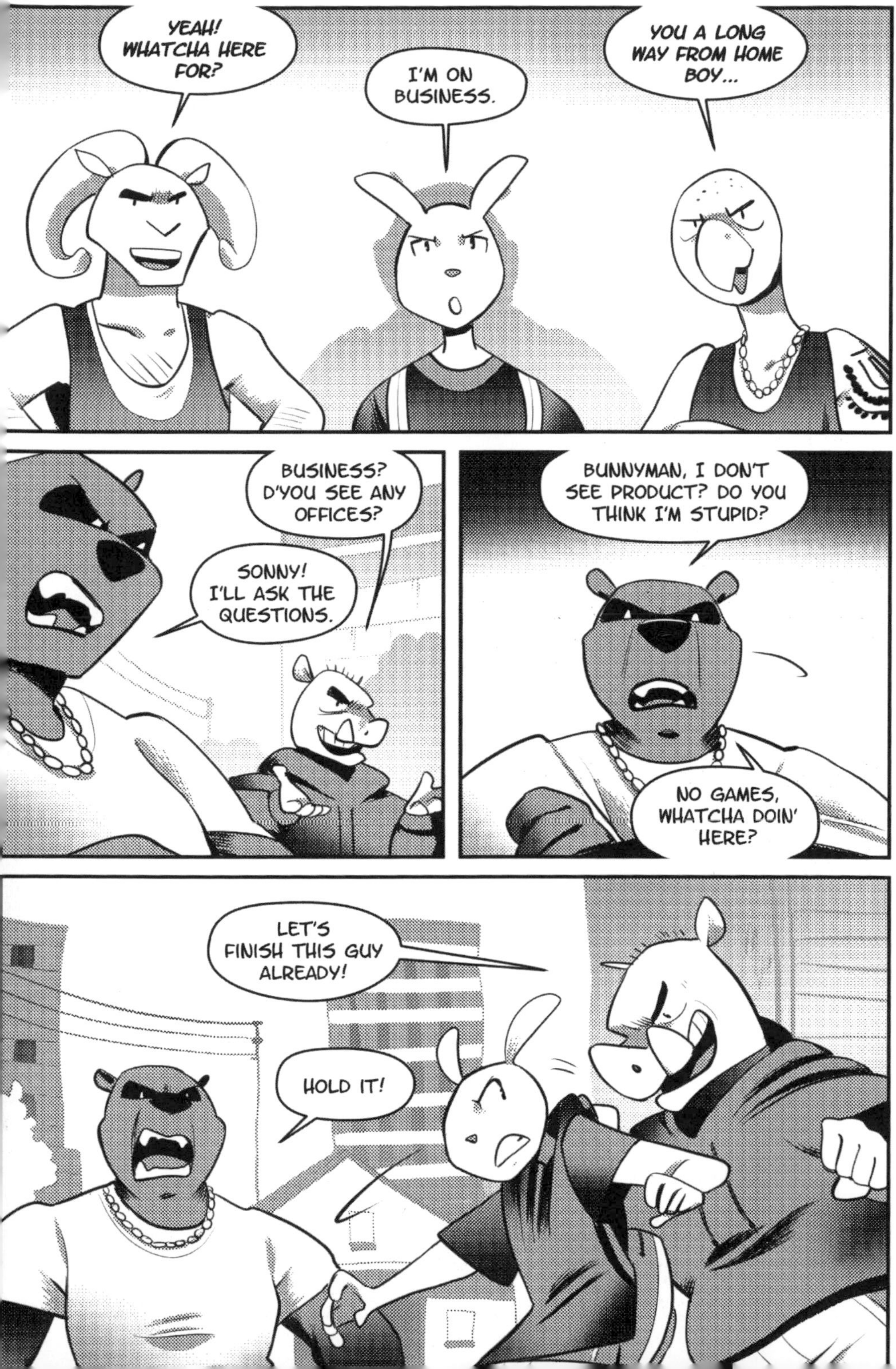
YEAH! WHATCHA HERE FOR?
I'M ON BUSINESS.
YOU A LONG WAY FROM HOME BOY...
BUSINESS? D'YOU SEE ANY OFFICES?
SONNY! I'LL ASK THE QUESTIONS.
BUNNYMAN, I DON'T SEE PRODUCT? DO YOU THINK I'M STUPID?
NO GAMES, WHATCHA DOIN' HERE?
LET'S FINISH THIS GUY ALREADY!
HOLD IT!

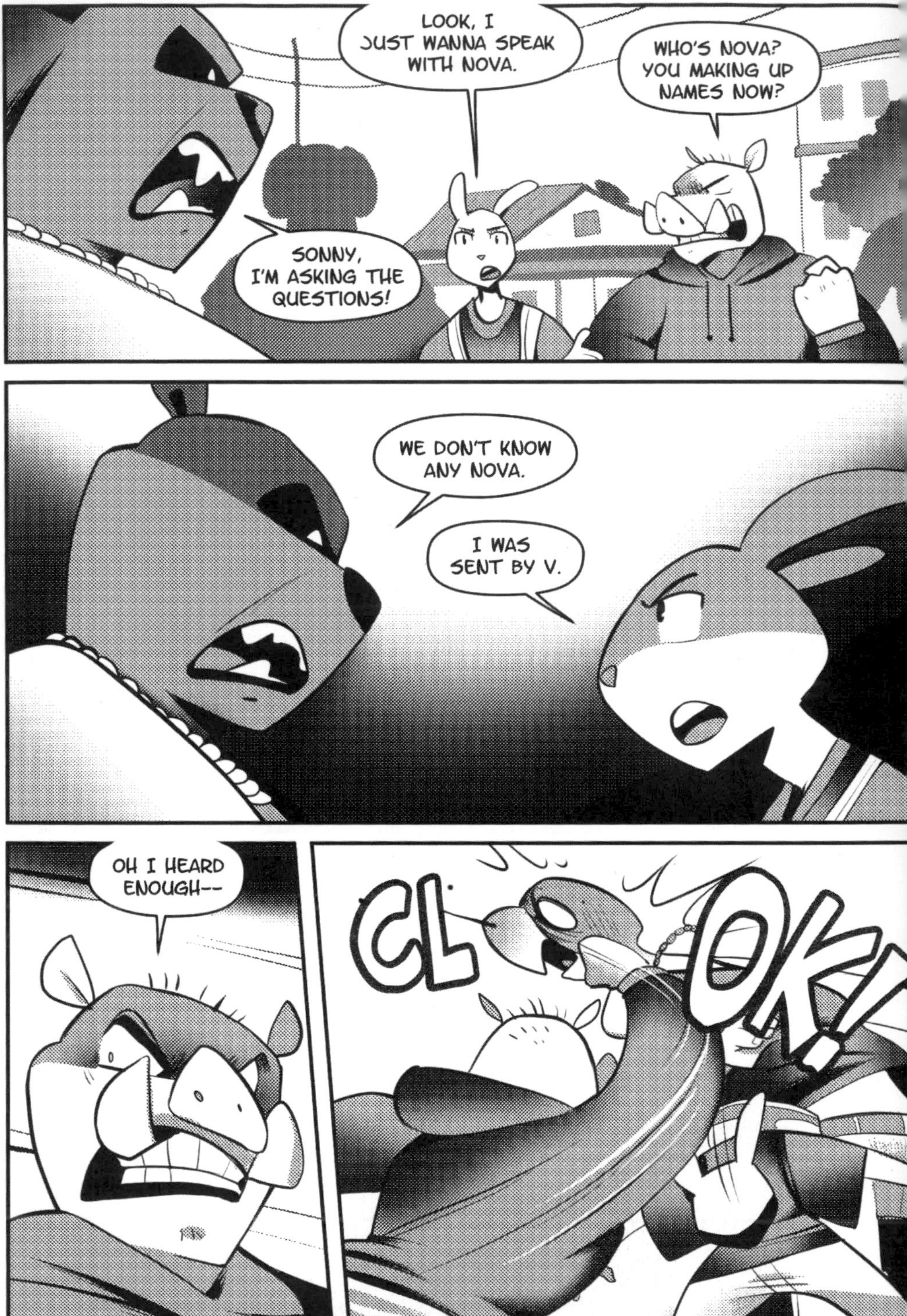
LOOK, I JUST WANNA SPEAK WITH NOVA.
WHO'S NOVA? YOU MAKING UP NAMES NOW?
SONNY, I'M ASKING THE QUESTIONS!
WE DON'T KNOW ANY NOVA.
I WAS SENT BY V.
OH I HEARD ENOUGH--
CLOK!

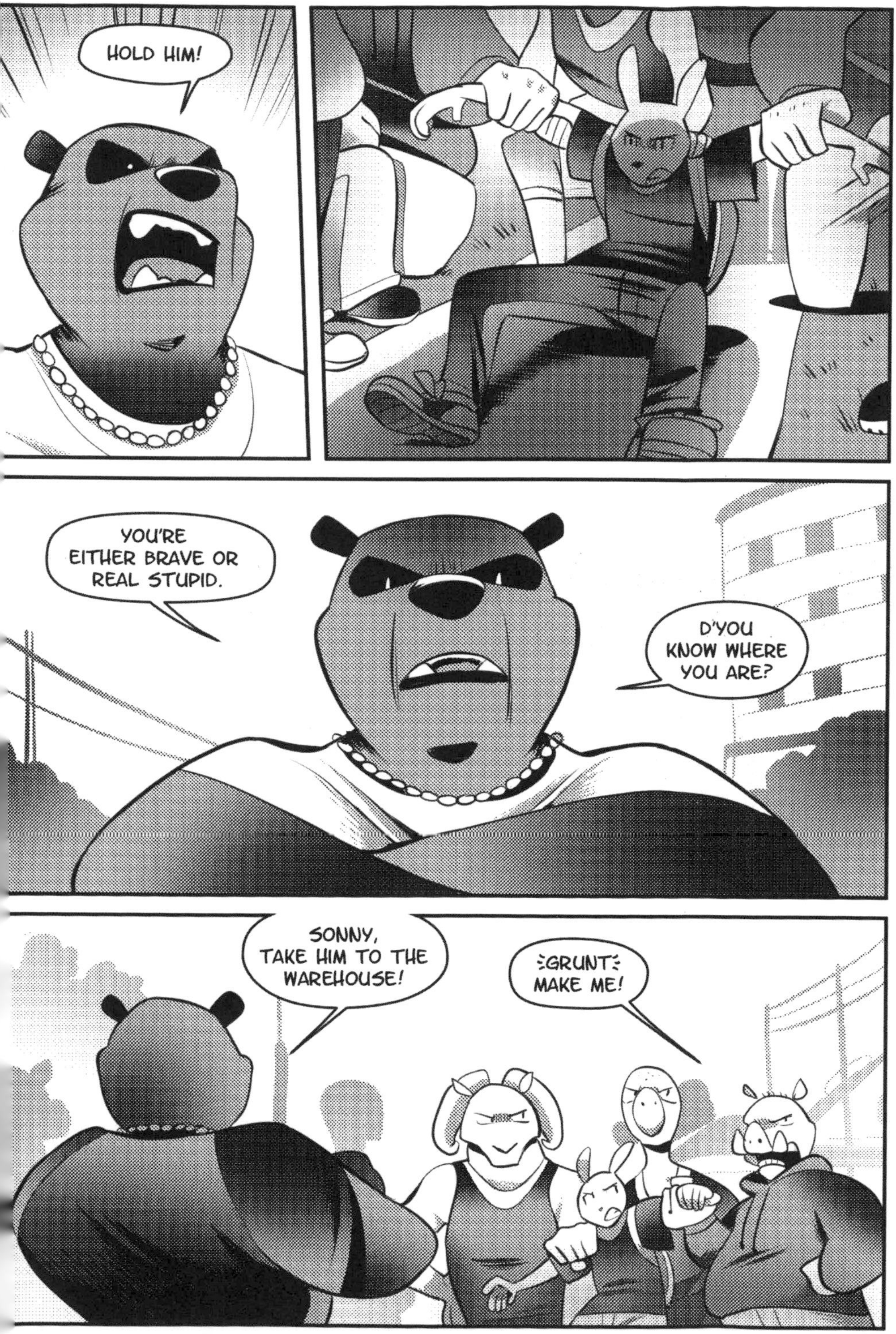
HOLD HIM!
YOU'RE EITHER BRAVE OR REAL STUPID.
D'YOU KNOW WHERE YOU ARE?
SONNY, TAKE HIM TO THE WAREHOUSE!
GRUNT MAKE ME!

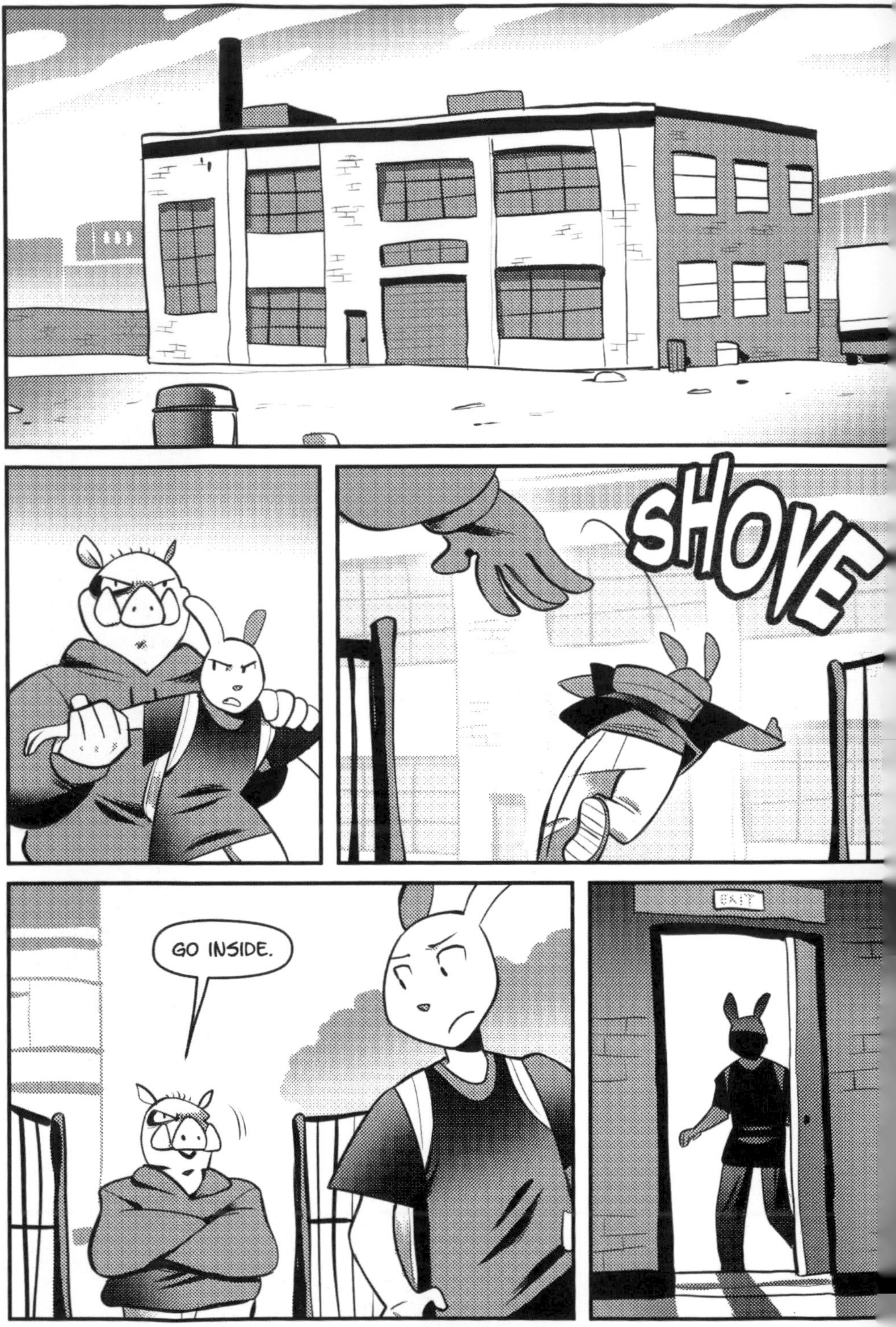
SHOVE
GO INSIDE.
EXIT

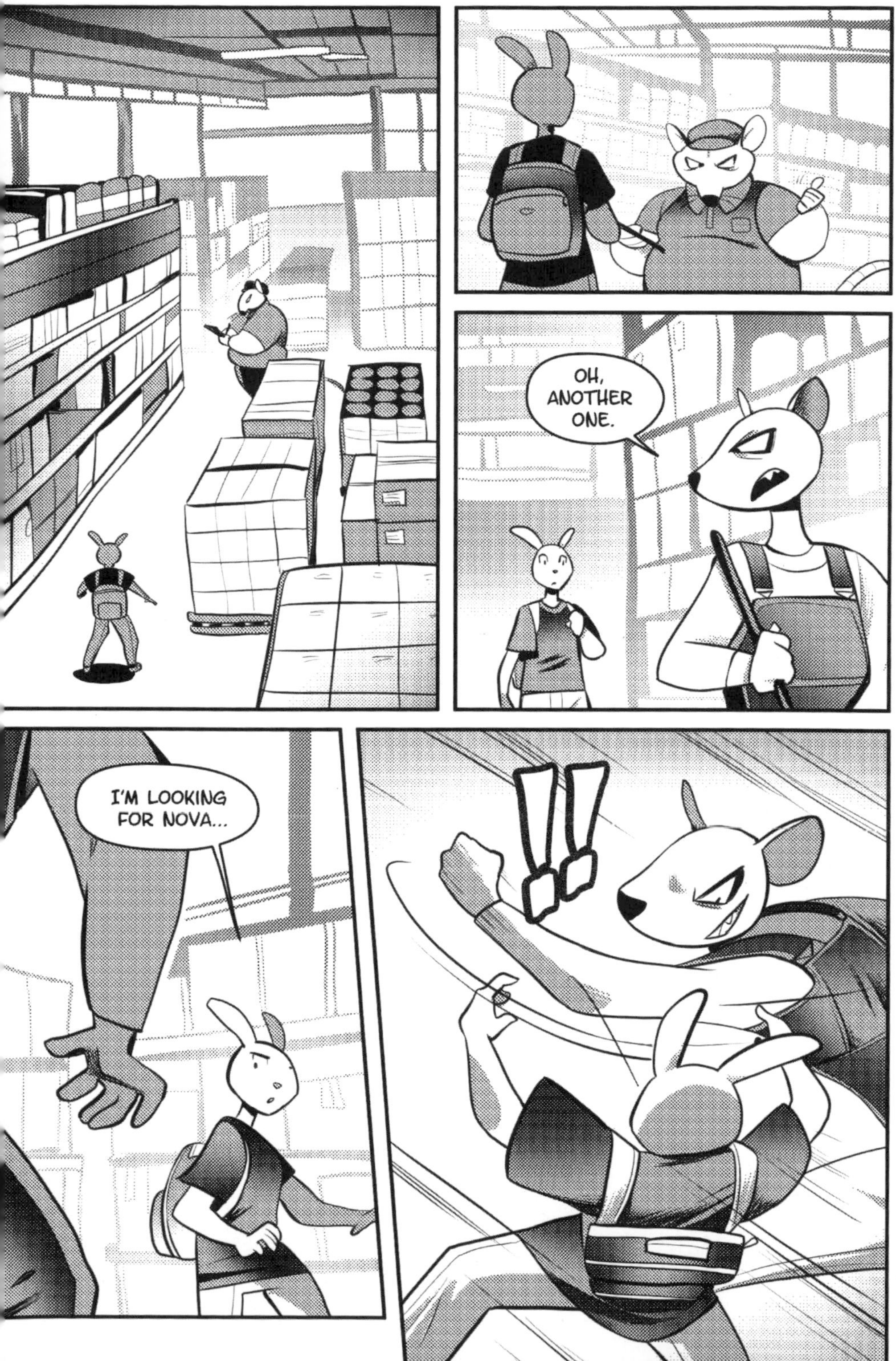
OH, ANOTHER ONE.
I'M LOOKING FOR NOVA...
!!

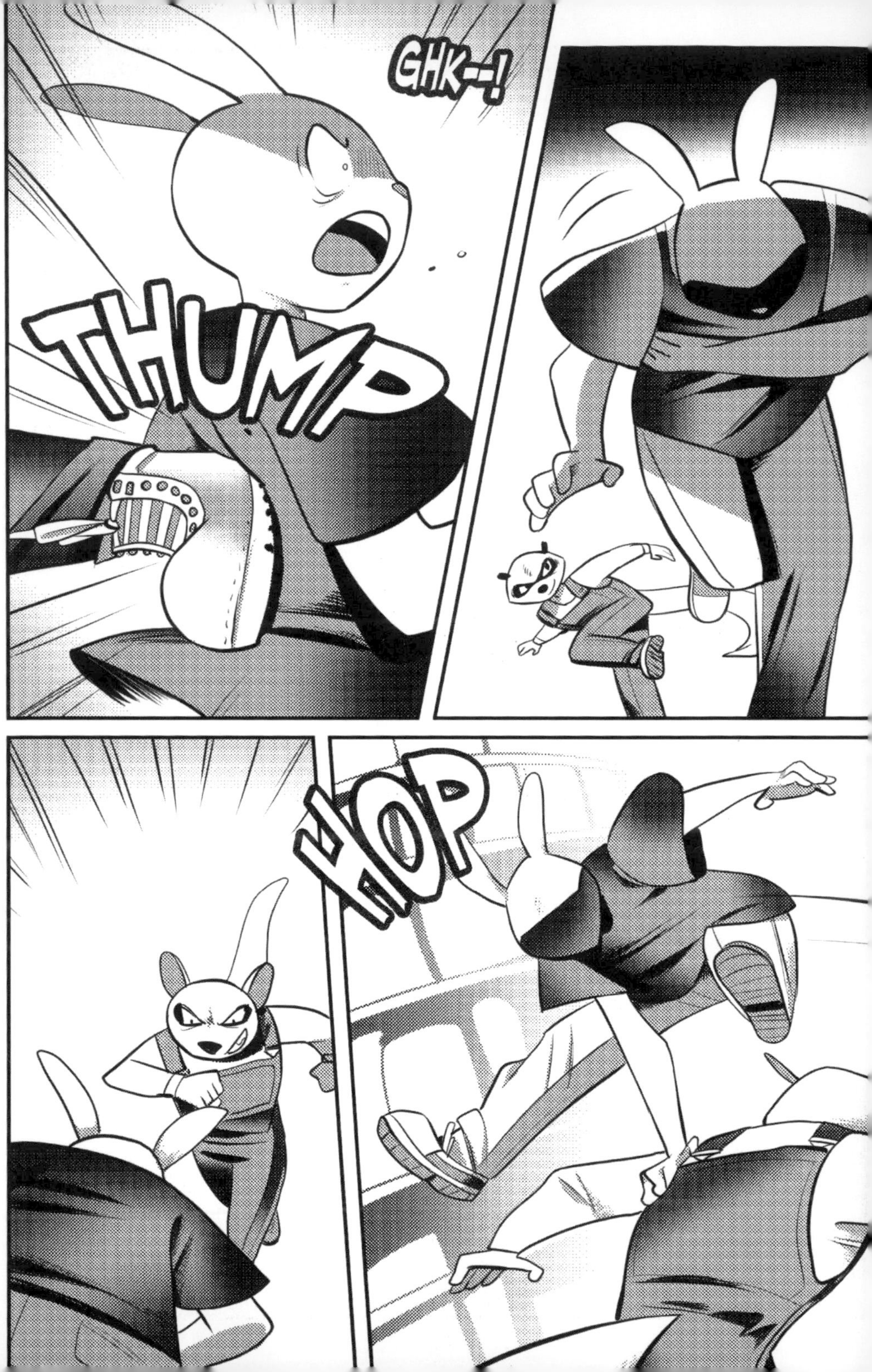

THUMP
GHK--!
HOP

CLAP

CLAP

CLAP

CRASH!

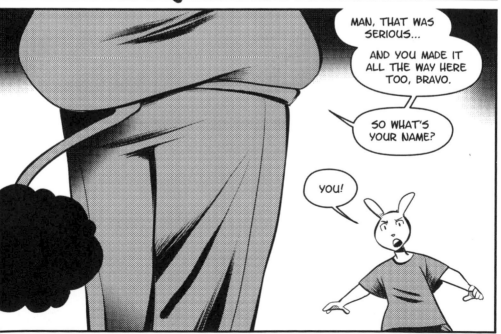

MAN, THAT WAS SERIOUS...

AND YOU MADE IT ALL THE WAY HERE TOO, BRAVO.

SO WHAT'S YOUR NAME?

YOU!

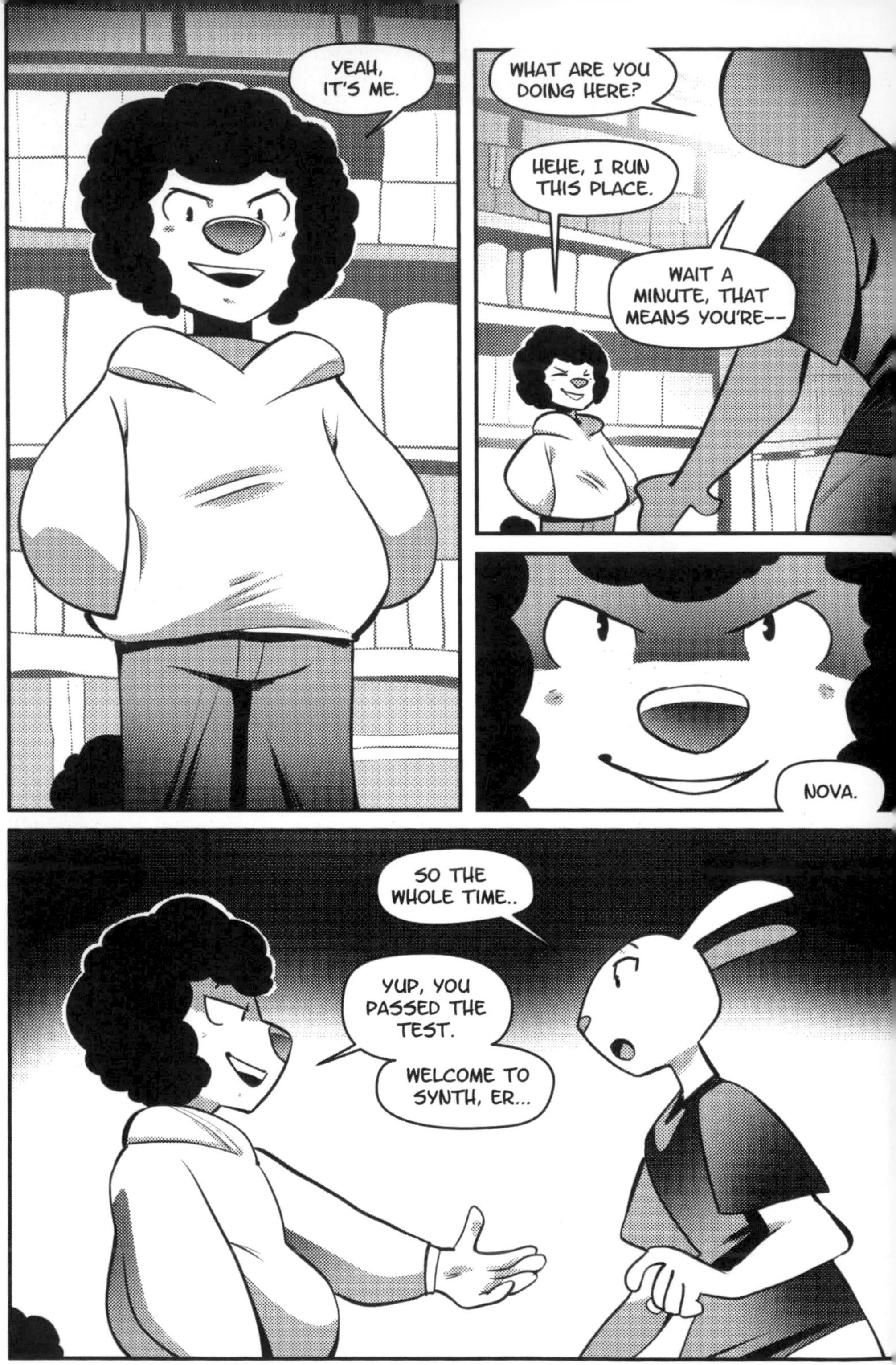
YEAH, IT'S ME.
WHAT ARE YOU DOING HERE?
HEHE, I RUN THIS PLACE.
WAIT A MINUTE, THAT MEANS YOU'RE--
NOVA.
SO THE WHOLE TIME..
YUP, YOU PASSED THE TEST.
WELCOME TO SYNTH, ER...

BLAKE, BLAKE SMITHE.

YOU'RE SERIOUS...

WE'RE GONNA CALL YOU *BLAKE SERIOUS*.

YEAH, KINDA CATCHY...

SO YOU WERE TESTING ME?

OLD MAN JIN SAID YOU WERE COMING.

SO?

C'MON, YOU GOTTA TEST PEOPLE RIGHT?

I WAS ALMOST KILLED!

PLEASE! THIS AIN'T CRIMSON.

CAN YOU COME TO SERVETON?

YEAH I GUESS.

HOW 'BOUT TOMORROW?

I NEED TO SEE THAT OLD CODGER ANYWAY.

45

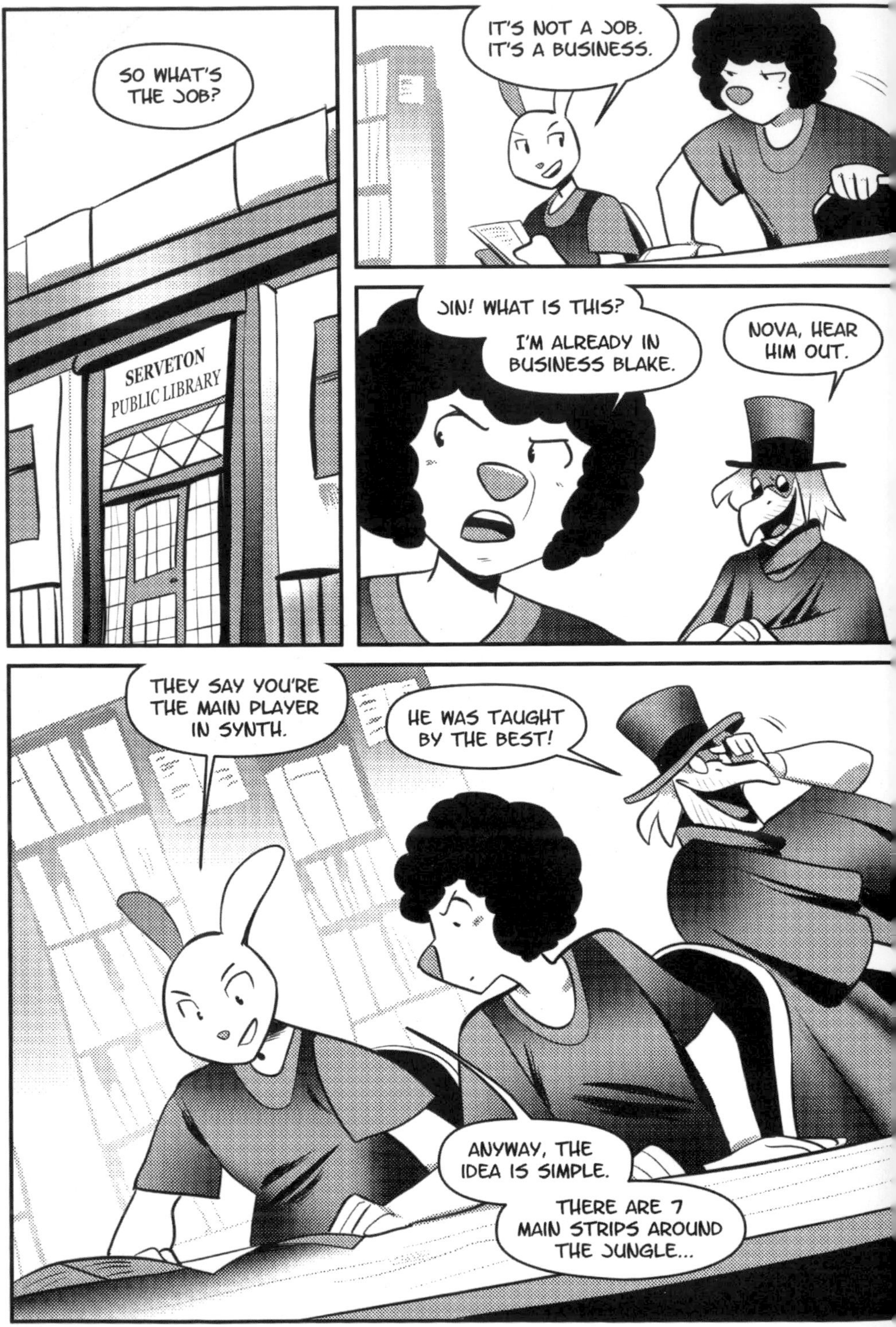
SO WHAT'S THE JOB?
SERVETON PUBLIC LIBRARY
IT'S NOT A JOB. IT'S A BUSINESS.
JIN! WHAT IS THIS?
I'M ALREADY IN BUSINESS BLAKE.
NOVA, HEAR HIM OUT.
THEY SAY YOU'RE THE MAIN PLAYER IN SYNTH.
HE WAS TAUGHT BY THE BEST!
ANYWAY, THE IDEA IS SIMPLE.
THERE ARE 7 MAIN STRIPS AROUND THE JUNGLE...

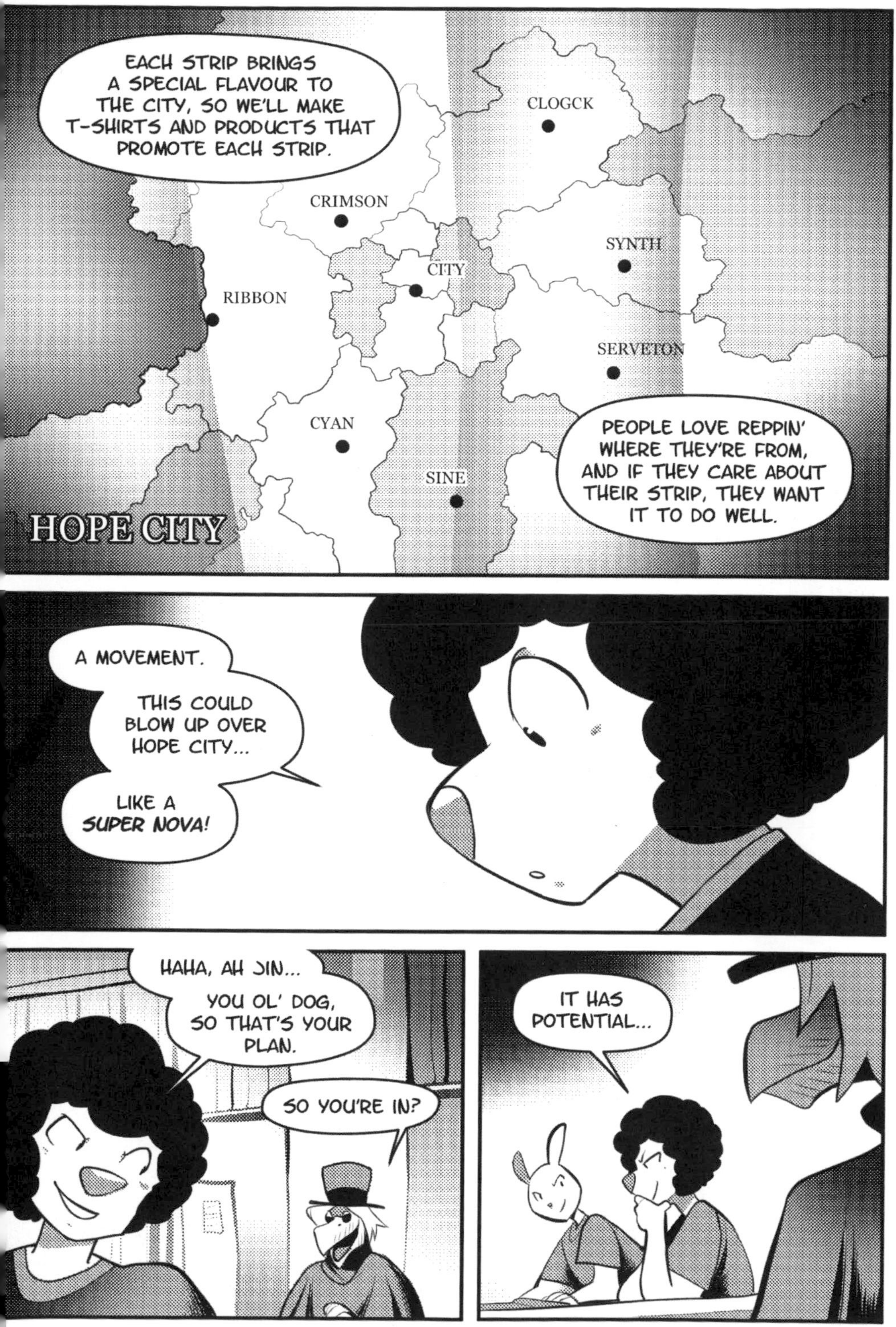
EACH STRIP BRINGS A SPECIAL FLAVOUR TO THE CITY, SO WE'LL MAKE T-SHIRTS AND PRODUCTS THAT PROMOTE EACH STRIP.
CLOGCK
CRIMSON
SYNTH
CITY
RIBBON
SERVETON
CYAN
SINE
HOPE CITY
PEOPLE LOVE REPPIN' WHERE THEY'RE FROM, AND IF THEY CARE ABOUT THEIR STRIP, THEY WANT IT TO DO WELL.
A MOVEMENT.
THIS COULD BLOW UP OVER HOPE CITY...
LIKE A *SUPER NOVA!*
HAHA, AH JIN...
YOU OL' DOG, SO THAT'S YOUR PLAN.
SO YOU'RE IN?
IT HAS POTENTIAL...

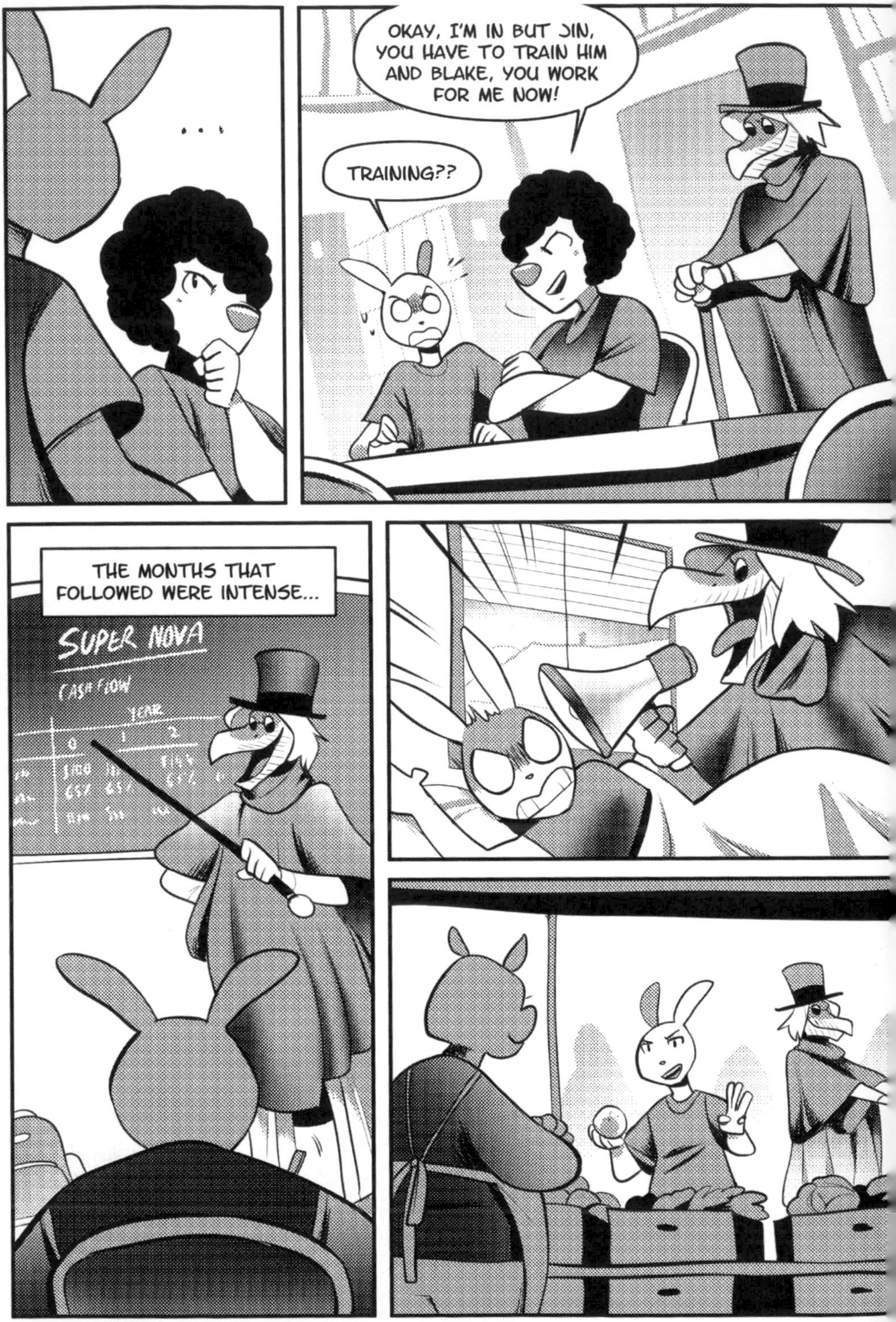
...
OKAY, I'M IN BUT JIN, YOU HAVE TO TRAIN HIM AND BLAKE, YOU WORK FOR ME NOW!
TRAINING??
THE MONTHS THAT FOLLOWED WERE INTENSE...
SUPER NOVA
CASH FLOW
YEAR
0
1
2

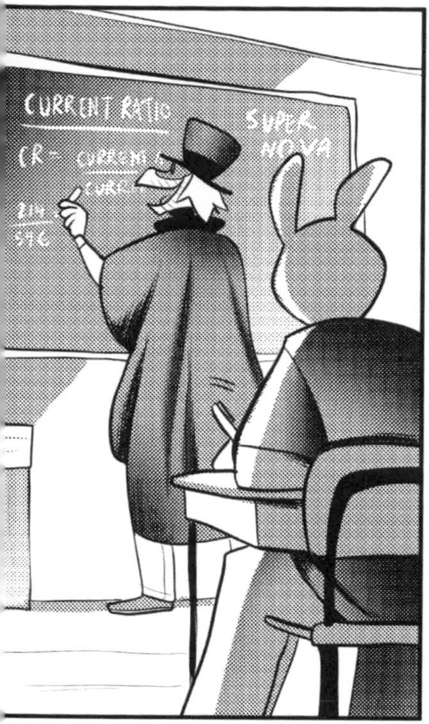
CURRENT RATIO
SUPER NOVA

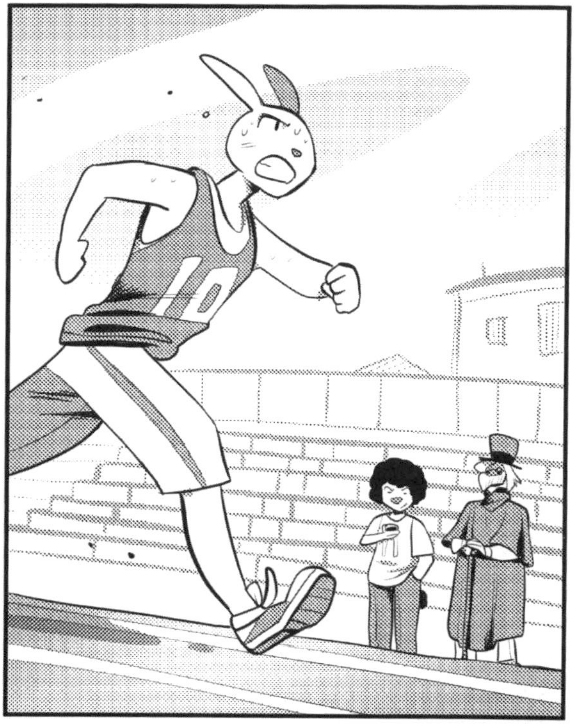

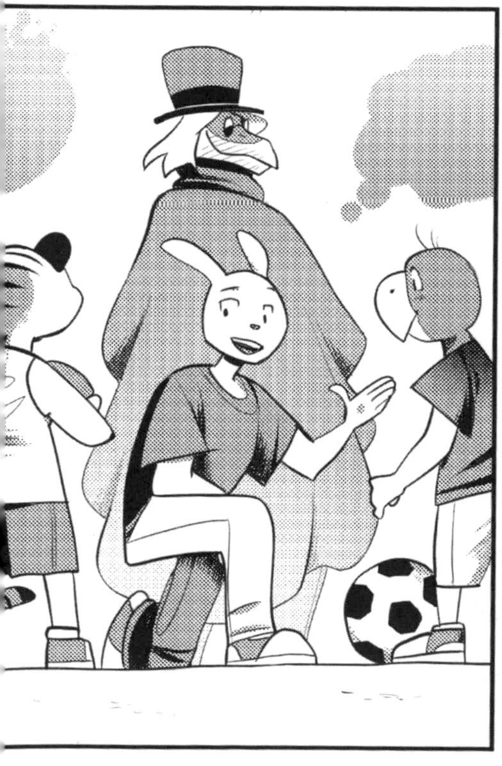

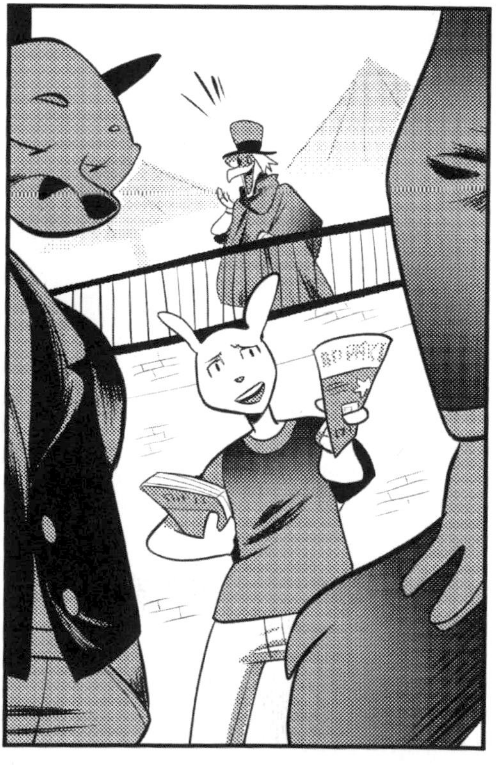

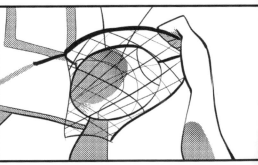

...BUT WORTH IT.

FIVE YEARS LATER

SERIOUS.

W'SUP?

SUPER NOVA IS FIVE YEARS OLD TODAY.

ARE YOU YOUNG MEN GOING TO EAT UP?

WOW, TIME FLIES...

SURE THING MAMA S.

... WHAT IS IT?

THE JUNGLE...

LET'S GO FOR IT.

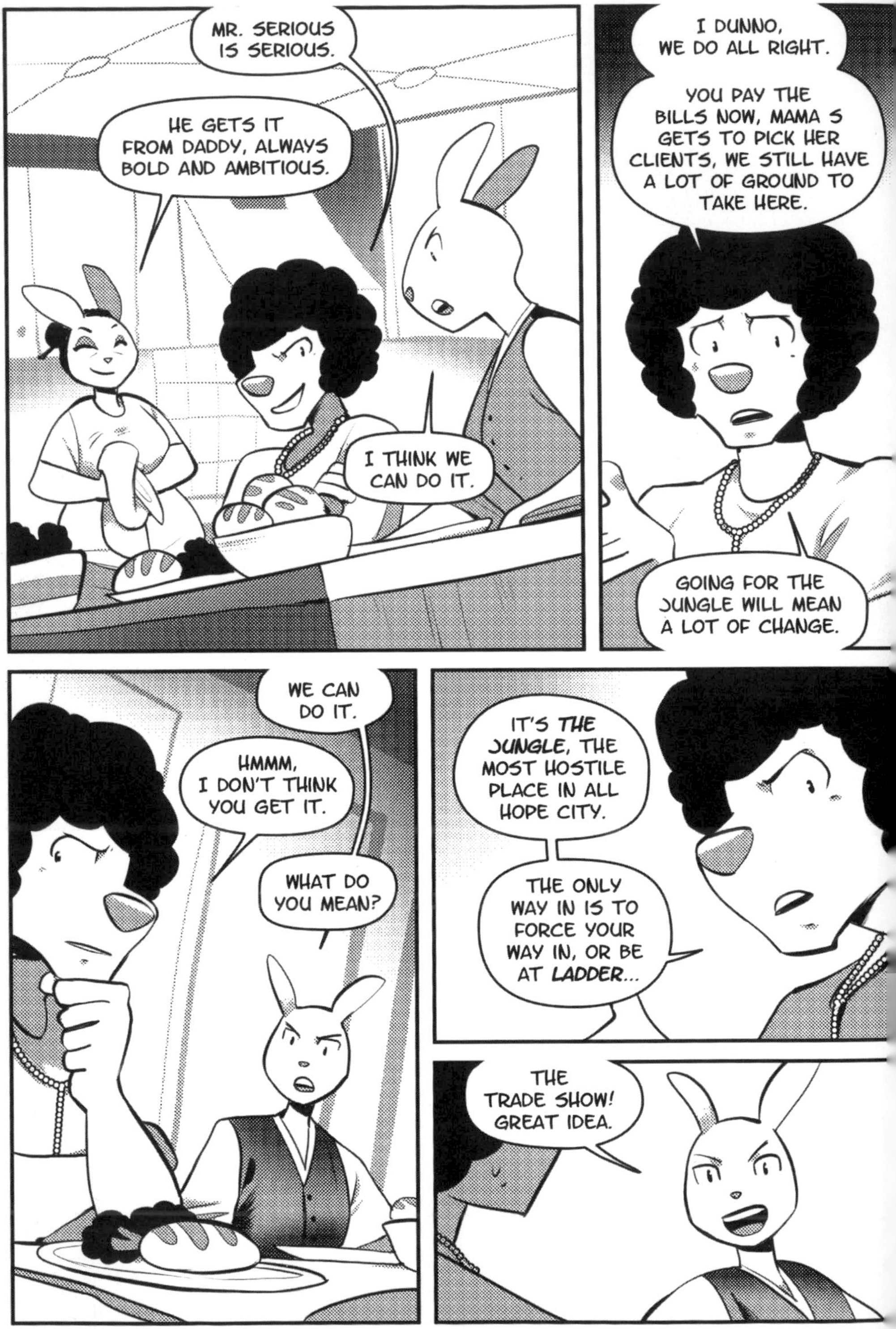
MR. SERIOUS IS SERIOUS.
HE GETS IT FROM DADDY, ALWAYS BOLD AND AMBITIOUS.
I THINK WE CAN DO IT.
I DUNNO, WE DO ALL RIGHT.
YOU PAY THE BILLS NOW, MAMA S GETS TO PICK HER CLIENTS, WE STILL HAVE A LOT OF GROUND TO TAKE HERE.
GOING FOR THE JUNGLE WILL MEAN A LOT OF CHANGE.
WE CAN DO IT.
HMMM, I DON'T THINK YOU GET IT.
WHAT DO YOU MEAN?
IT'S *THE JUNGLE*, THE MOST HOSTILE PLACE IN ALL HOPE CITY.
THE ONLY WAY IN IS TO FORCE YOUR WAY IN, OR BE AT *LADDER*...
THE TRADE SHOW! GREAT IDEA.

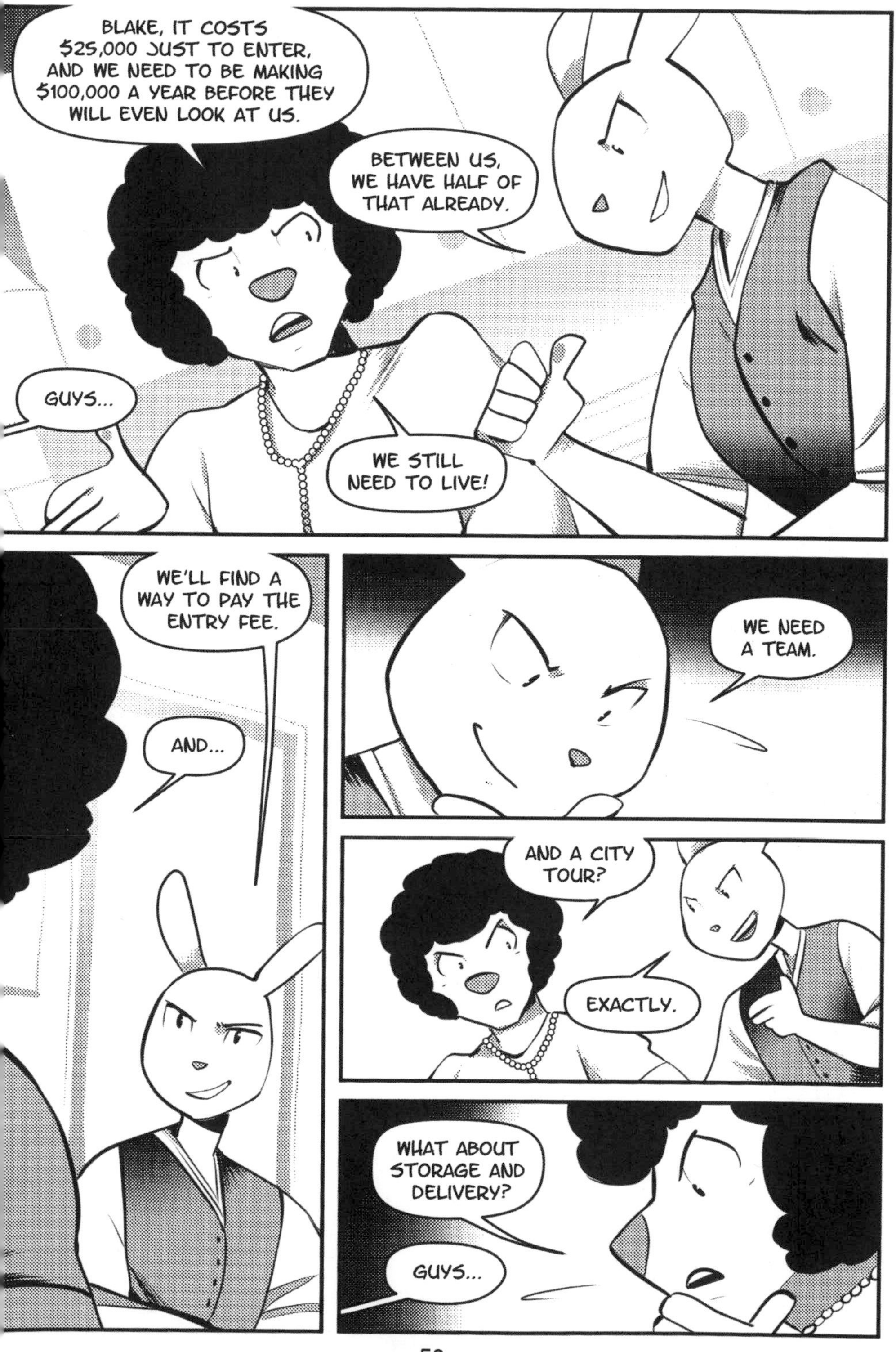
BLAKE, IT COSTS $25,000 JUST TO ENTER, AND WE NEED TO BE MAKING $100,000 A YEAR BEFORE THEY WILL EVEN LOOK AT US.
BETWEEN US, WE HAVE HALF OF THAT ALREADY.
GUYS...
WE STILL NEED TO LIVE!
WE'LL FIND A WAY TO PAY THE ENTRY FEE.
AND...
WE NEED A TEAM.
AND A CITY TOUR?
EXACTLY.
WHAT ABOUT STORAGE AND DELIVERY?
GUYS...

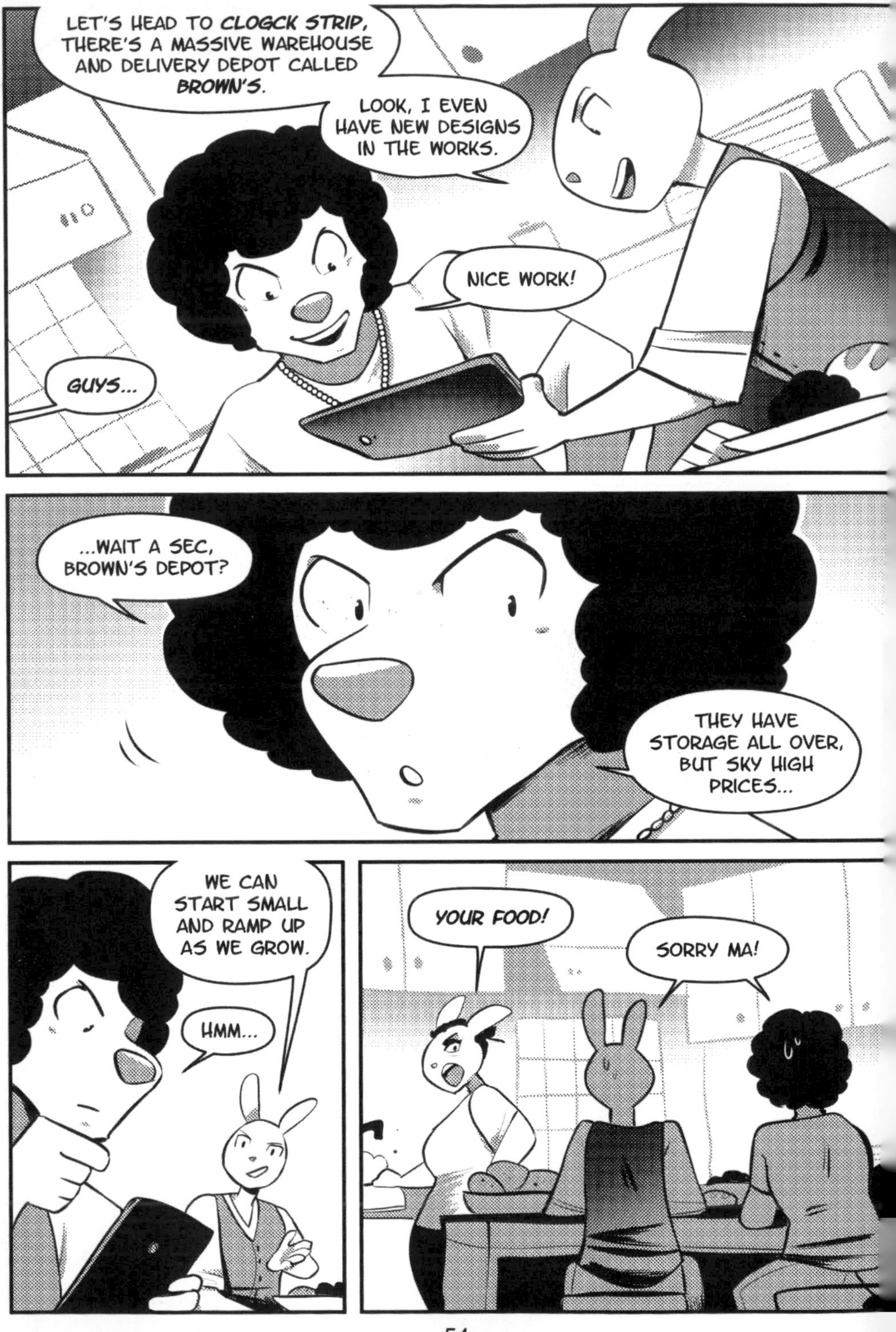
LET'S HEAD TO CLOGCK STRIP, THERE'S A MASSIVE WAREHOUSE AND DELIVERY DEPOT CALLED BROWN'S.
LOOK, I EVEN HAVE NEW DESIGNS IN THE WORKS.
NICE WORK!
GUYS...
...WAIT A SEC, BROWN'S DEPOT?
THEY HAVE STORAGE ALL OVER, BUT SKY HIGH PRICES...
WE CAN START SMALL AND RAMP UP AS WE GROW.
HMM...
YOUR FOOD!
SORRY MA!

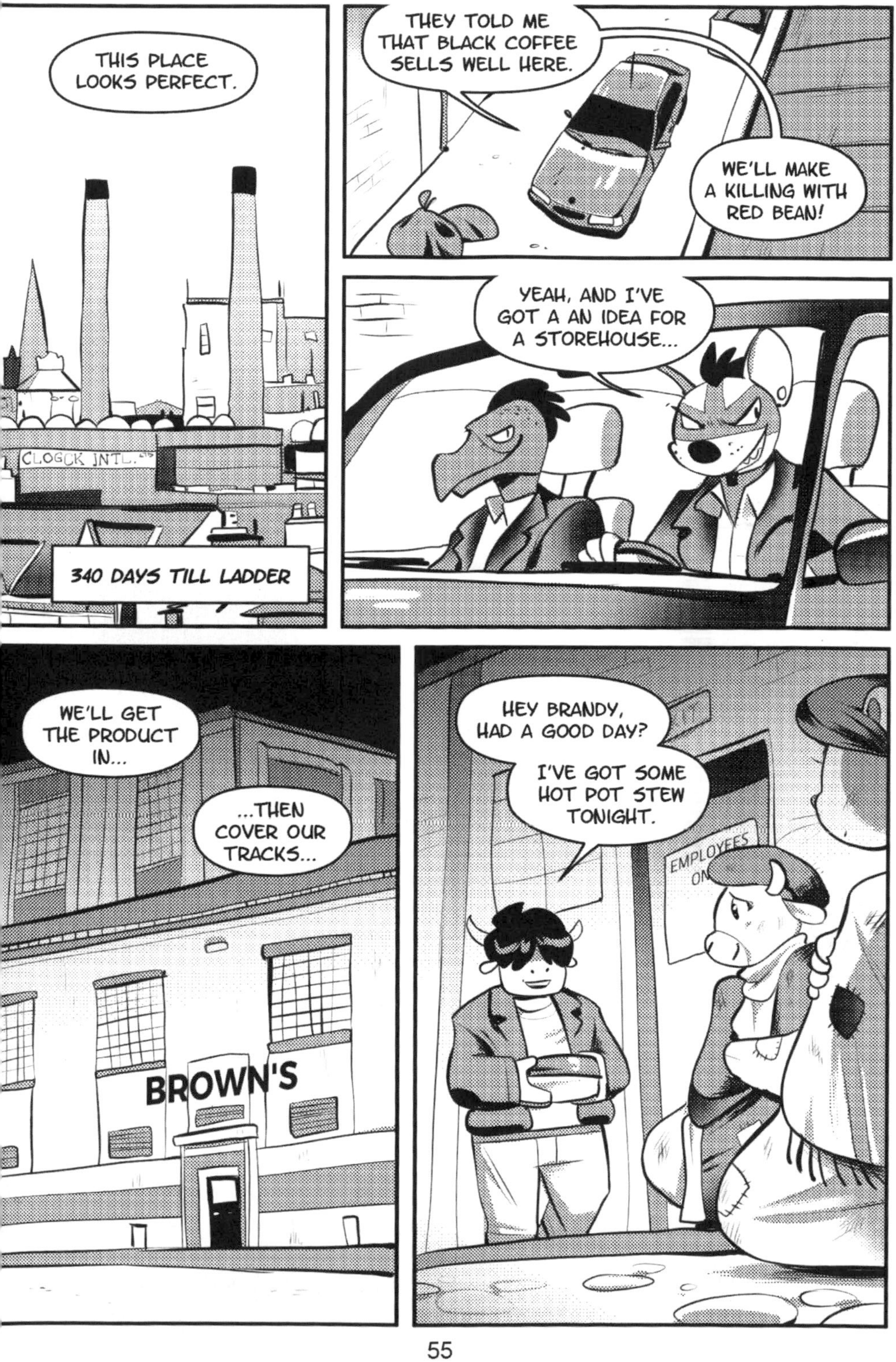
THIS PLACE LOOKS PERFECT.
CLOGCK INTL.
340 DAYS TILL LADDER
THEY TOLD ME THAT BLACK COFFEE SELLS WELL HERE.
WE'LL MAKE A KILLING WITH RED BEAN!
YEAH, AND I'VE GOT A AN IDEA FOR A STOREHOUSE...
WE'LL GET THE PRODUCT IN...
...THEN COVER OUR TRACKS...
BROWN'S
HEY BRANDY, HAD A GOOD DAY?
I'VE GOT SOME HOT POT STEW TONIGHT.

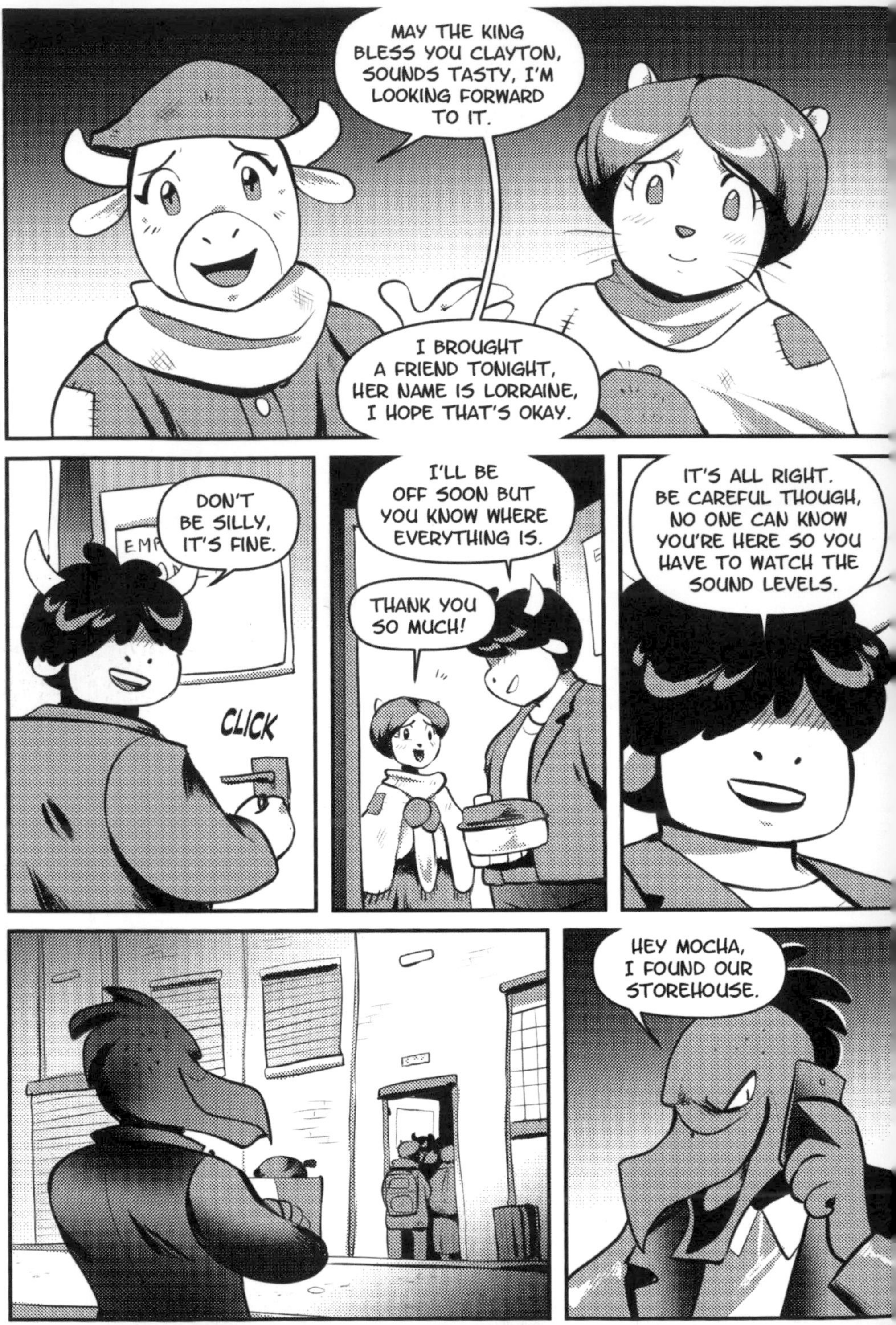
MAY THE KING BLESS YOU CLAYTON, SOUNDS TASTY, I'M LOOKING FORWARD TO IT.
I BROUGHT A FRIEND TONIGHT, HER NAME IS LORRAINE, I HOPE THAT'S OKAY.
DON'T BE SILLY, IT'S FINE.
CLICK
I'LL BE OFF SOON BUT YOU KNOW WHERE EVERYTHING IS.
THANK YOU SO MUCH!
IT'S ALL RIGHT. BE CAREFUL THOUGH, NO ONE CAN KNOW YOU'RE HERE SO YOU HAVE TO WATCH THE SOUND LEVELS.
HEY MOCHA, I FOUND OUR STOREHOUSE.

WE MOVE IT
TOMORROW...

WHERE
DO YOU THINK
YOU'RE GOING?

PLEASE,
I DON'T HAVE
ANYTHING!

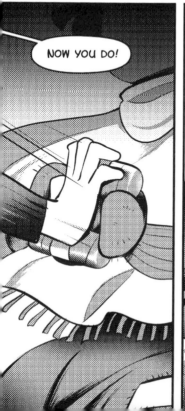

NOW YOU DO!

TAKE THESE BEANS TO THE
WAREHOUSE. WHEN YOU'RE DONE
COME BACK FOR THE REST.

MY BUDDY IS WATCHING,
IF YOU TRY ANYTHING FUNNY,
WE'LL DECAFFEINATE YOU!

GULP!

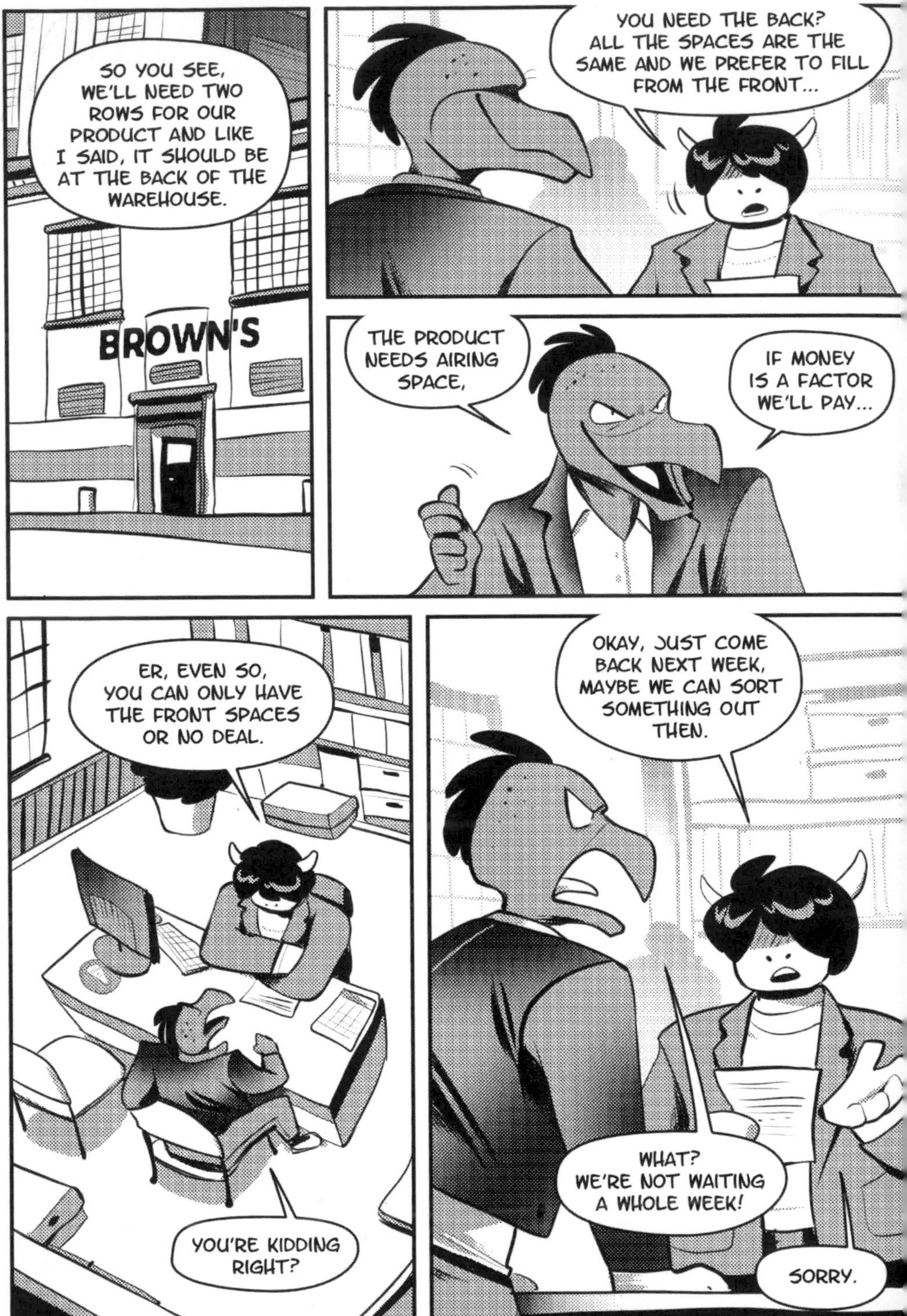
SO YOU SEE, WE'LL NEED TWO ROWS FOR OUR PRODUCT AND LIKE I SAID, IT SHOULD BE AT THE BACK OF THE WAREHOUSE.
BROWN'S
YOU NEED THE BACK? ALL THE SPACES ARE THE SAME AND WE PREFER TO FILL FROM THE FRONT...
THE PRODUCT NEEDS AIRING SPACE,
IF MONEY IS A FACTOR WE'LL PAY...
ER, EVEN SO, YOU CAN ONLY HAVE THE FRONT SPACES OR NO DEAL.
YOU'RE KIDDING RIGHT?
OKAY, JUST COME BACK NEXT WEEK, MAYBE WE CAN SORT SOMETHING OUT THEN.
WHAT? WE'RE NOT WAITING A WHOLE WEEK!
SORRY.

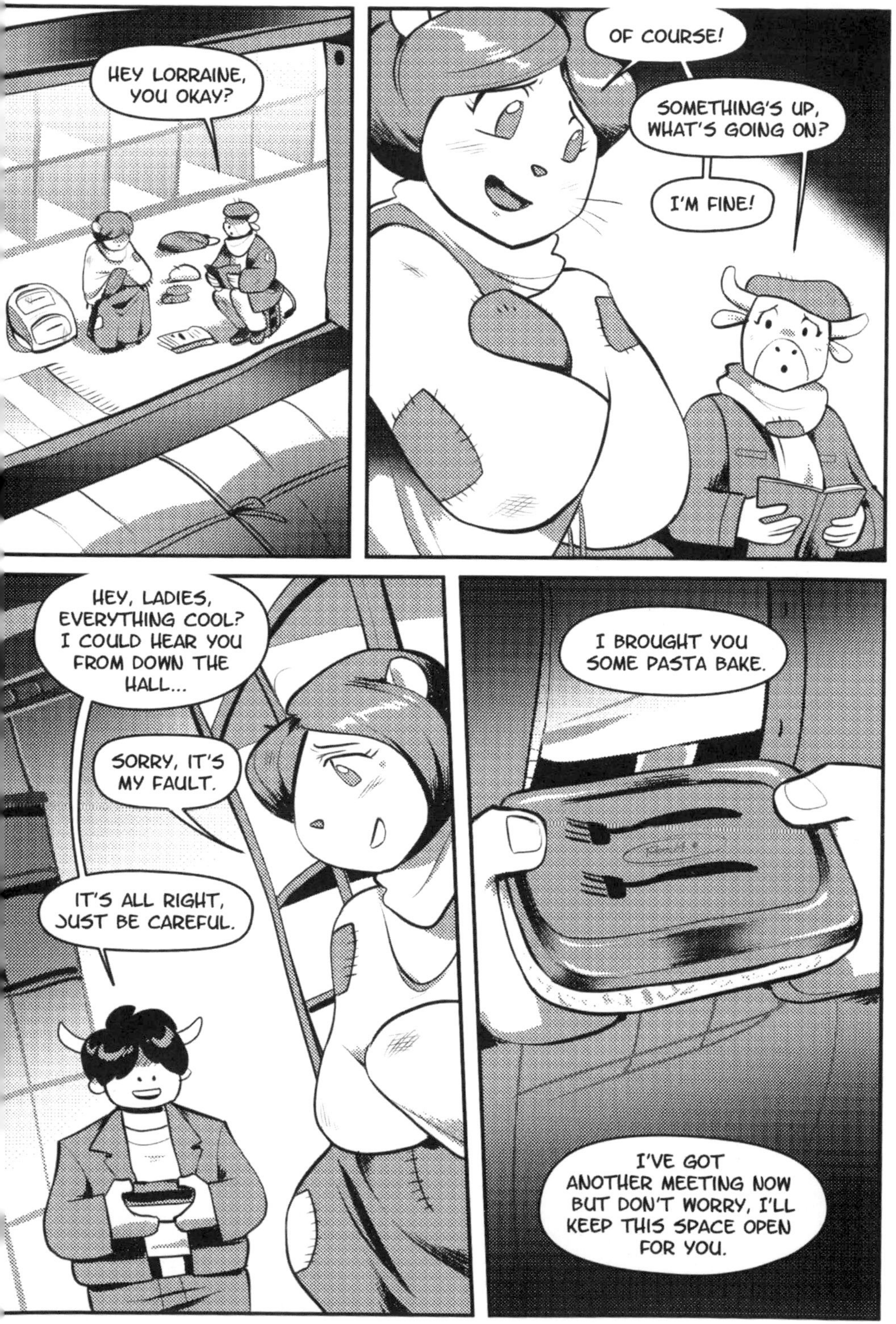
HEY LORRAINE, YOU OKAY?
OF COURSE!
SOMETHING'S UP, WHAT'S GOING ON?
I'M FINE!
HEY, LADIES, EVERYTHING COOL? I COULD HEAR YOU FROM DOWN THE HALL...
SORRY, IT'S MY FAULT.
IT'S ALL RIGHT, JUST BE CAREFUL.
I BROUGHT YOU SOME PASTA BAKE.
I'VE GOT ANOTHER MEETING NOW BUT DON'T WORRY, I'LL KEEP THIS SPACE OPEN FOR YOU.

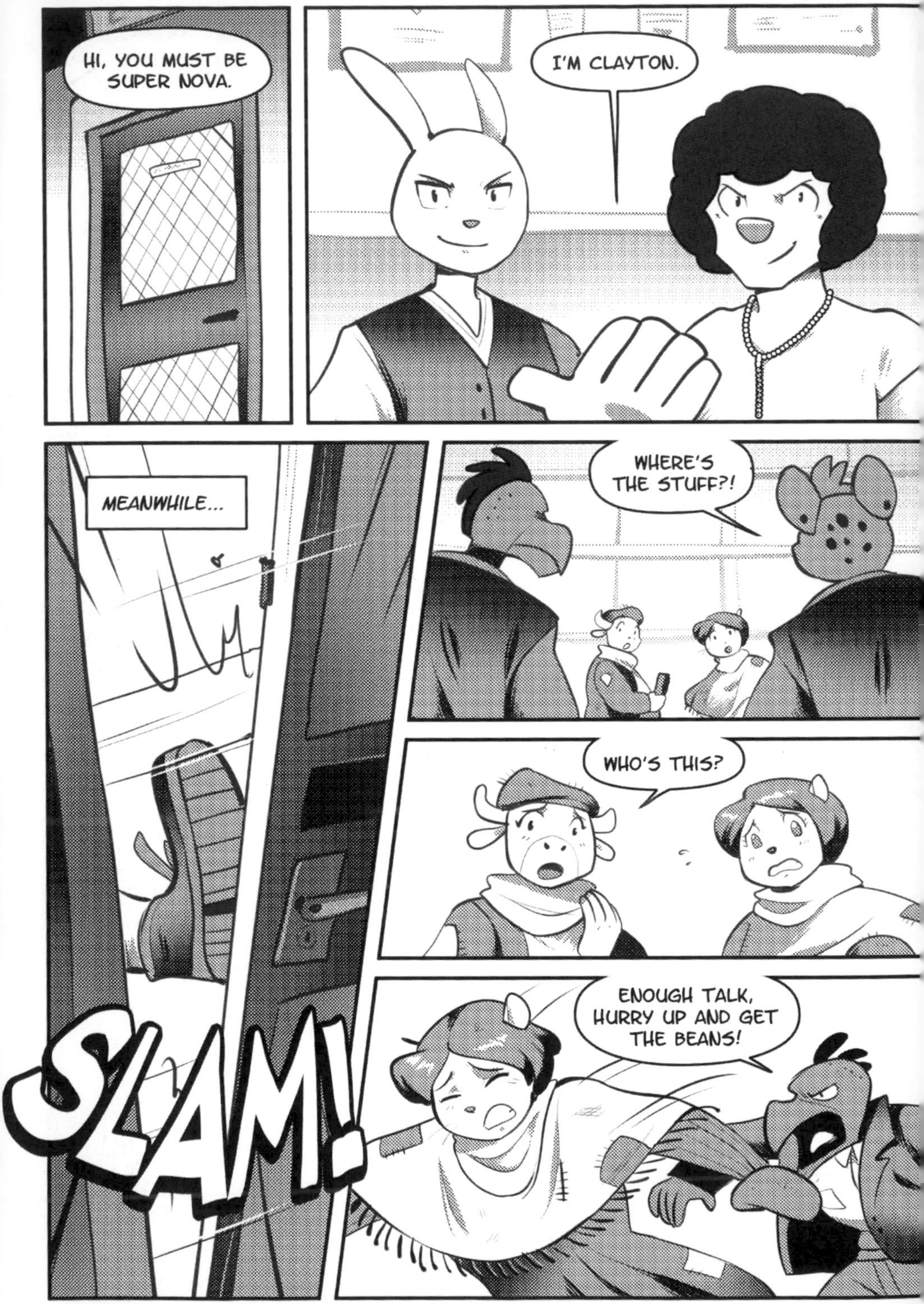
HI, YOU MUST BE SUPER NOVA.
I'M CLAYTON.
MEANWHILE...
WHERE'S THE STUFF?!
WHO'S THIS?
SLAM!
ENOUGH TALK, HURRY UP AND GET THE BEANS!

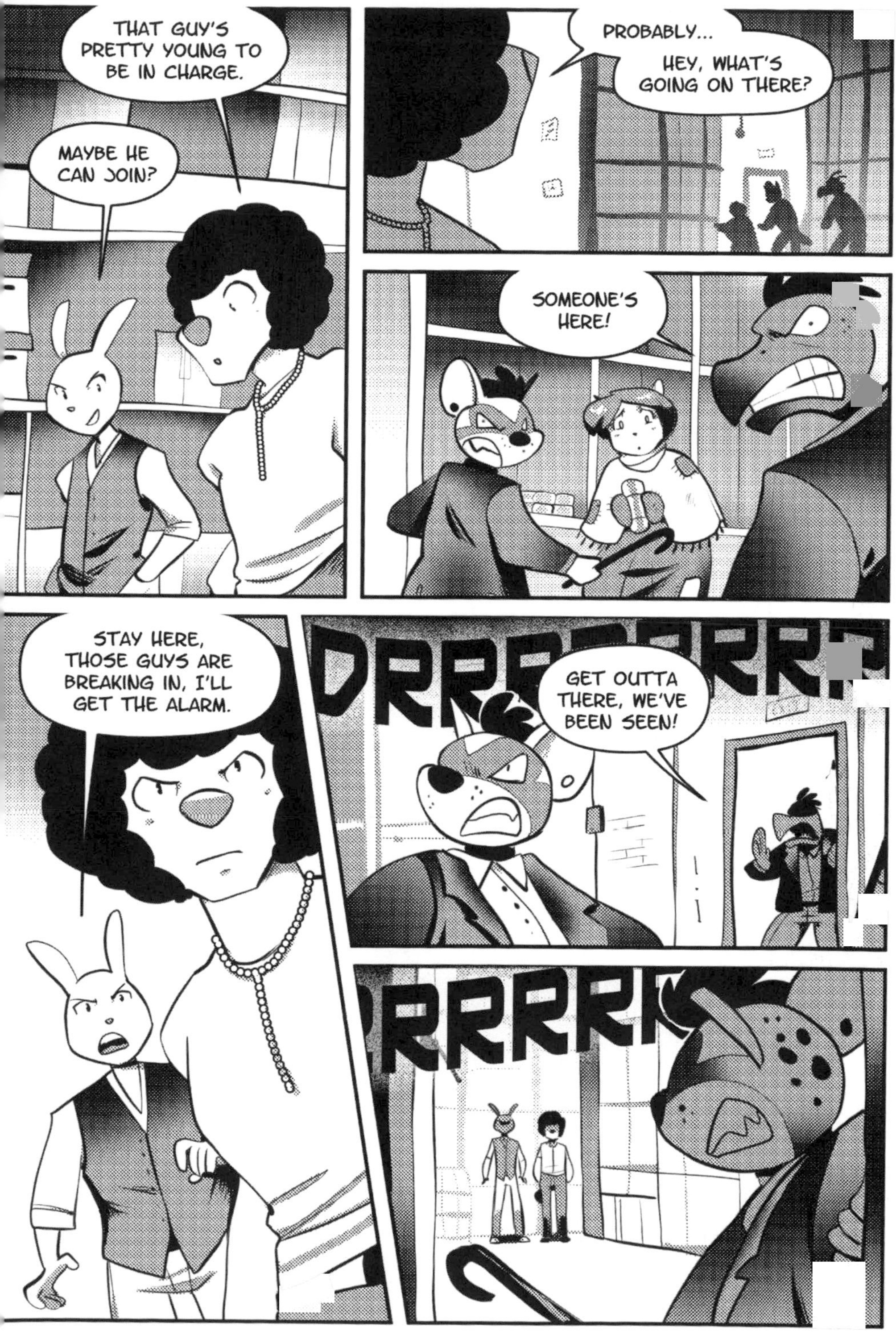
THAT GUY'S PRETTY YOUNG TO BE IN CHARGE.
MAYBE HE CAN JOIN?
PROBABLY...
HEY, WHAT'S GOING ON THERE?
SOMEONE'S HERE!
STAY HERE, THOSE GUYS ARE BREAKING IN, I'LL GET THE ALARM.
DRRRRRRRRR
GET OUTTA THERE, WE'VE BEEN SEEN!
RRRRRR

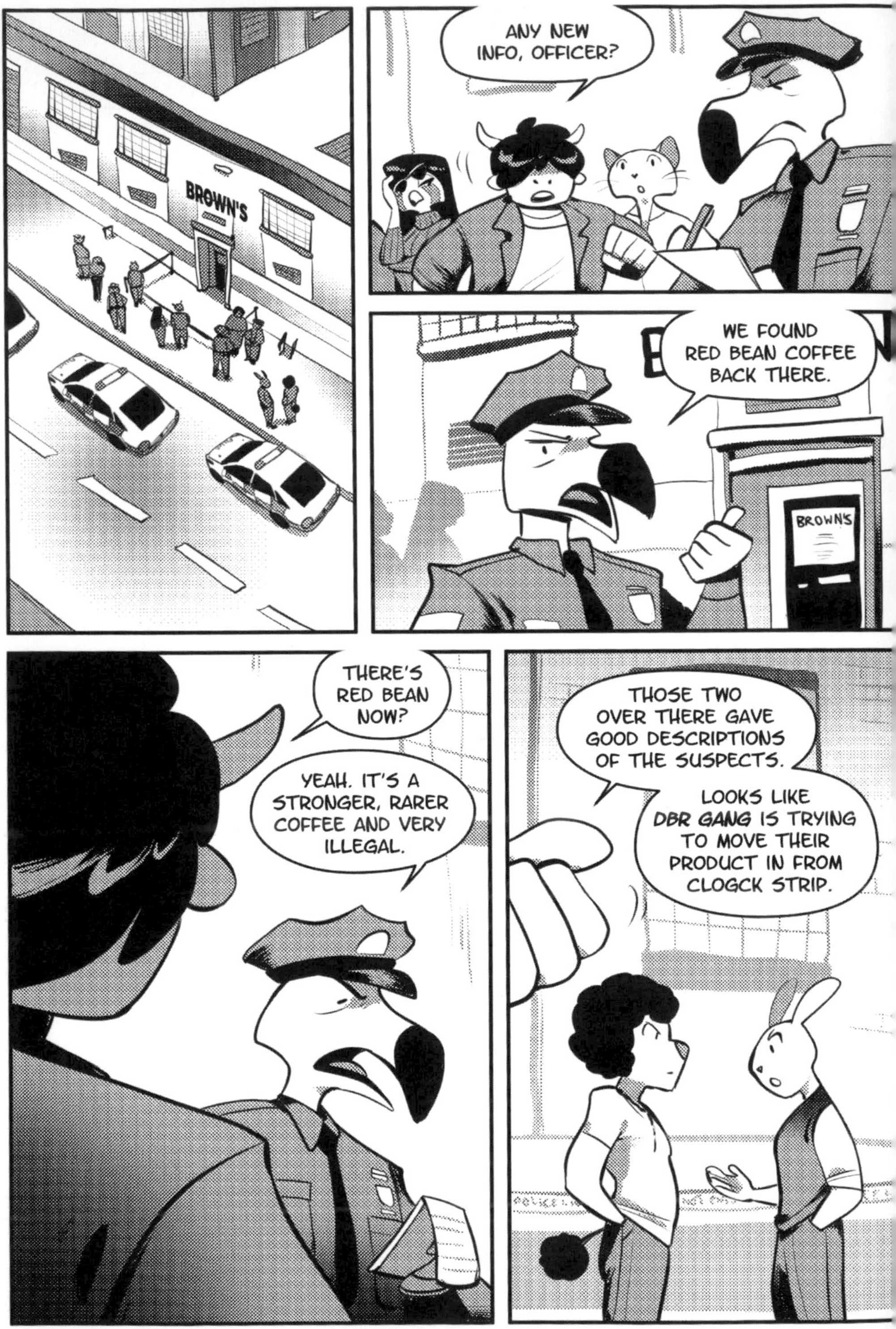
BROWN'S
ANY NEW INFO, OFFICER?
WE FOUND RED BEAN COFFEE BACK THERE.
BROWN'S
THERE'S RED BEAN NOW?
YEAH. IT'S A STRONGER, RARER COFFEE AND VERY ILLEGAL.
THOSE TWO OVER THERE GAVE GOOD DESCRIPTIONS OF THE SUSPECTS.
LOOKS LIKE *DBR GANG* IS TRYING TO MOVE THEIR PRODUCT IN FROM CLOGCK STRIP.

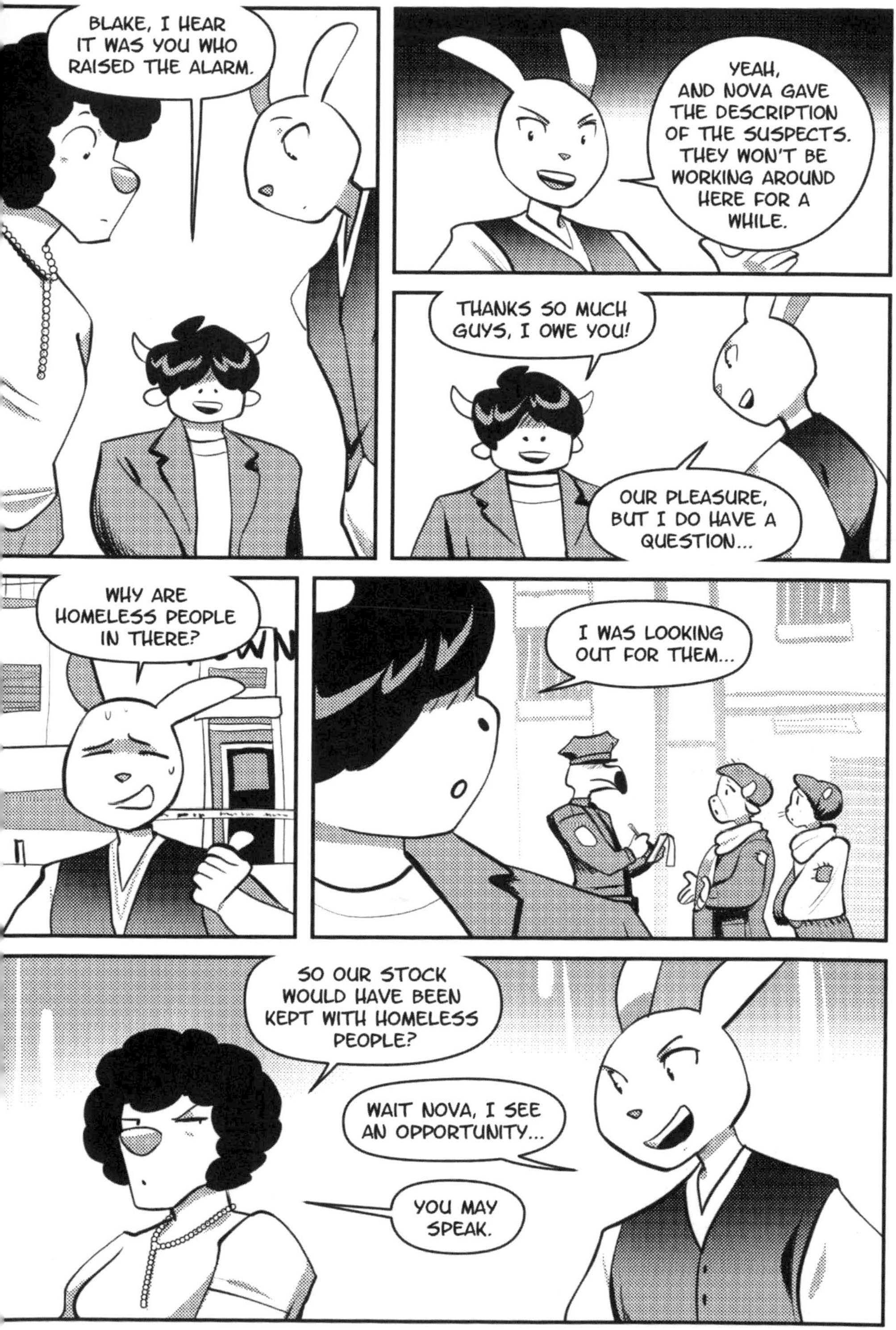
BLAKE, I HEAR IT WAS YOU WHO RAISED THE ALARM.
YEAH, AND NOVA GAVE THE DESCRIPTION OF THE SUSPECTS. THEY WON'T BE WORKING AROUND HERE FOR A WHILE.
THANKS SO MUCH GUYS, I OWE YOU!
OUR PLEASURE, BUT I DO HAVE A QUESTION...
WHY ARE HOMELESS PEOPLE IN THERE?
I WAS LOOKING OUT FOR THEM...
SO OUR STOCK WOULD HAVE BEEN KEPT WITH HOMELESS PEOPLE?
WAIT NOVA, I SEE AN OPPORTUNITY...
YOU MAY SPEAK.

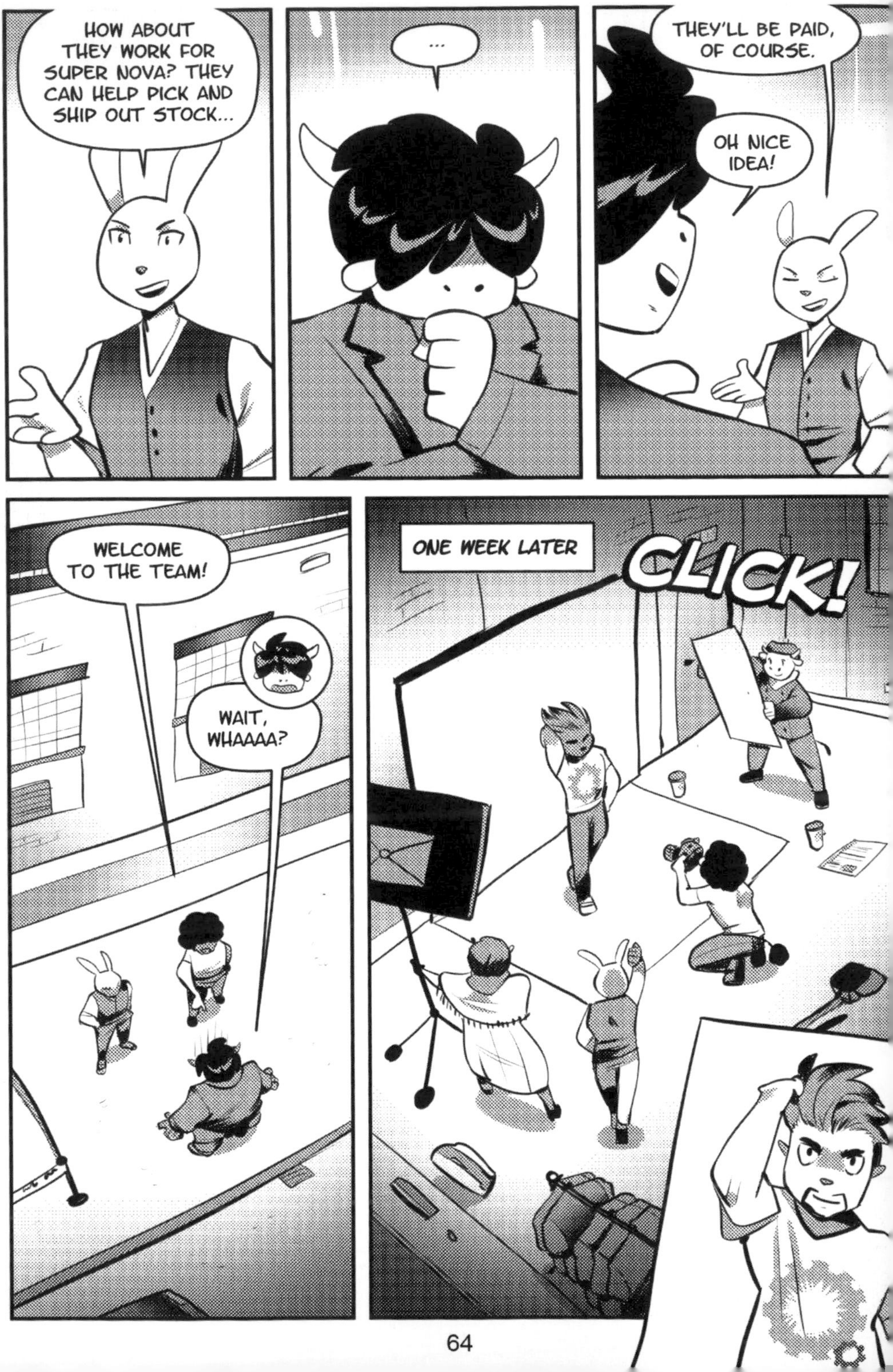
HOW ABOUT THEY WORK FOR SUPER NOVA? THEY CAN HELP PICK AND SHIP OUT STOCK...
...
THEY'LL BE PAID, OF COURSE.
OH NICE IDEA!
WELCOME TO THE TEAM!
WAIT, WHAAAA?
ONE WEEK LATER
CLICK!

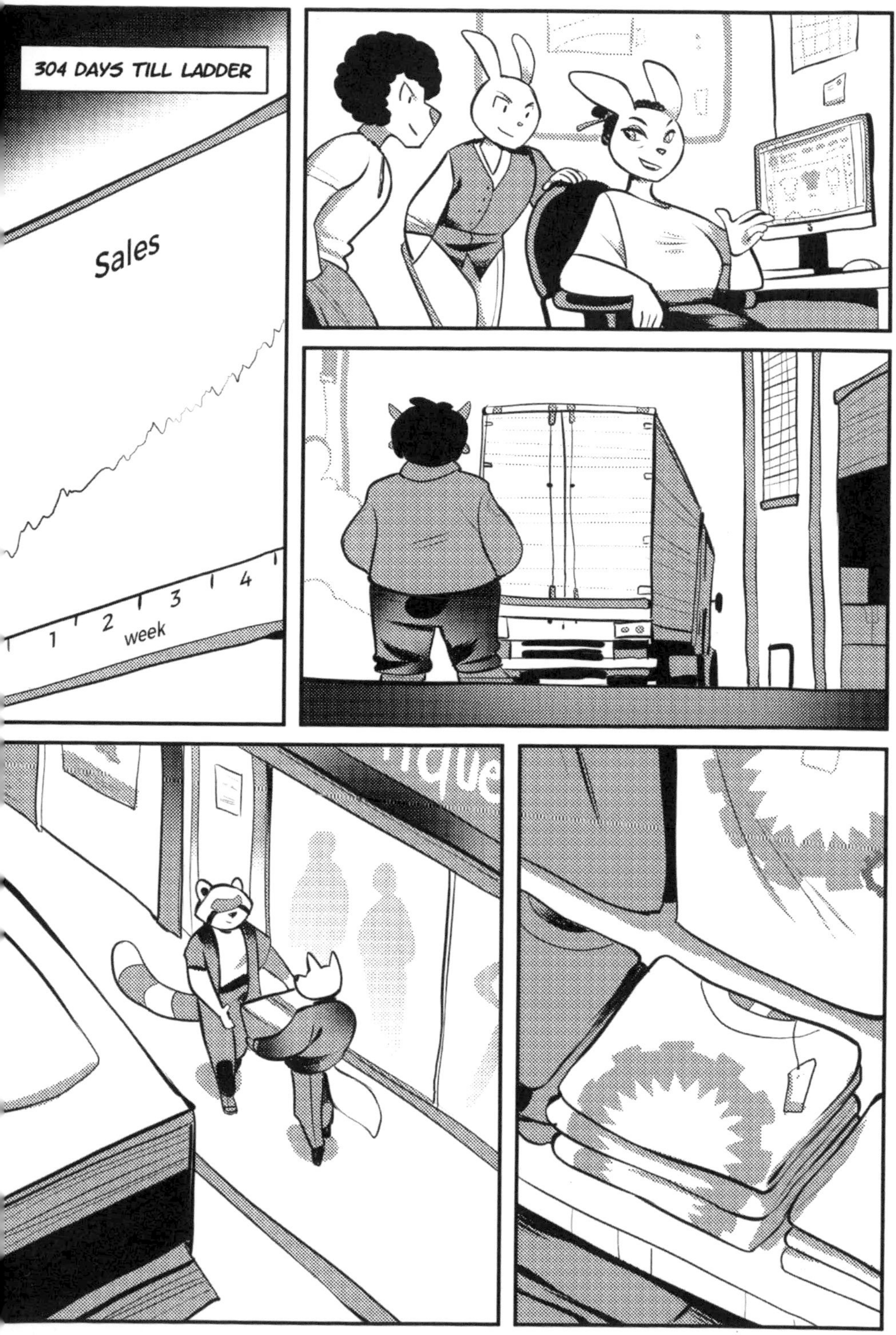
304 DAYS TILL LADDER
Sales
1
2
3
4
week

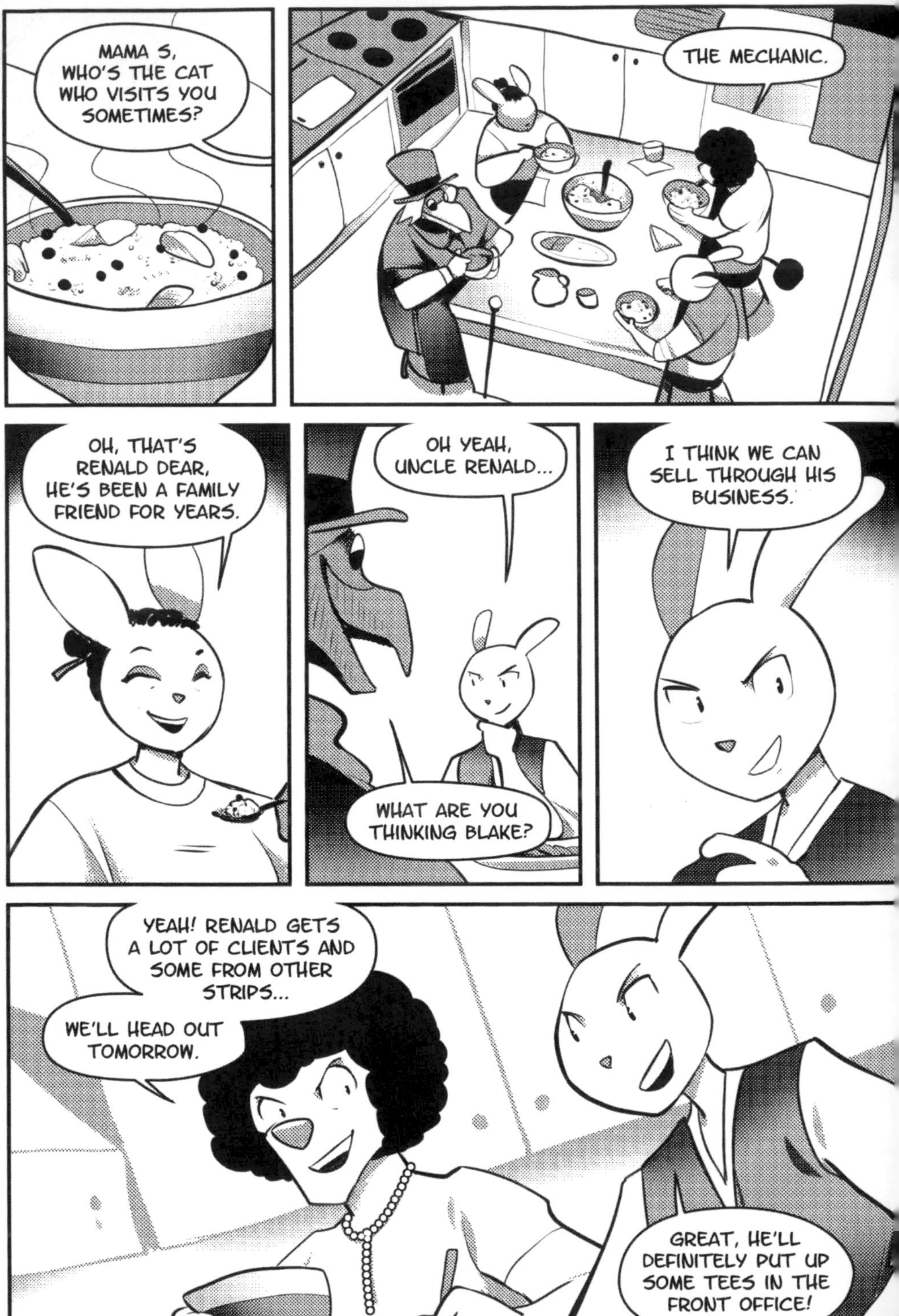
MAMA S, WHO'S THE CAT WHO VISITS YOU SOMETIMES?
THE MECHANIC.
OH, THAT'S RENALD DEAR, HE'S BEEN A FAMILY FRIEND FOR YEARS.
OH YEAH, UNCLE RENALD...
WHAT ARE YOU THINKING BLAKE?
I THINK WE CAN SELL THROUGH HIS BUSINESS.
YEAH! RENALD GETS A LOT OF CLIENTS AND SOME FROM OTHER STRIPS...
WE'LL HEAD OUT TOMORROW.
GREAT, HE'LL DEFINITELY PUT UP SOME TEES IN THE FRONT OFFICE!

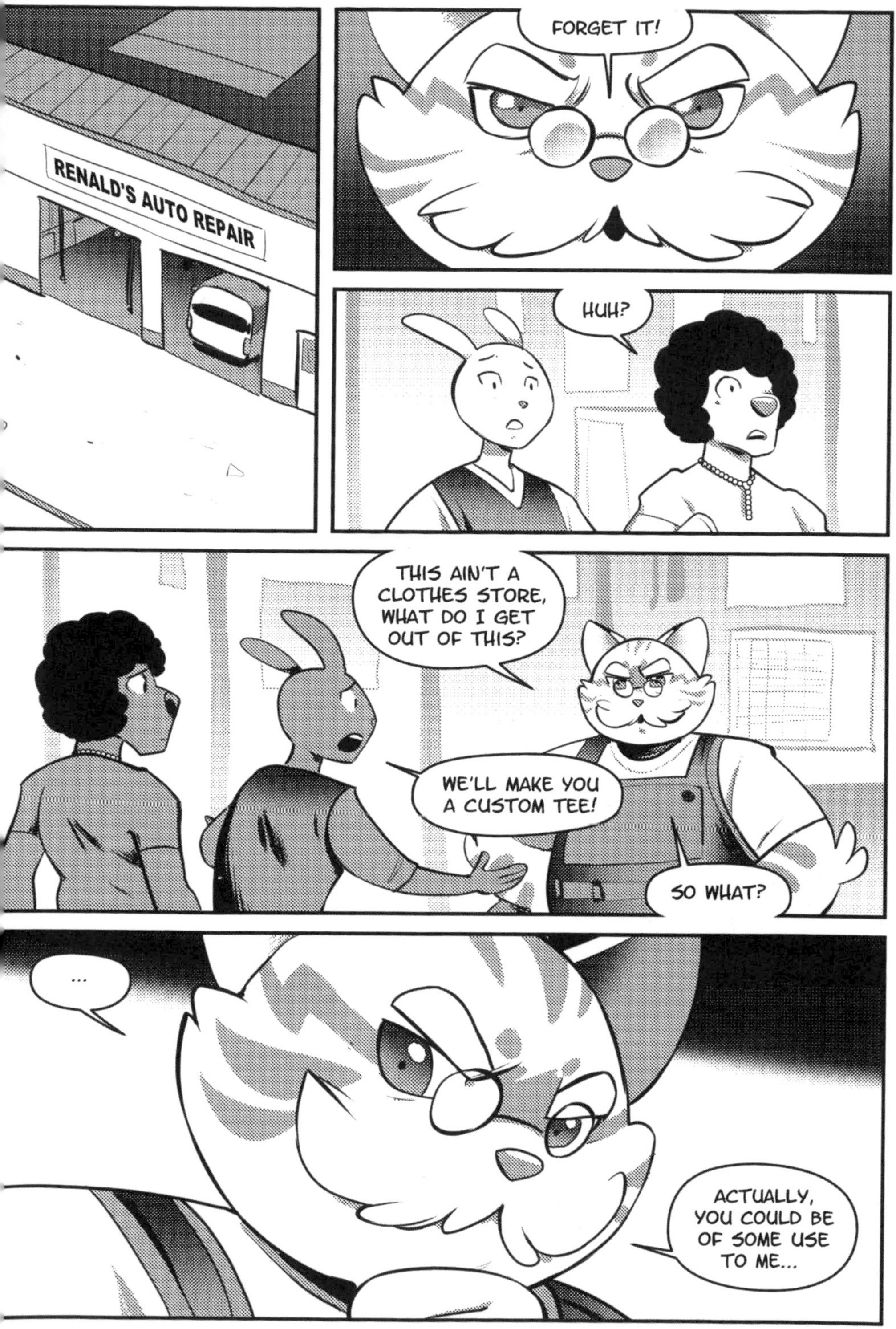
RENALD'S AUTO REPAIR
FORGET IT!
HUH?
THIS AIN'T A CLOTHES STORE, WHAT DO I GET OUT OF THIS?
WE'LL MAKE YOU A CUSTOM TEE!
SO WHAT?
...
ACTUALLY, YOU COULD BE OF SOME USE TO ME...

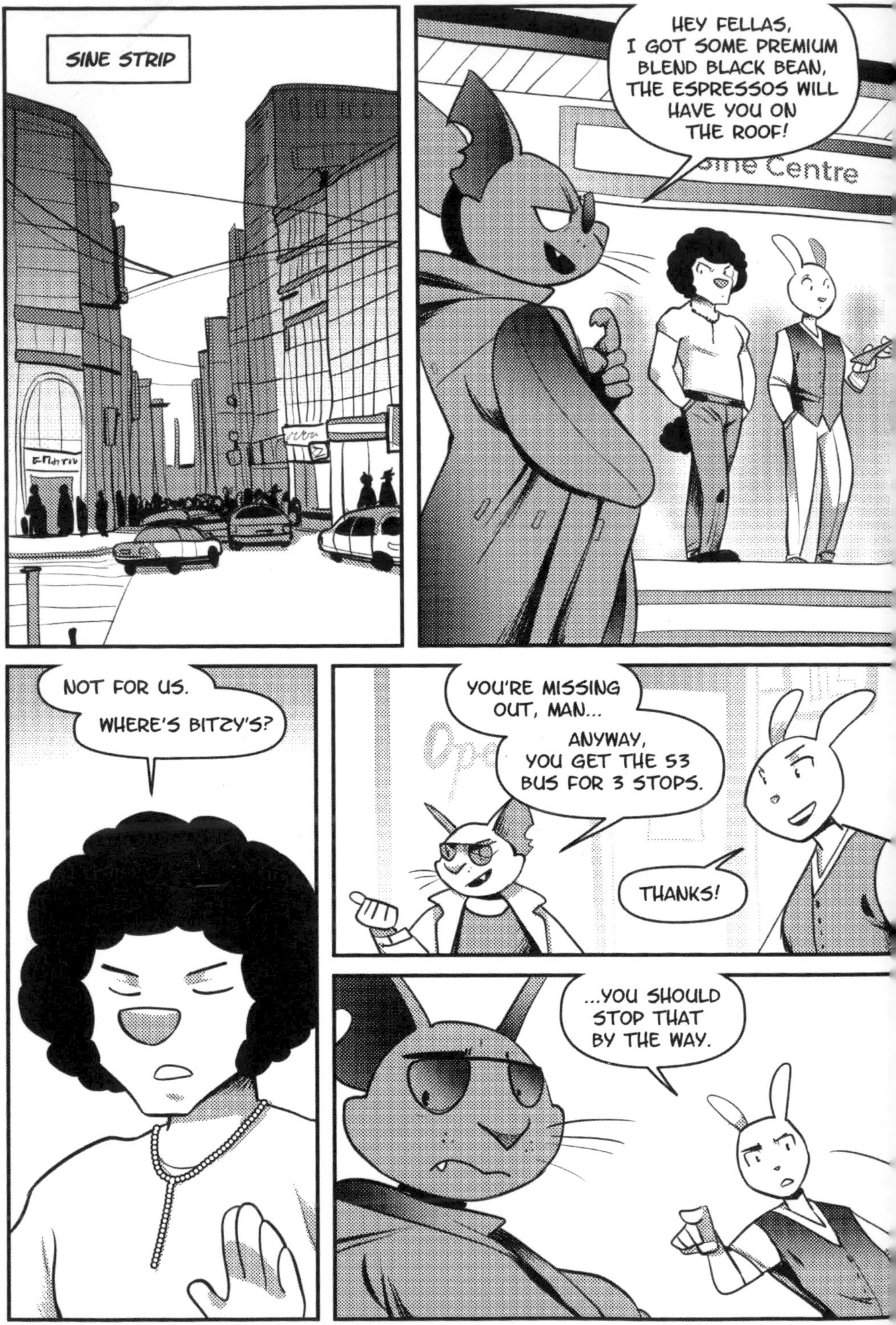
SINE STRIP
HEY FELLAS, I GOT SOME PREMIUM BLEND BLACK BEAN, THE ESPRESSOS WILL HAVE YOU ON THE ROOF!
NOT FOR US.
WHERE'S BITZY'S?
YOU'RE MISSING OUT, MAN...
ANYWAY, YOU GET THE 53 BUS FOR 3 STOPS.
THANKS!
...YOU SHOULD STOP THAT BY THE WAY.

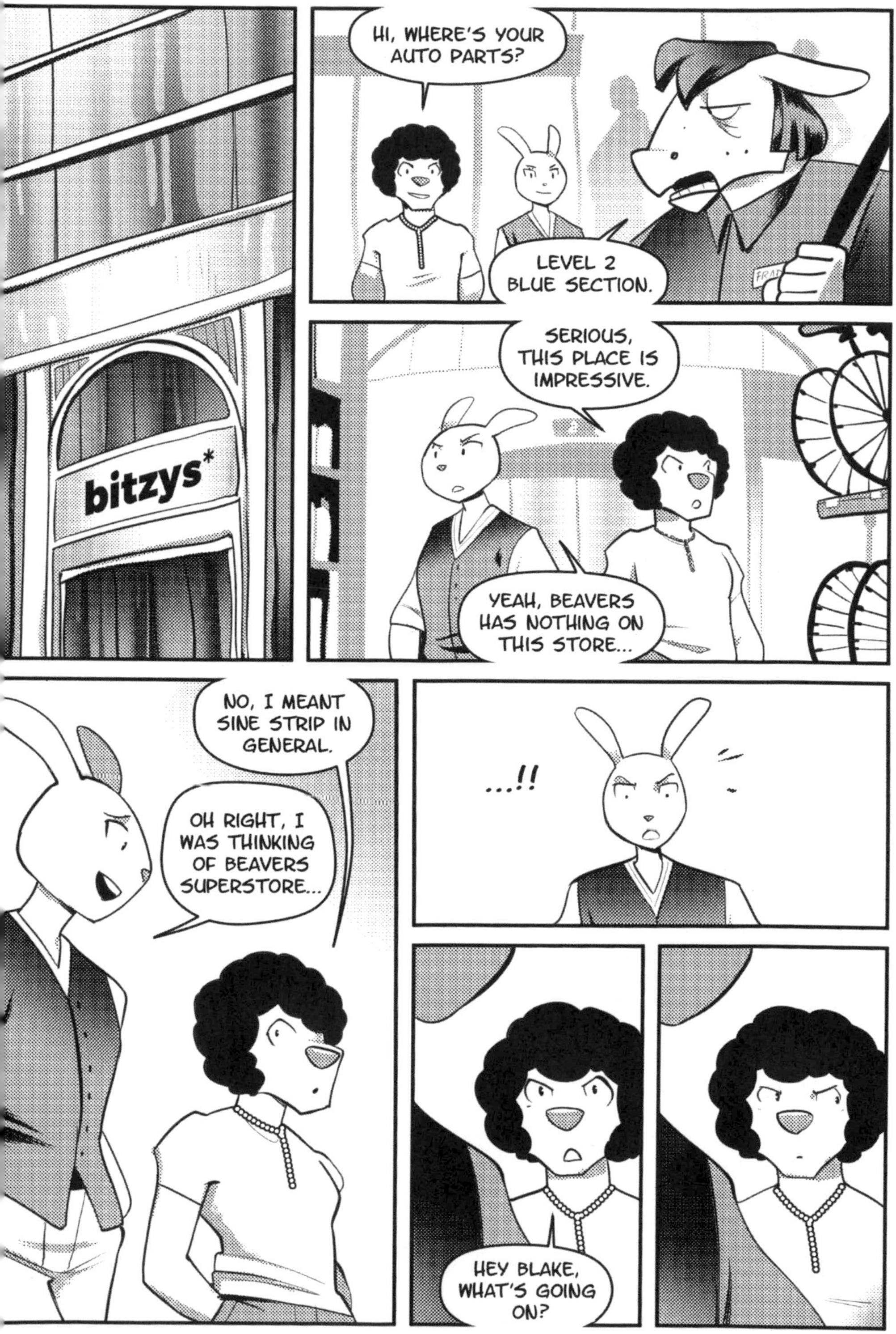
bitzys*
HI, WHERE'S YOUR AUTO PARTS?
LEVEL 2 BLUE SECTION.
SERIOUS, THIS PLACE IS IMPRESSIVE.
YEAH, BEAVERS HAS NOTHING ON THIS STORE...
NO, I MEANT SINE STRIP IN GENERAL.
OH RIGHT, I WAS THINKING OF BEAVERS SUPERSTORE...
...!!
HEY BLAKE, WHAT'S GOING ON?

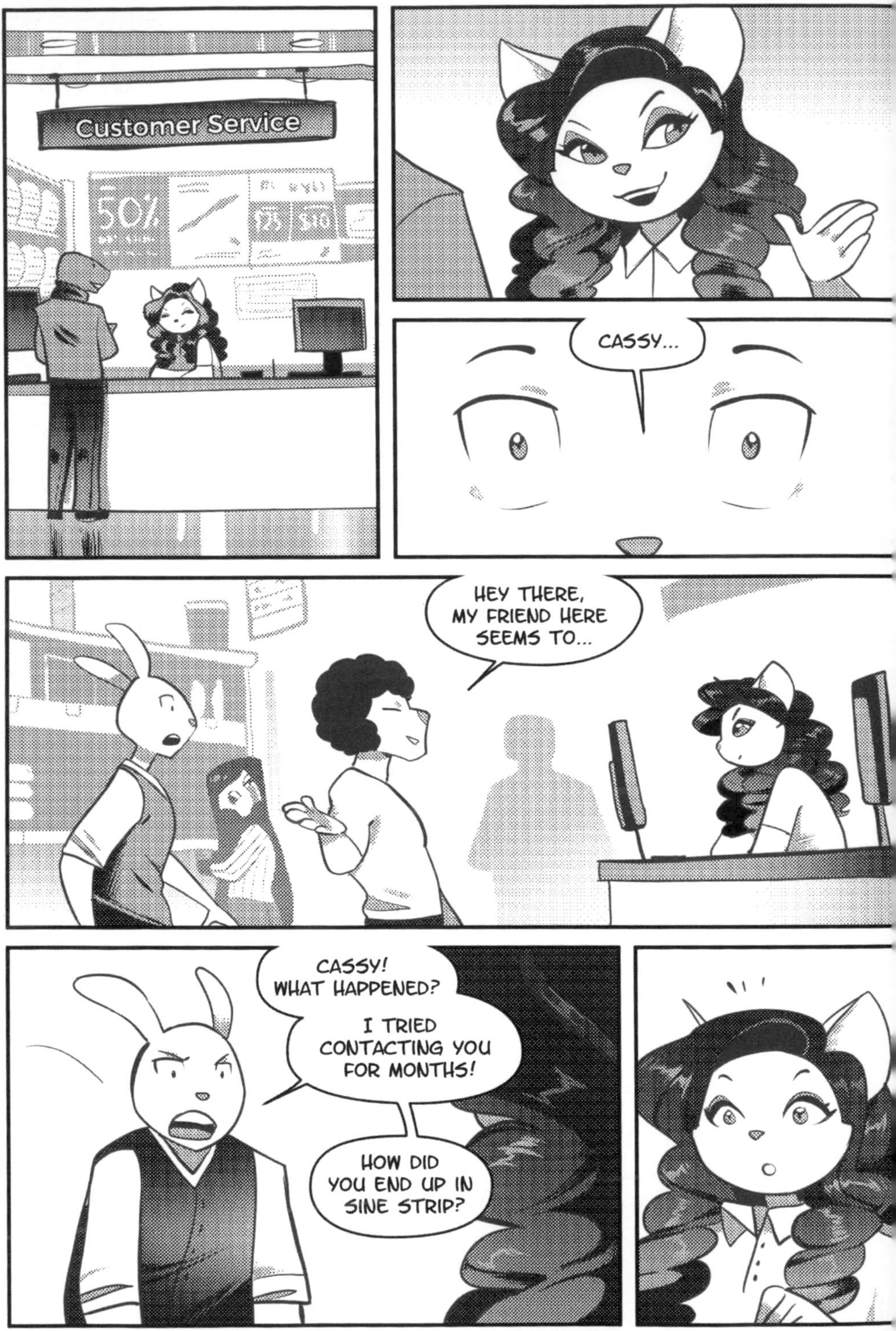
Customer Service
50%
CASSY...
HEY THERE, MY FRIEND HERE SEEMS TO...
CASSY! WHAT HAPPENED?
I TRIED CONTACTING YOU FOR MONTHS!
HOW DID YOU END UP IN SINE STRIP?

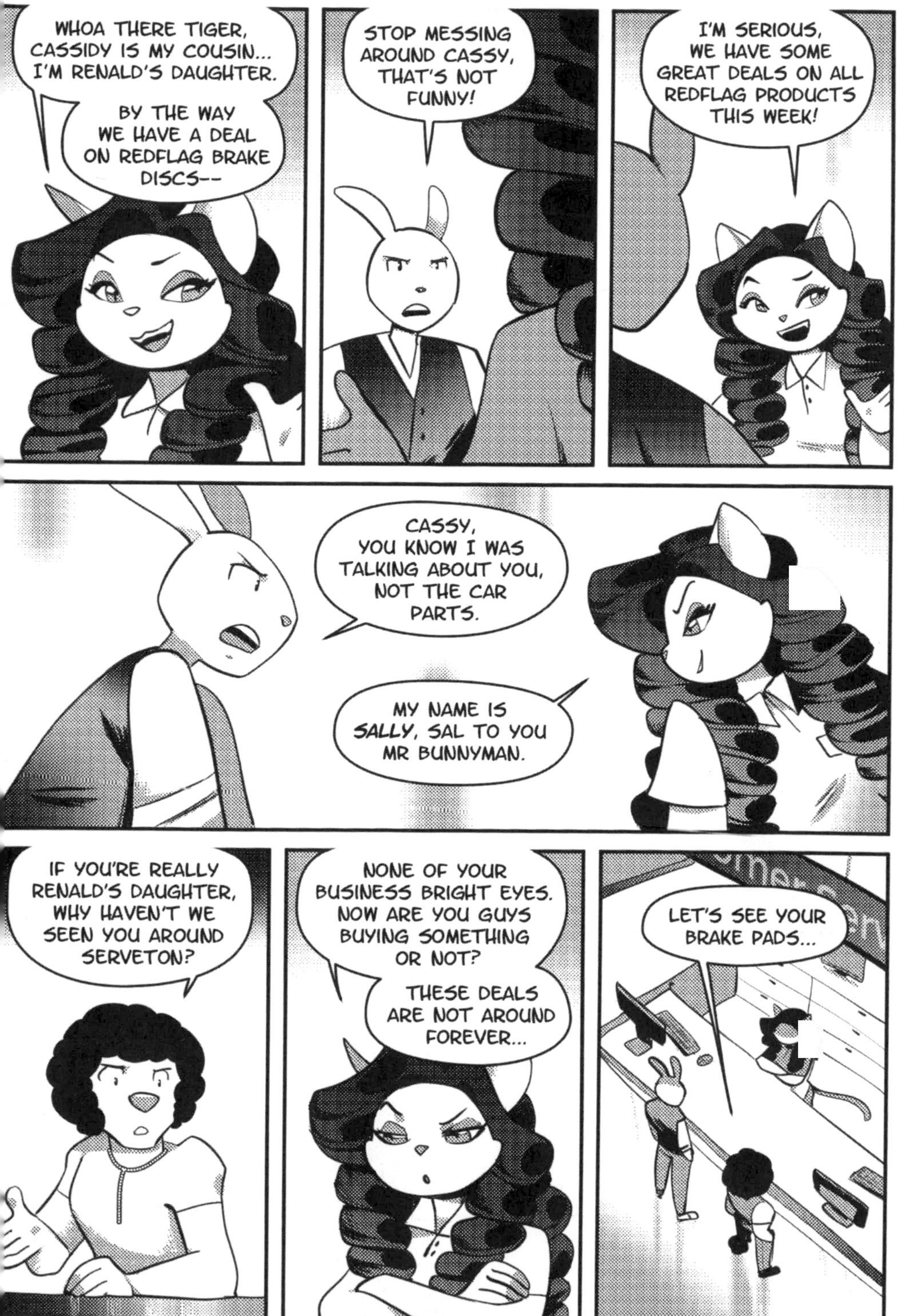
WHOA THERE TIGER, CASSIDY IS MY COUSIN... I'M RENALD'S DAUGHTER.
BY THE WAY WE HAVE A DEAL ON REDFLAG BRAKE DISCS--
STOP MESSING AROUND CASSY, THAT'S NOT FUNNY!
I'M SERIOUS, WE HAVE SOME GREAT DEALS ON ALL REDFLAG PRODUCTS THIS WEEK!
CASSY, YOU KNOW I WAS TALKING ABOUT YOU, NOT THE CAR PARTS.
MY NAME IS *SALLY*, SAL TO YOU MR BUNNYMAN.
IF YOU'RE REALLY RENALD'S DAUGHTER, WHY HAVEN'T WE SEEN YOU AROUND SERVETON?
NONE OF YOUR BUSINESS BRIGHT EYES. NOW ARE YOU GUYS BUYING SOMETHING OR NOT?
THESE DEALS ARE NOT AROUND FOREVER...
LET'S SEE YOUR BRAKE PADS...

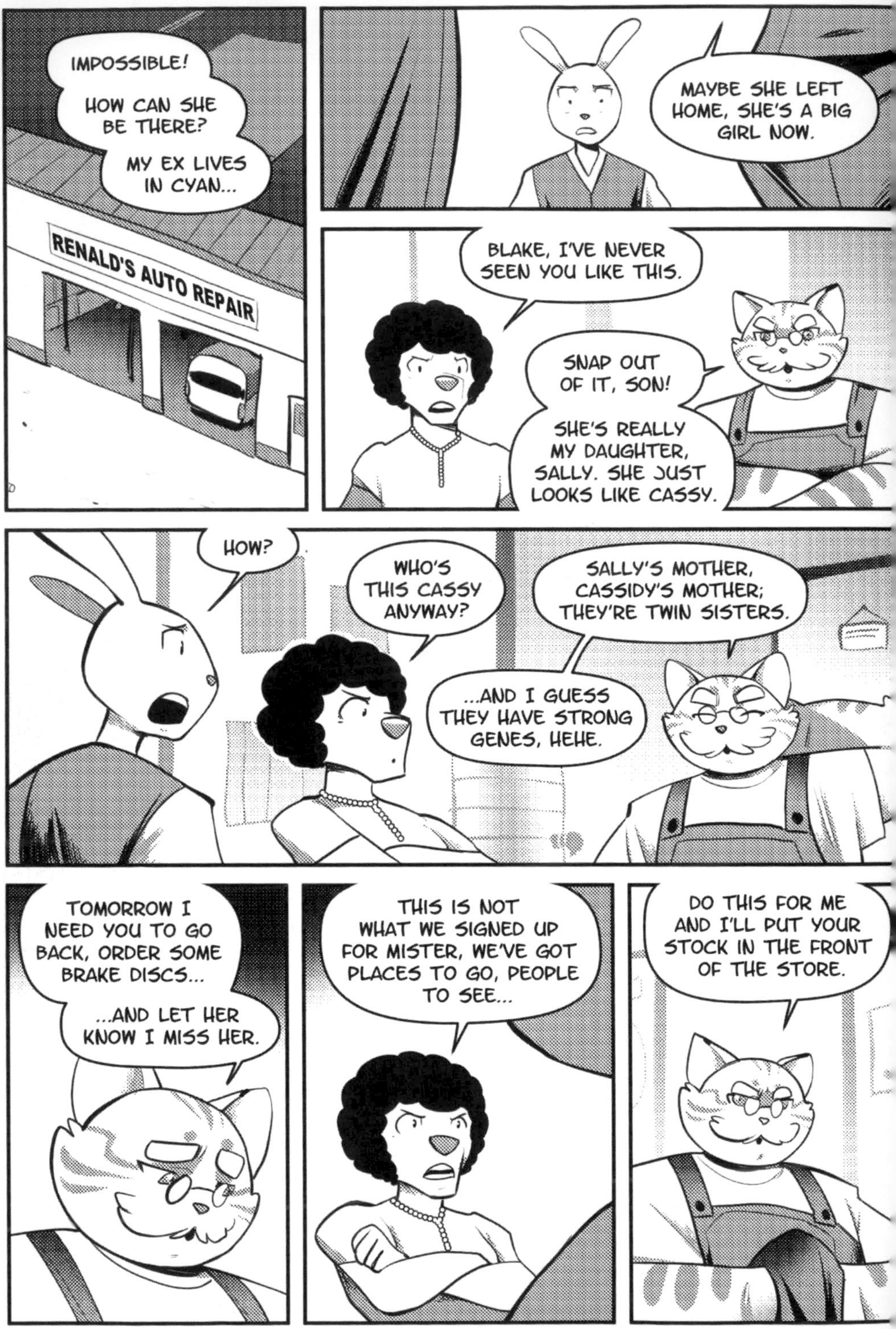
IMPOSSIBLE!
HOW CAN SHE BE THERE?
MY EX LIVES IN CYAN...
RENALD'S AUTO REPAIR
MAYBE SHE LEFT HOME, SHE'S A BIG GIRL NOW.
BLAKE, I'VE NEVER SEEN YOU LIKE THIS.
SNAP OUT OF IT, SON!
SHE'S REALLY MY DAUGHTER, SALLY. SHE JUST LOOKS LIKE CASSY.
HOW?
WHO'S THIS CASSY ANYWAY?
SALLY'S MOTHER, CASSIDY'S MOTHER; THEY'RE TWIN SISTERS.
...AND I GUESS THEY HAVE STRONG GENES, HEHE.
TOMORROW I NEED YOU TO GO BACK, ORDER SOME BRAKE DISCS...
...AND LET HER KNOW I MISS HER.
THIS IS NOT WHAT WE SIGNED UP FOR MISTER, WE'VE GOT PLACES TO GO, PEOPLE TO SEE...
DO THIS FOR ME AND I'LL PUT YOUR STOCK IN THE FRONT OF THE STORE.

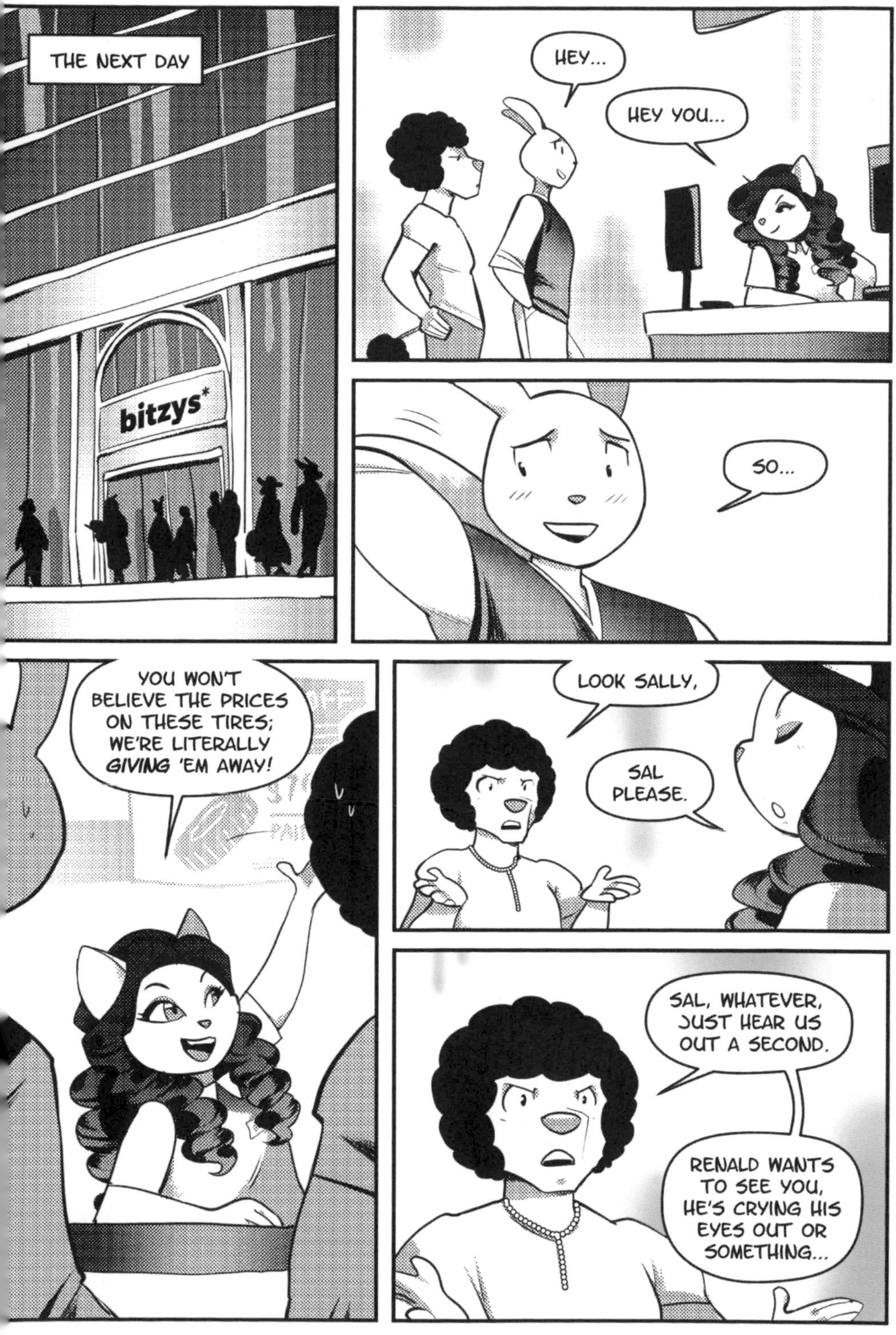
THE NEXT DAY
bitzys*
HEY...
HEY YOU...
SO...
YOU WON'T BELIEVE THE PRICES ON THESE TIRES; WE'RE LITERALLY *GIVING* 'EM AWAY!
LOOK SALLY,
SAL PLEASE.
SAL, WHATEVER, JUST HEAR US OUT A SECOND.
RENALD WANTS TO SEE YOU, HE'S CRYING HIS EYES OUT OR SOMETHING...

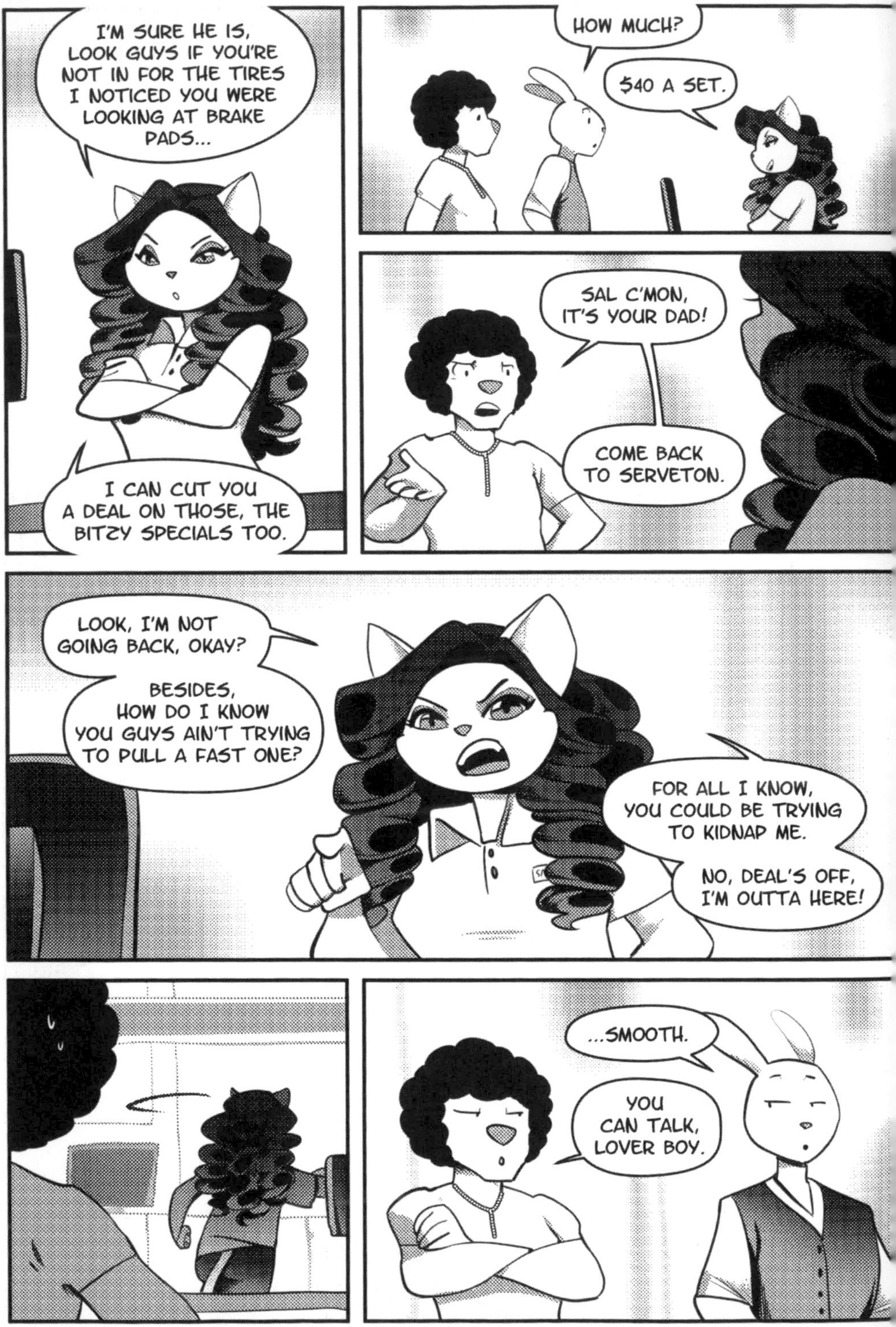
I'M SURE HE IS, LOOK GUYS IF YOU'RE NOT IN FOR THE TIRES I NOTICED YOU WERE LOOKING AT BRAKE PADS...
I CAN CUT YOU A DEAL ON THOSE, THE BITZY SPECIALS TOO.
HOW MUCH?
$40 A SET.
SAL C'MON, IT'S YOUR DAD!
COME BACK TO SERVETON.
LOOK, I'M NOT GOING BACK, OKAY?
BESIDES, HOW DO I KNOW YOU GUYS AIN'T TRYING TO PULL A FAST ONE?
FOR ALL I KNOW, YOU COULD BE TRYING TO KIDNAP ME.
NO, DEAL'S OFF, I'M OUTTA HERE!
...SMOOTH.
YOU CAN TALK, LOVER BOY.

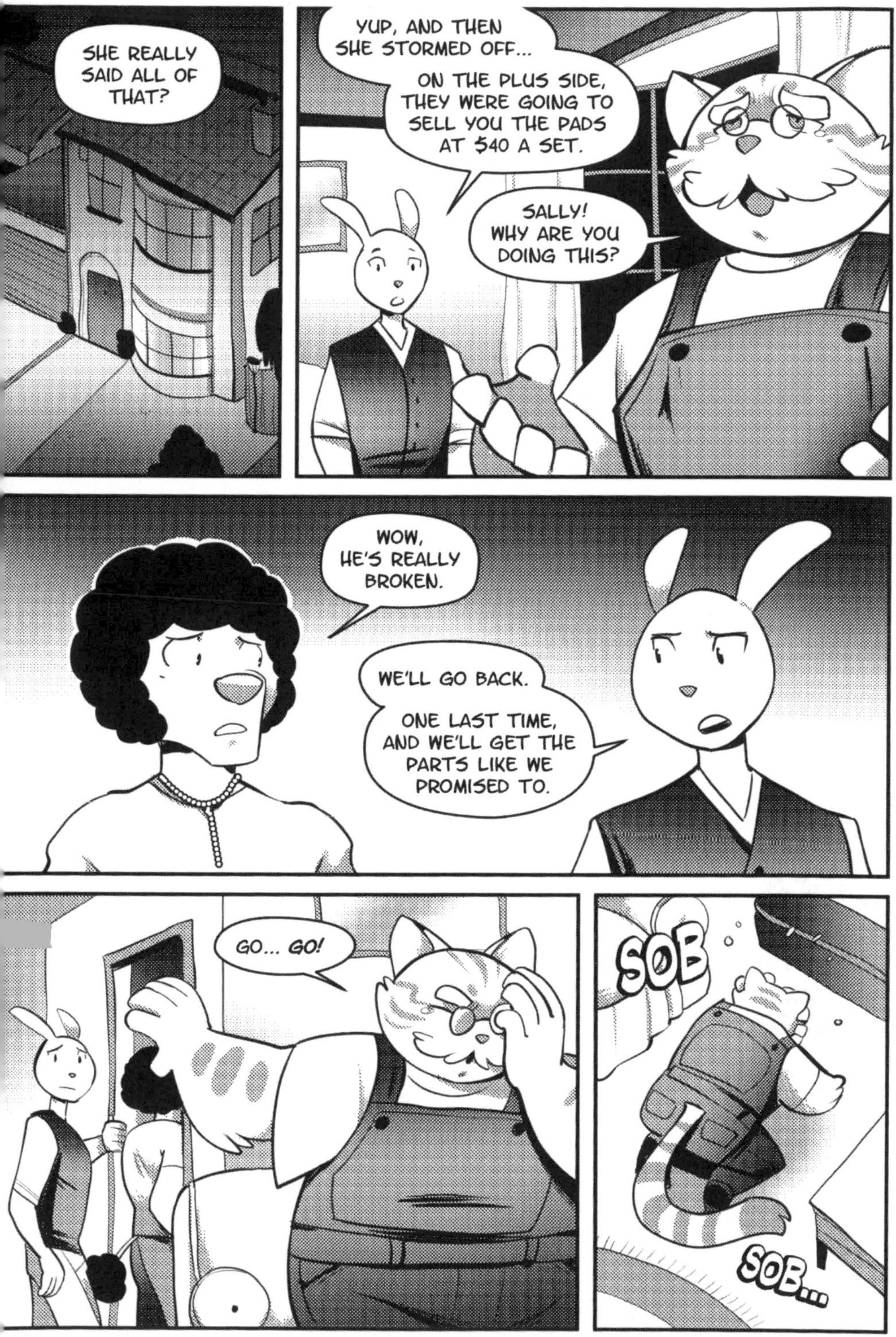

SHE REALLY SAID ALL OF THAT?
YUP, AND THEN SHE STORMED OFF...
ON THE PLUS SIDE, THEY WERE GOING TO SELL YOU THE PADS AT $40 A SET.
SALLY! WHY ARE YOU DOING THIS?
WOW, HE'S REALLY BROKEN.
WE'LL GO BACK.
ONE LAST TIME, AND WE'LL GET THE PARTS LIKE WE PROMISED TO.
GO... GO!
SOB
SOB...

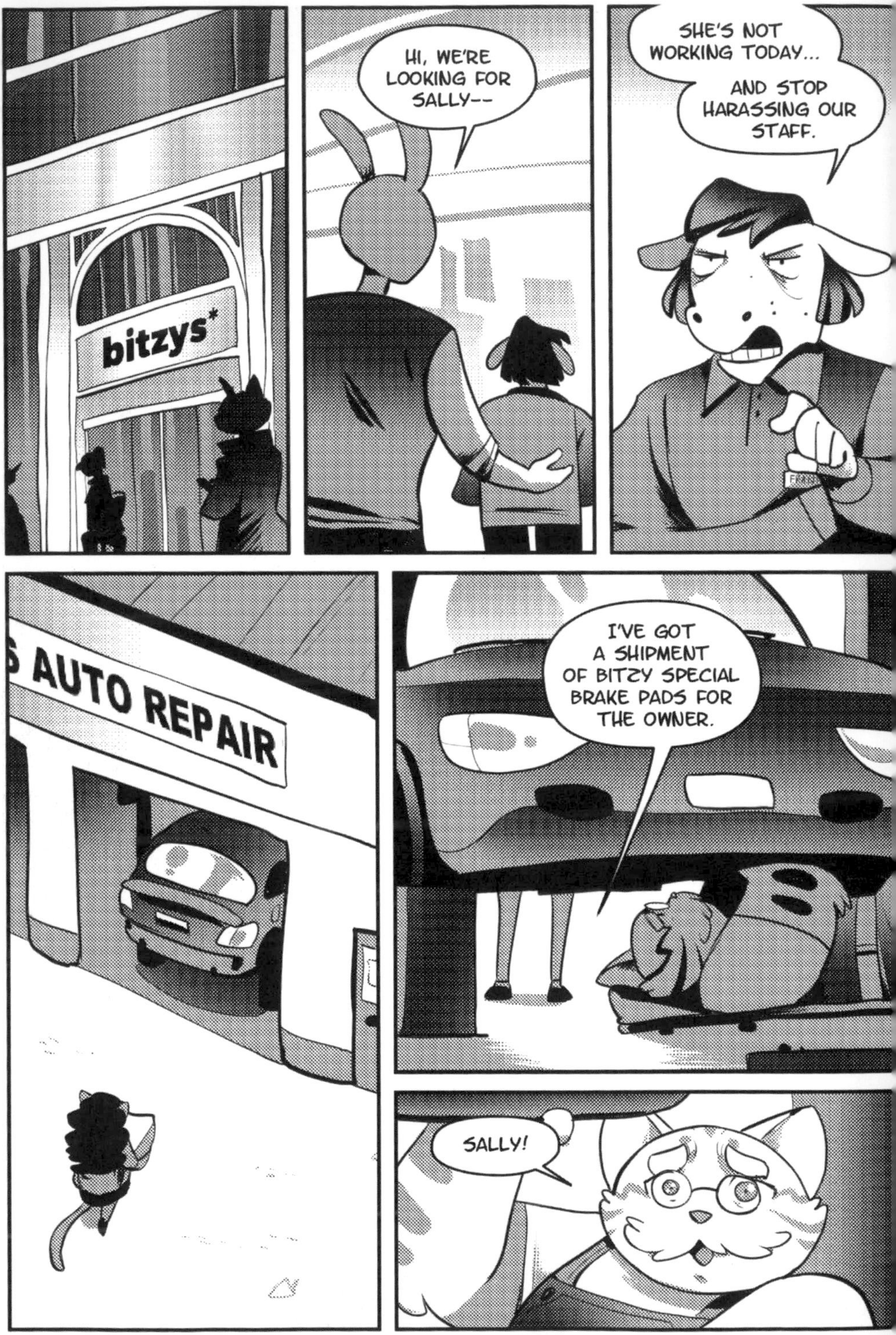
bitzys*
HI, WE'RE LOOKING FOR SALLY--
SHE'S NOT WORKING TODAY...
AND STOP HARASSING OUR STAFF.
S AUTO REPAIR
I'VE GOT A SHIPMENT OF BITZY SPECIAL BRAKE PADS FOR THE OWNER.
SALLY!

I'M TELLING YOU THIS NEWS IS PROBABLY GONNA KILL HIM.

WE DIDN'T EVEN GET THE BRAKE PADS...

HA HA HA HA HA

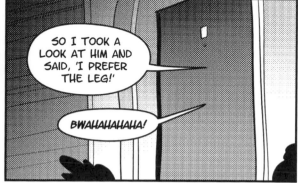

SO I TOOK A LOOK AT HIM AND SAID, 'I PREFER THE LEG!'

BWAHAHAHAHA!

WHAT'S THIS?

OH GUYS, COME ON IN!

I OWE YOU BIG TIME, YOU'VE BROUGHT BACK MY SALLY.

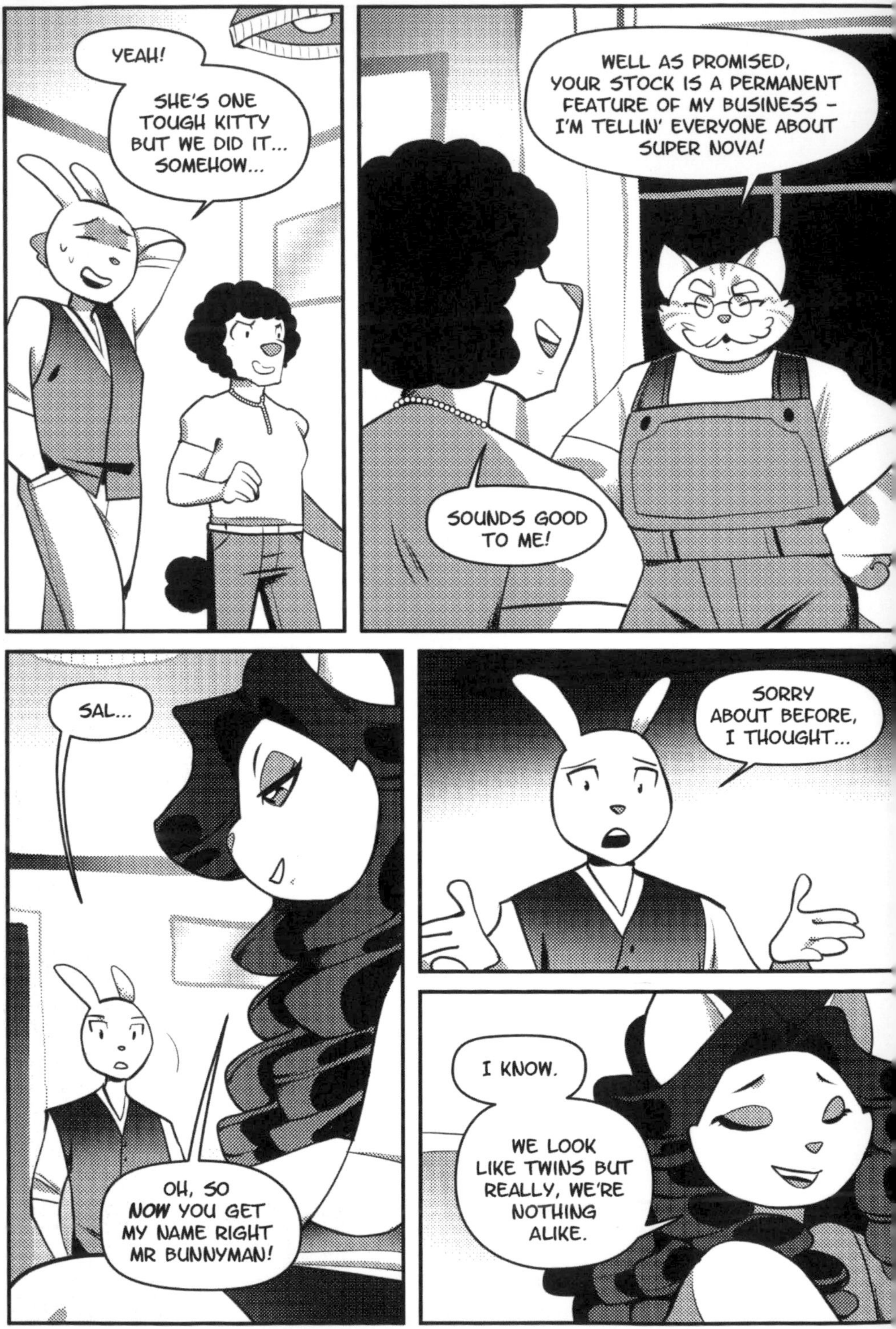
YEAH!
SHE'S ONE TOUGH KITTY BUT WE DID IT... SOMEHOW...
WELL AS PROMISED, YOUR STOCK IS A PERMANENT FEATURE OF MY BUSINESS – I'M TELLIN' EVERYONE ABOUT SUPER NOVA!
SOUNDS GOOD TO ME!
SAL...
OH, SO NOW YOU GET MY NAME RIGHT MR BUNNYMAN!
SORRY ABOUT BEFORE, I THOUGHT...
I KNOW.
WE LOOK LIKE TWINS BUT REALLY, WE'RE NOTHING ALIKE.

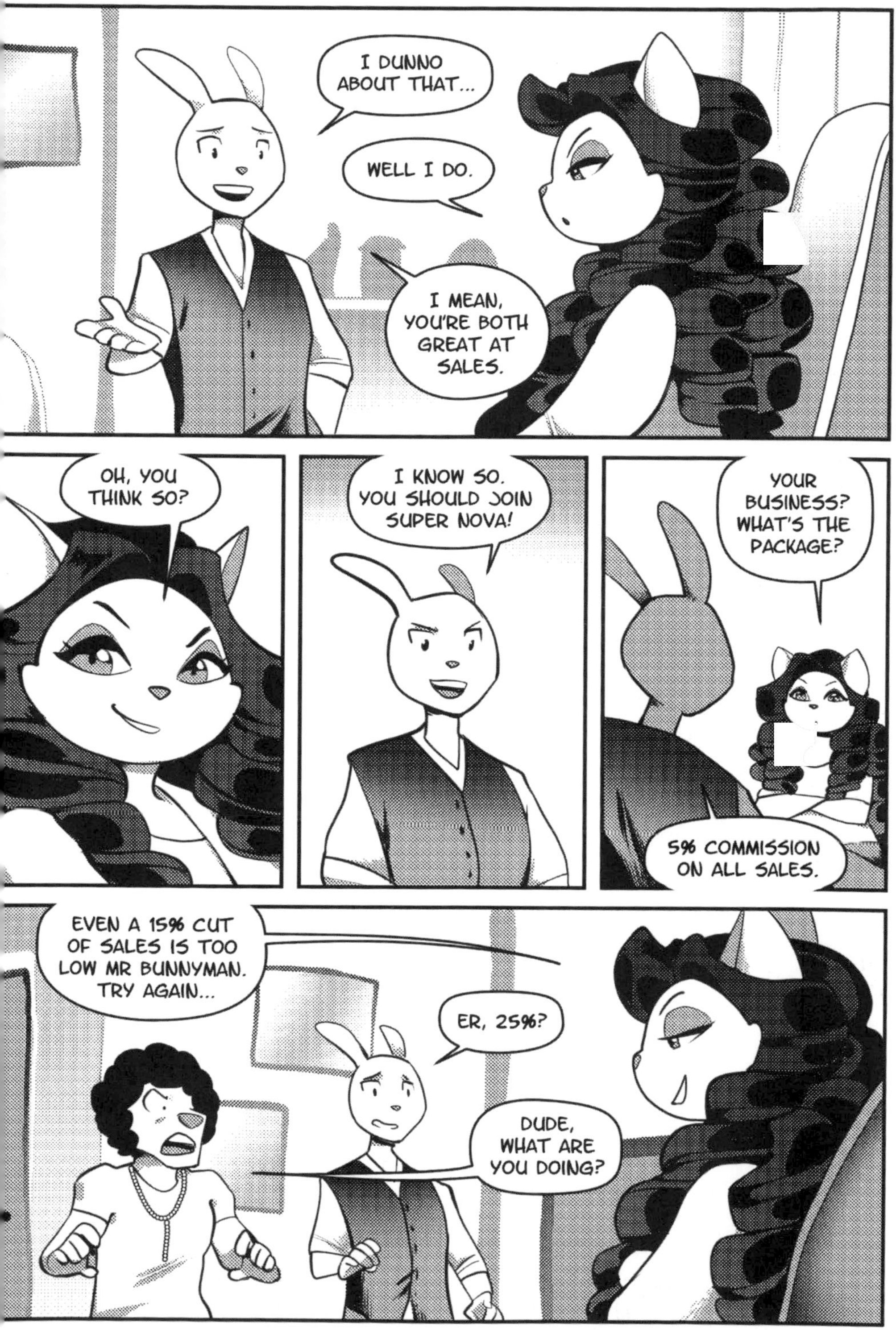
I DUNNO ABOUT THAT...
WELL I DO.
I MEAN, YOU'RE BOTH GREAT AT SALES.
OH, YOU THINK SO?
I KNOW SO. YOU SHOULD JOIN SUPER NOVA!
YOUR BUSINESS? WHAT'S THE PACKAGE?
5% COMMISSION ON ALL SALES.
EVEN A 15% CUT OF SALES IS TOO LOW MR BUNNYMAN. TRY AGAIN...
ER, 25%?
DUDE, WHAT ARE YOU DOING?

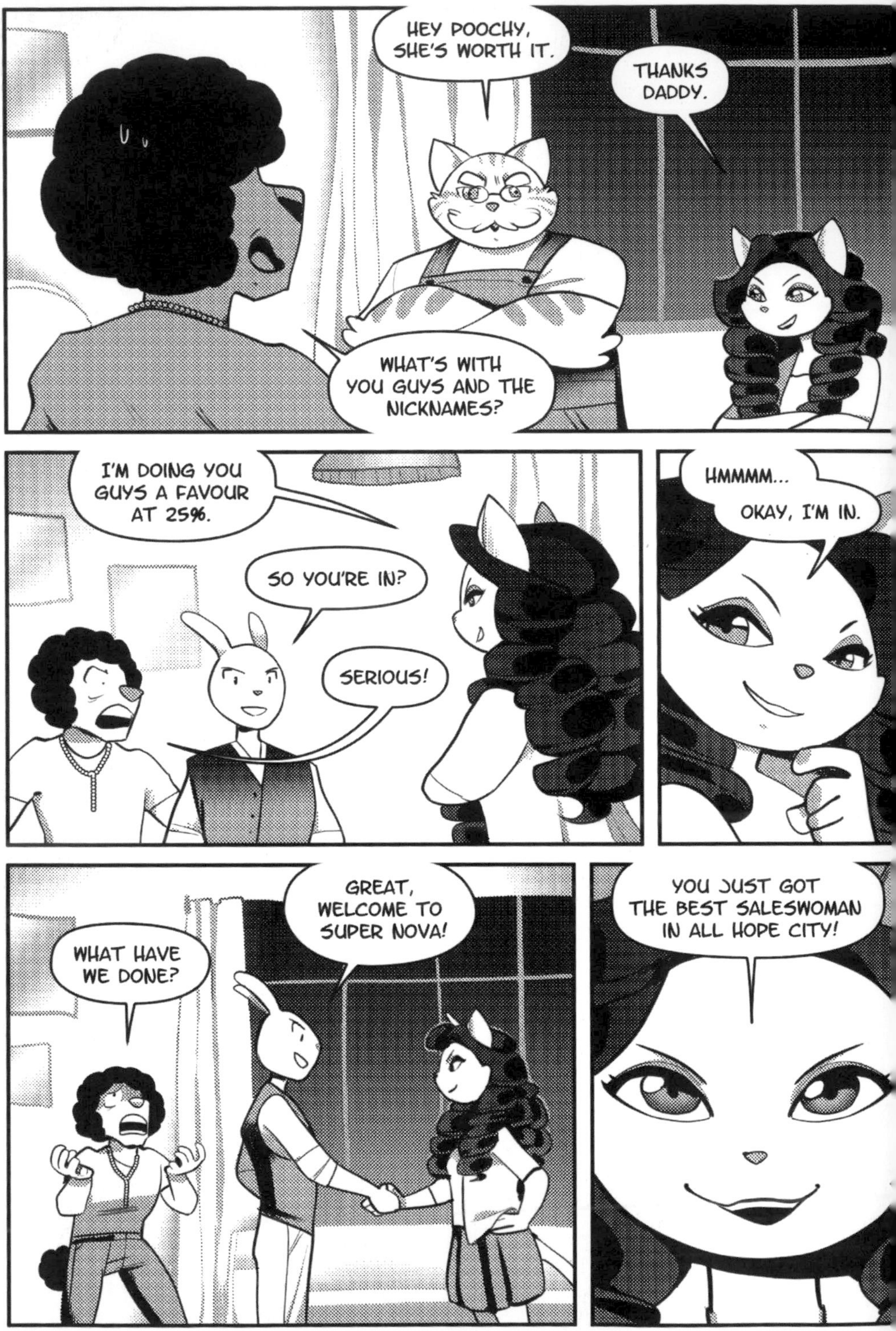
HEY POOCHY, SHE'S WORTH IT.
THANKS DADDY.
WHAT'S WITH YOU GUYS AND THE NICKNAMES?
I'M DOING YOU GUYS A FAVOUR AT 25%.
SO YOU'RE IN?
SERIOUS!
HMMMM...
OKAY, I'M IN.
WHAT HAVE WE DONE?
GREAT, WELCOME TO SUPER NOVA!
YOU JUST GOT THE BEST SALESWOMAN IN ALL HOPE CITY!

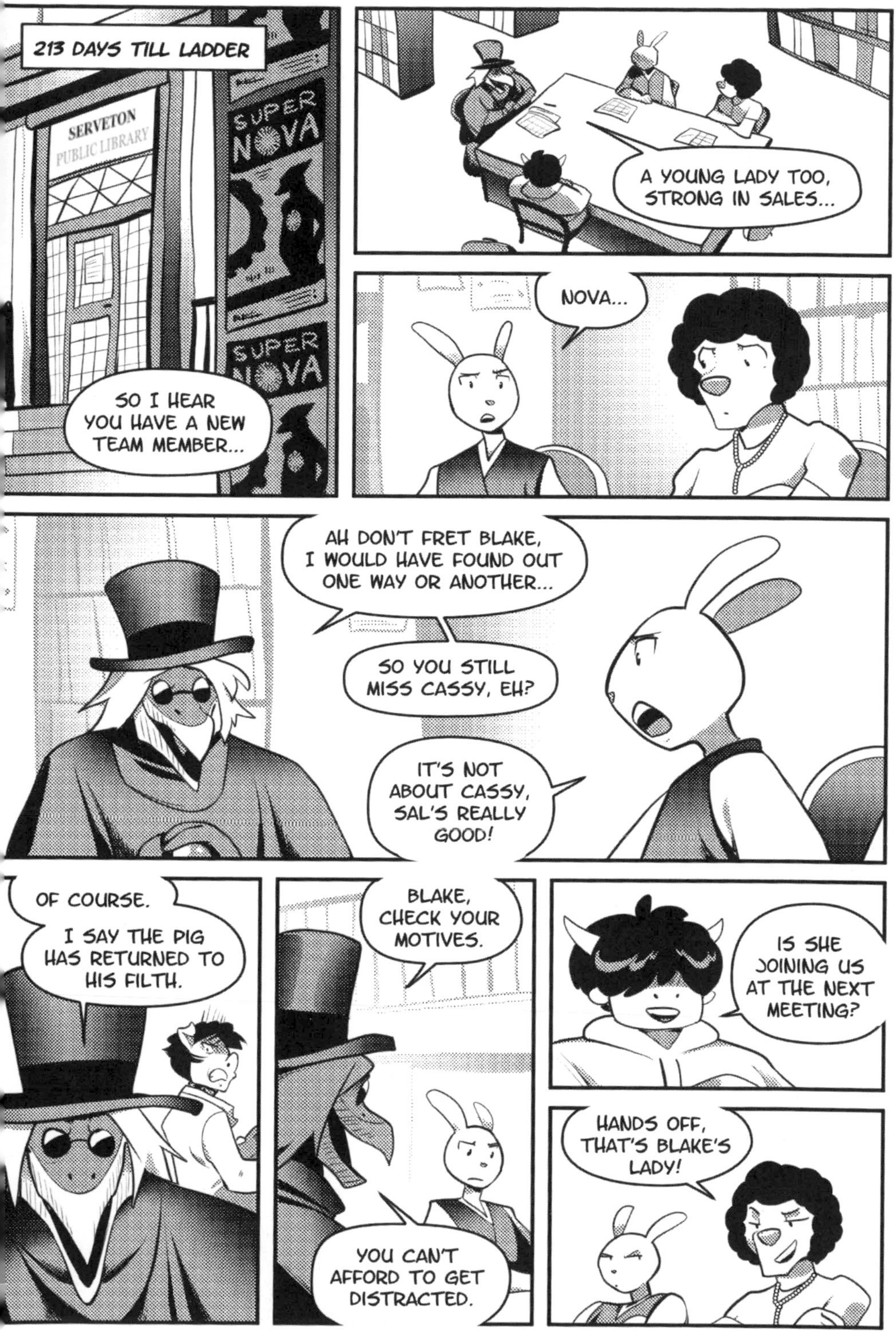
213 DAYS TILL LADDER
SERVETON PUBLIC LIBRARY
SUPER NOVA
SUPER NOVA
SO I HEAR YOU HAVE A NEW TEAM MEMBER...
A YOUNG LADY TOO, STRONG IN SALES...
NOVA...
AH DON'T FRET BLAKE, I WOULD HAVE FOUND OUT ONE WAY OR ANOTHER...
SO YOU STILL MISS CASSY, EH?
IT'S NOT ABOUT CASSY, SAL'S REALLY GOOD!
OF COURSE.
I SAY THE PIG HAS RETURNED TO HIS FILTH.
BLAKE, CHECK YOUR MOTIVES.
YOU CAN'T AFFORD TO GET DISTRACTED.
IS SHE JOINING US AT THE NEXT MEETING?
HANDS OFF, THAT'S BLAKE'S LADY!

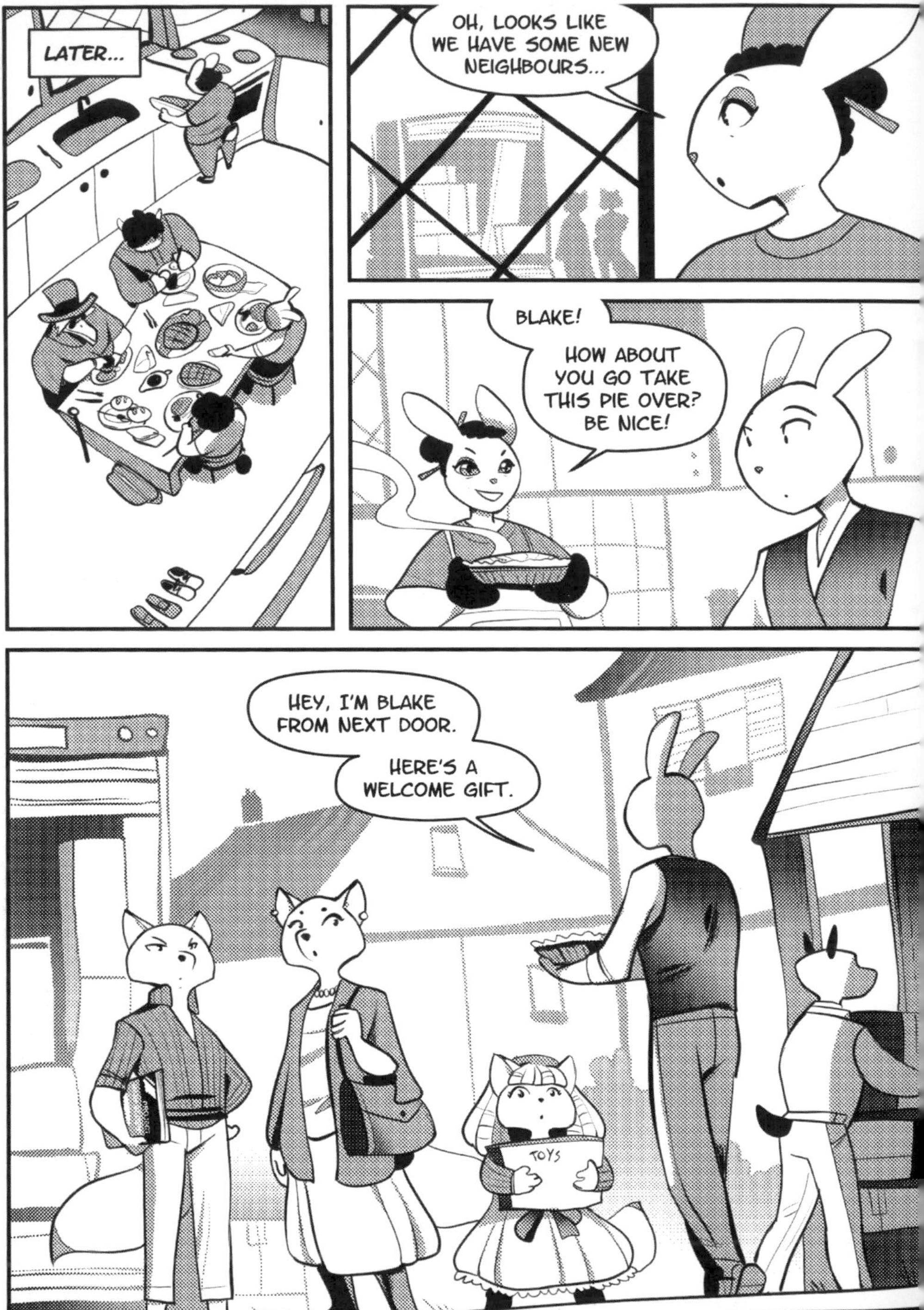
LATER...
OH, LOOKS LIKE WE HAVE SOME NEW NEIGHBOURS...
BLAKE!
HOW ABOUT YOU GO TAKE THIS PIE OVER? BE NICE!
HEY, I'M BLAKE FROM NEXT DOOR.
HERE'S A WELCOME GIFT.
TOYS

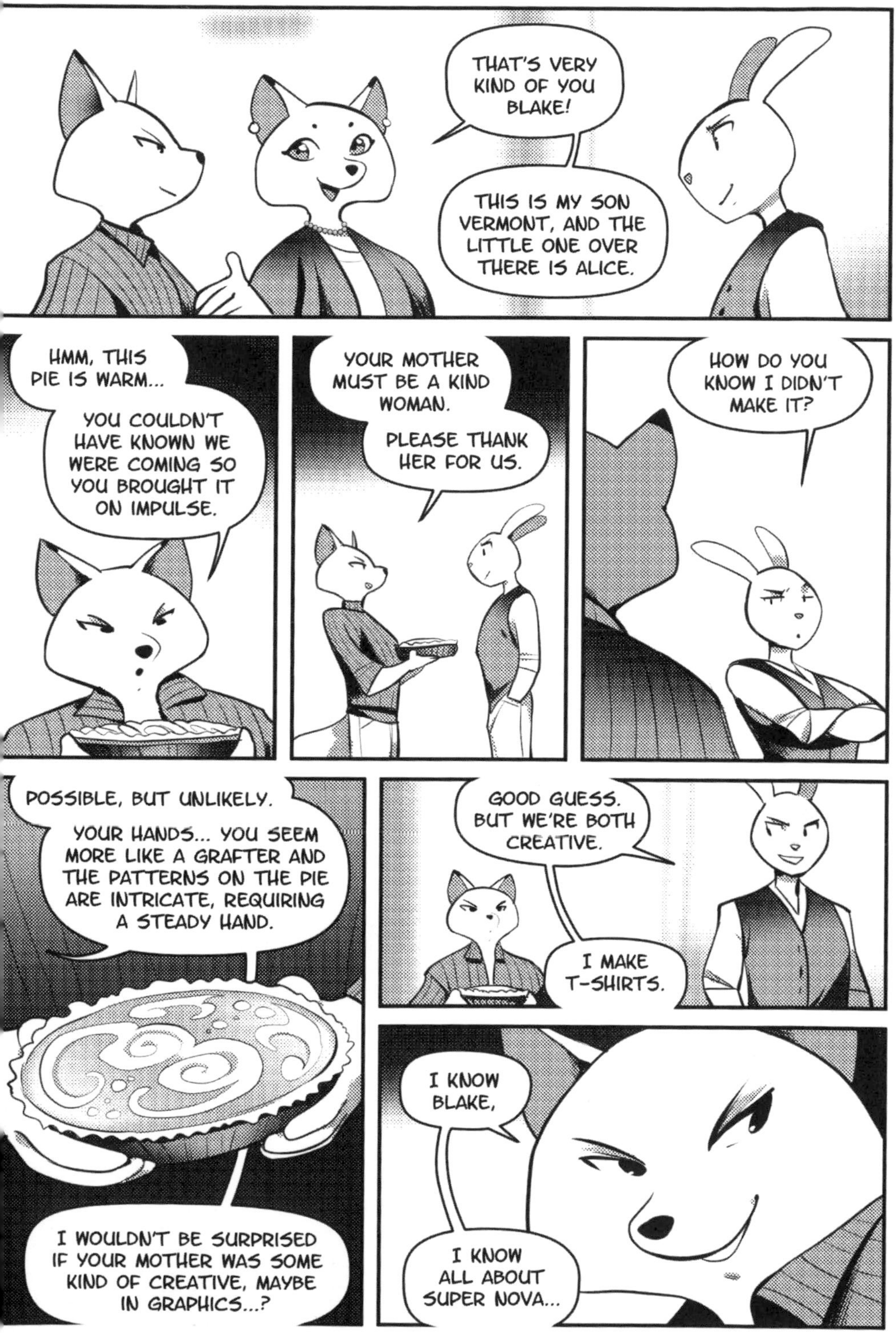
THAT'S VERY KIND OF YOU BLAKE!
THIS IS MY SON VERMONT, AND THE LITTLE ONE OVER THERE IS ALICE.
HMM, THIS PIE IS WARM...
YOU COULDN'T HAVE KNOWN WE WERE COMING SO YOU BROUGHT IT ON IMPULSE.
YOUR MOTHER MUST BE A KIND WOMAN.
PLEASE THANK HER FOR US.
HOW DO YOU KNOW I DIDN'T MAKE IT?
POSSIBLE, BUT UNLIKELY.
YOUR HANDS... YOU SEEM MORE LIKE A GRAFTER AND THE PATTERNS ON THE PIE ARE INTRICATE, REQUIRING A STEADY HAND.
I WOULDN'T BE SURPRISED IF YOUR MOTHER WAS SOME KIND OF CREATIVE, MAYBE IN GRAPHICS...?
GOOD GUESS. BUT WE'RE BOTH CREATIVE.
I MAKE T-SHIRTS.
I KNOW BLAKE,
I KNOW ALL ABOUT SUPER NOVA...

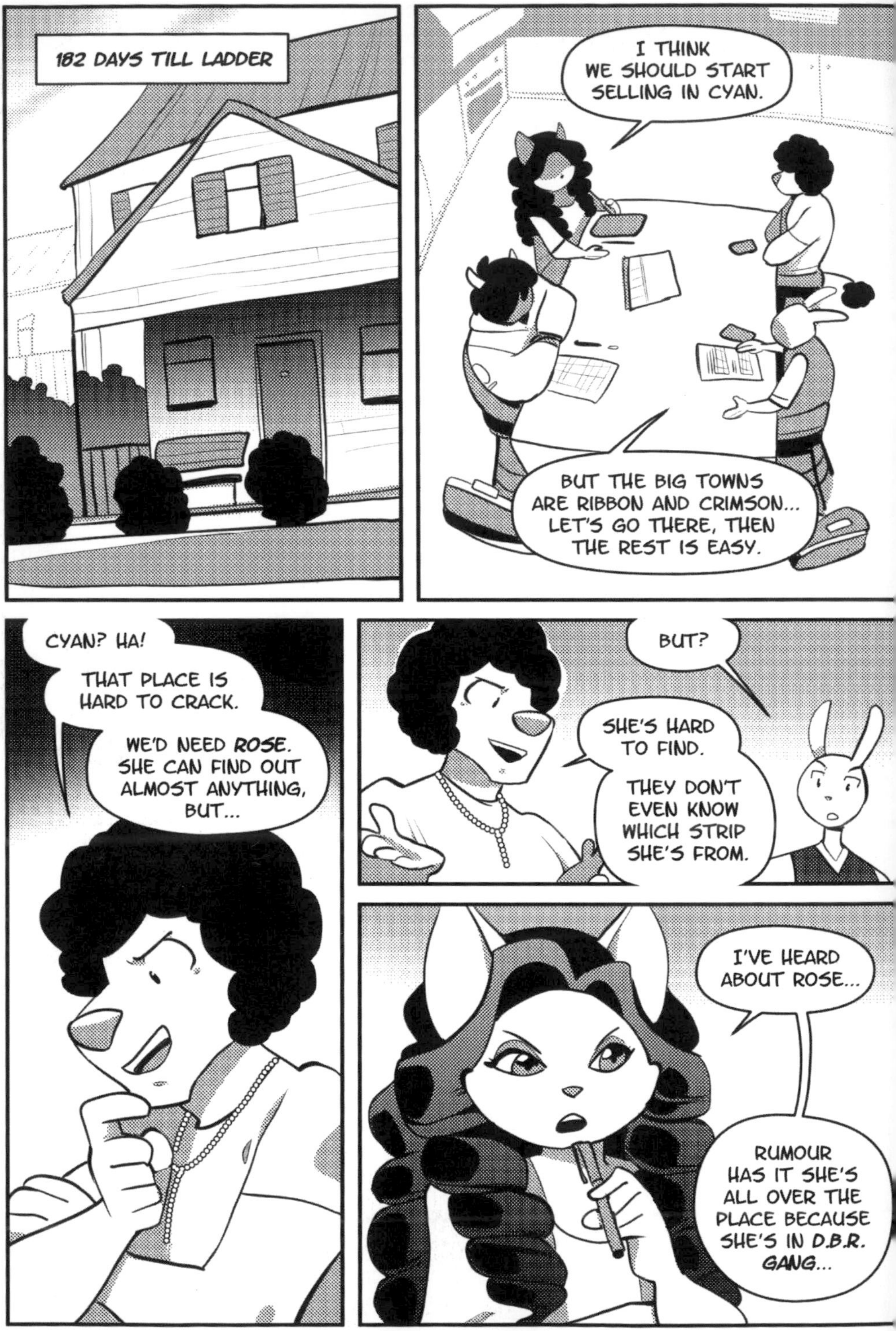
182 DAYS TILL LADDER
I THINK WE SHOULD START SELLING IN CYAN.
BUT THE BIG TOWNS ARE RIBBON AND CRIMSON... LET'S GO THERE, THEN THE REST IS EASY.
CYAN? HA!
THAT PLACE IS HARD TO CRACK.
WE'D NEED ***ROSE***. SHE CAN FIND OUT ALMOST ANYTHING, BUT...
BUT?
SHE'S HARD TO FIND.
THEY DON'T EVEN KNOW WHICH STRIP SHE'S FROM.
I'VE HEARD ABOUT ROSE...
RUMOUR HAS IT SHE'S ALL OVER THE PLACE BECAUSE SHE'S IN *D.B.R. GANG*...

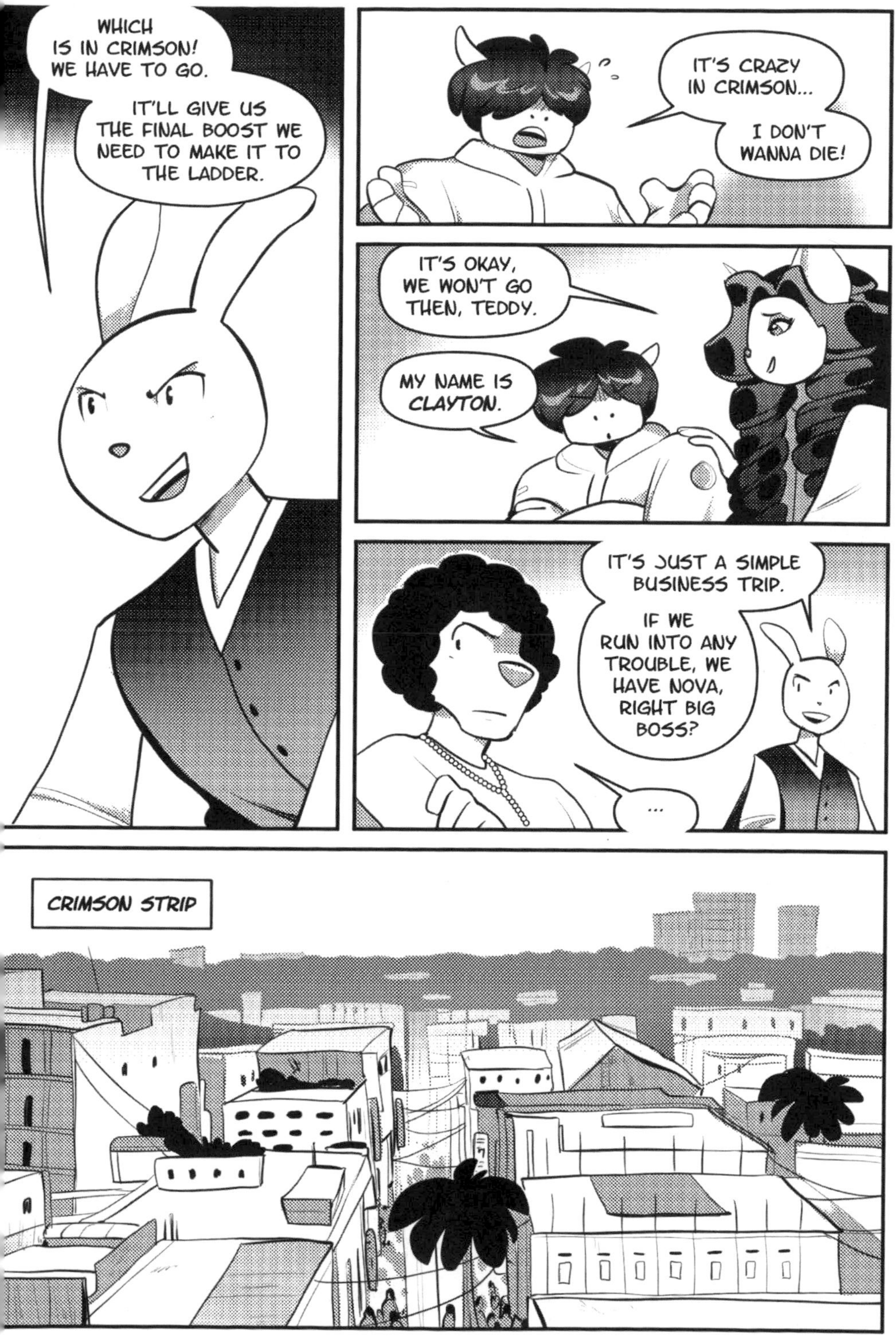
WHICH IS IN CRIMSON! WE HAVE TO GO.
IT'LL GIVE US THE FINAL BOOST WE NEED TO MAKE IT TO THE LADDER.
IT'S CRAZY IN CRIMSON...
I DON'T WANNA DIE!
IT'S OKAY, WE WON'T GO THEN, TEDDY.
MY NAME IS CLAYTON.
IT'S JUST A SIMPLE BUSINESS TRIP.
IF WE RUN INTO ANY TROUBLE, WE HAVE NOVA, RIGHT BIG BOSS?
...
CRIMSON STRIP

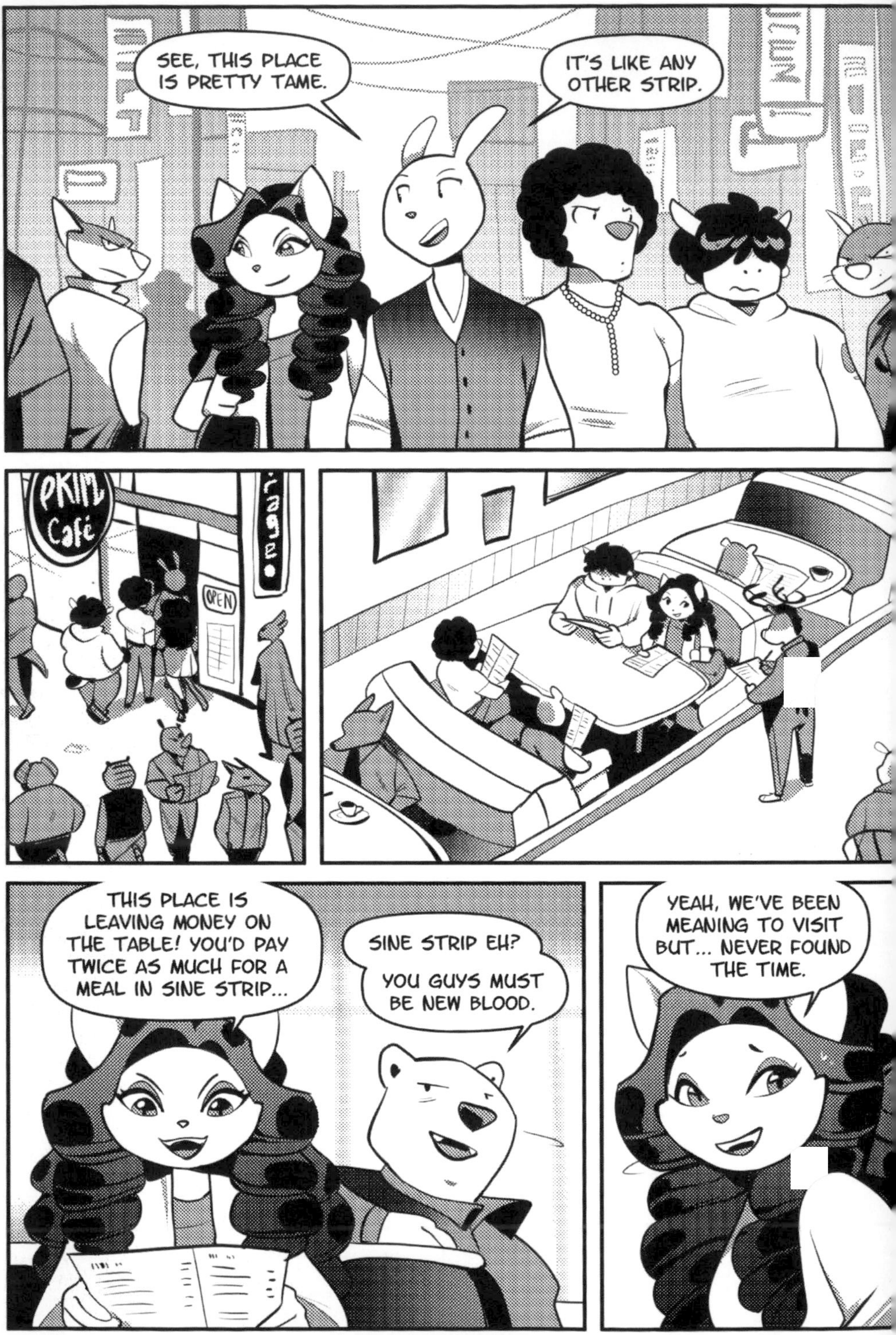
SEE, THIS PLACE IS PRETTY TAME.
IT'S LIKE ANY OTHER STRIP.
OPEN
THIS PLACE IS LEAVING MONEY ON THE TABLE! YOU'D PAY TWICE AS MUCH FOR A MEAL IN SINE STRIP...
SINE STRIP EH?
YOU GUYS MUST BE NEW BLOOD.
YEAH, WE'VE BEEN MEANING TO VISIT BUT... NEVER FOUND THE TIME.

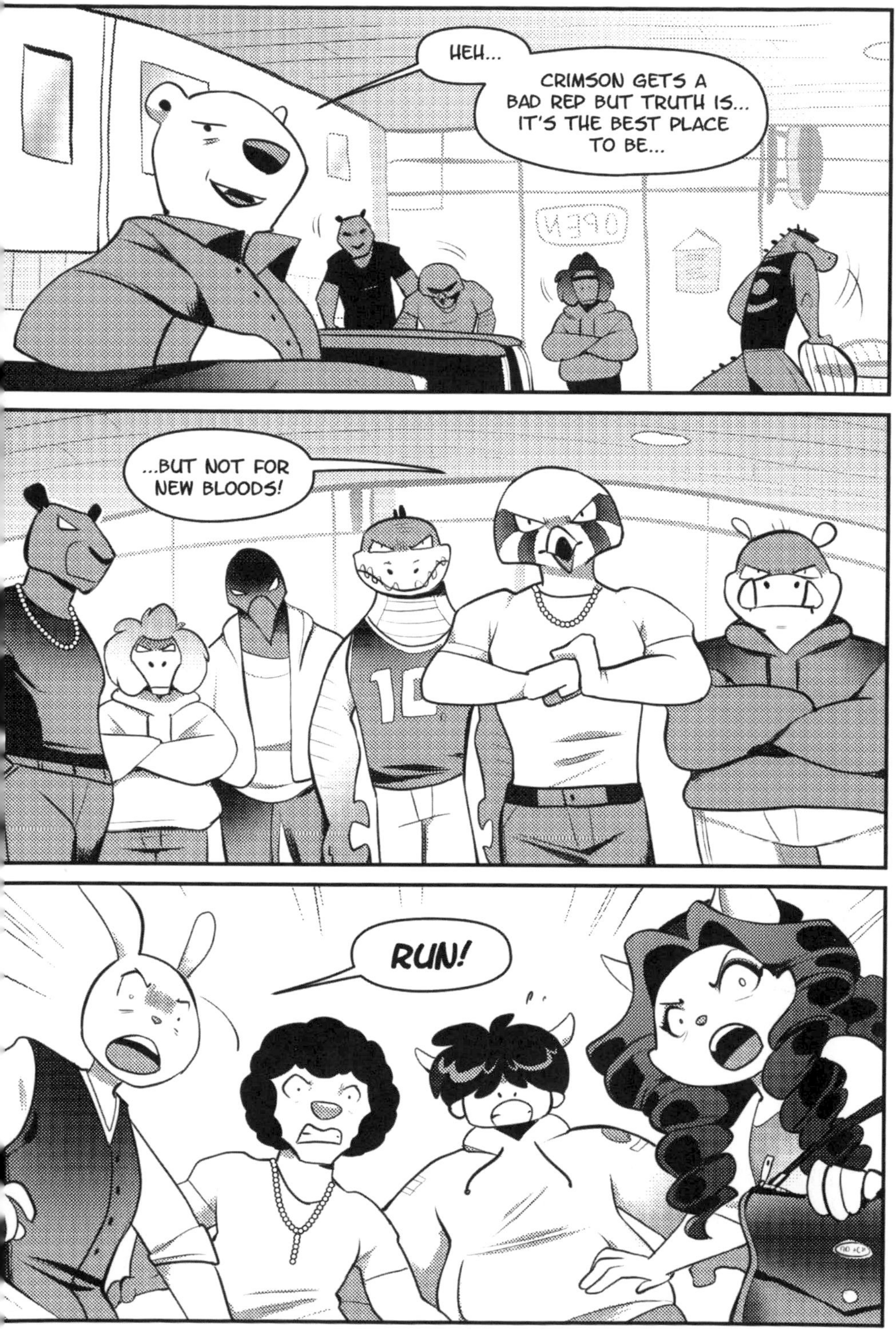
HEH...
CRIMSON GETS A BAD REP BUT TRUTH IS... IT'S THE BEST PLACE TO BE...
OPEN
...BUT NOT FOR NEW BLOODS!
RUN!

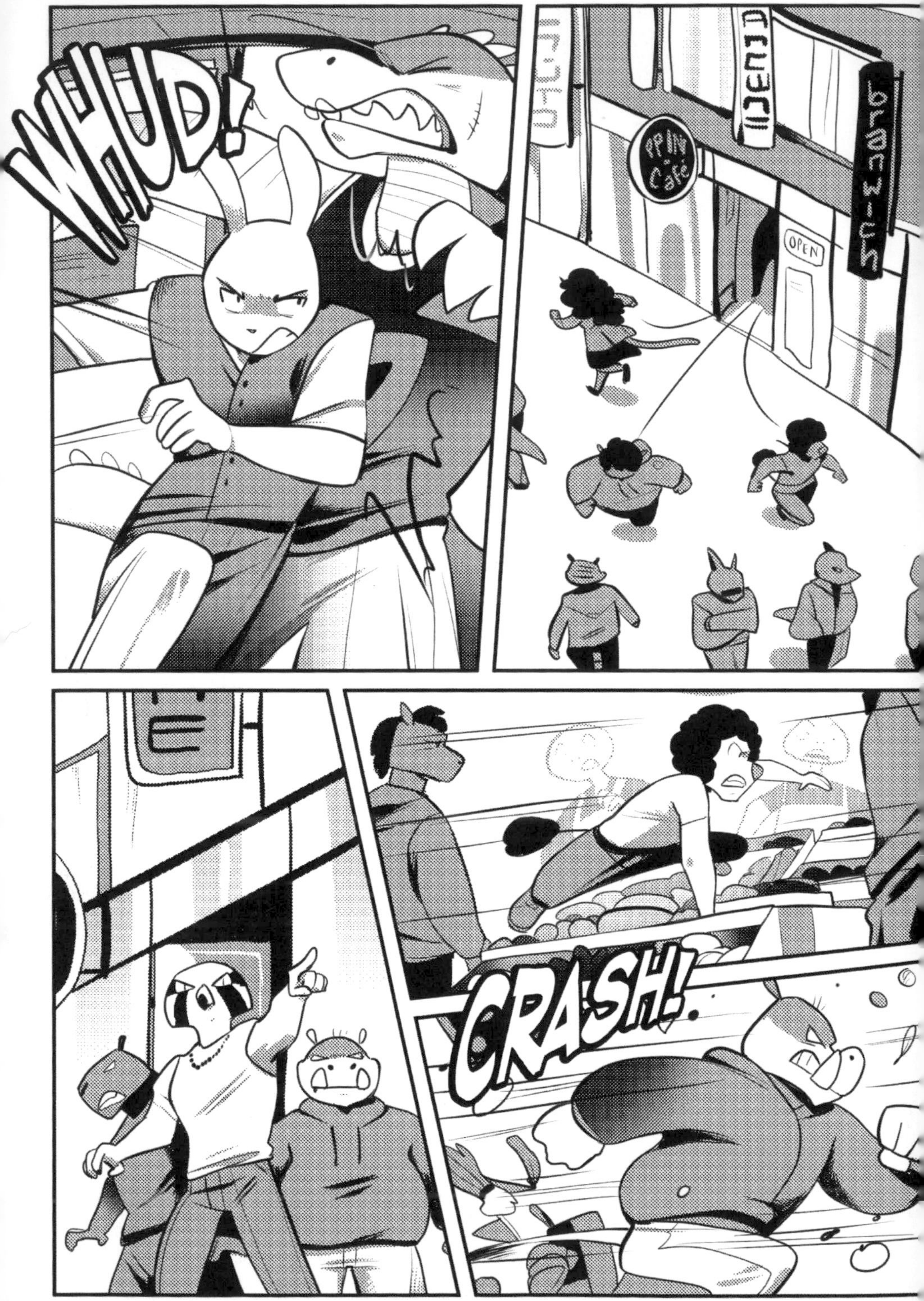
WHUD!
OPEN
CRASH!

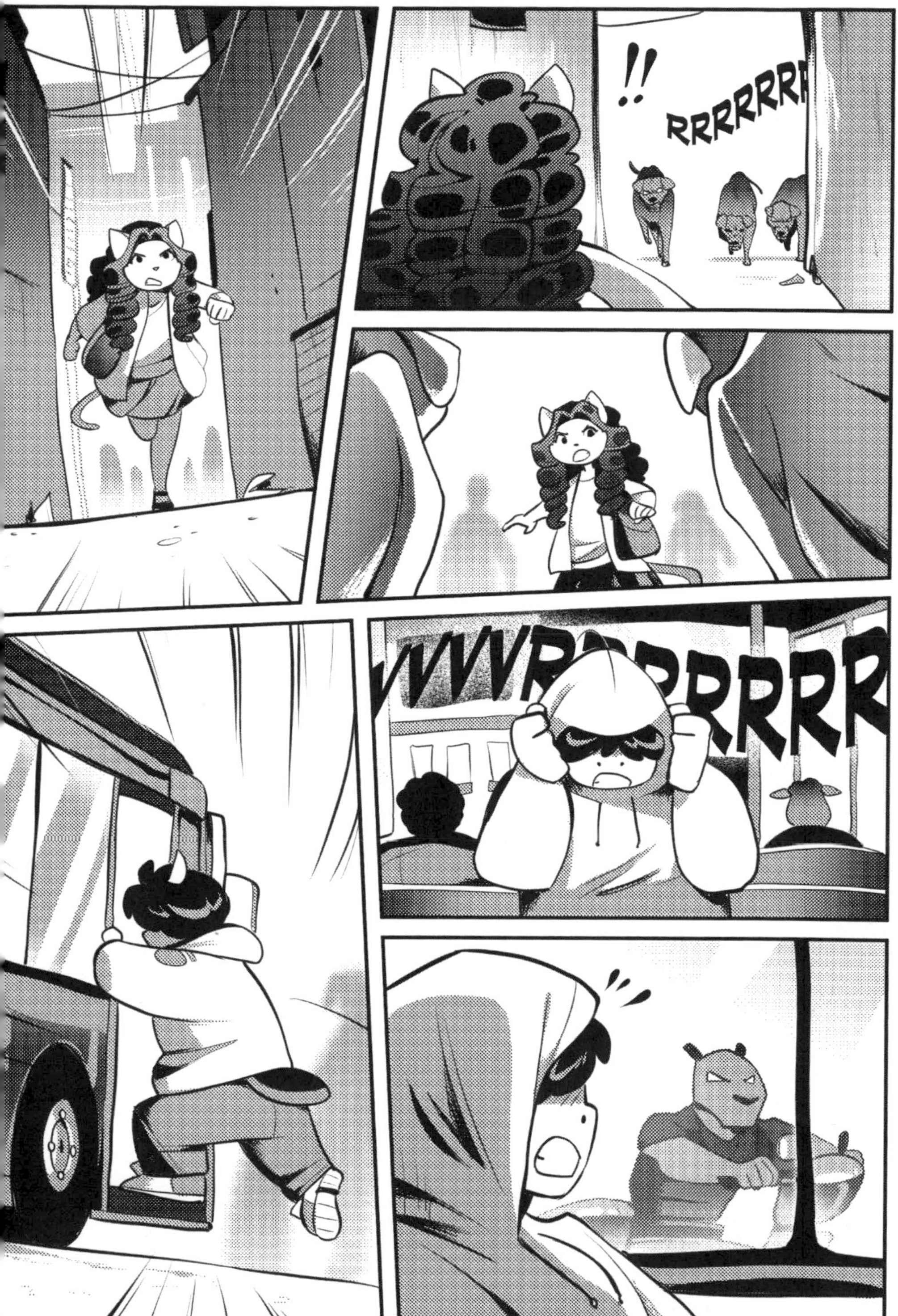
!!
RRRRRRR
VVVVRRRRRRRRR

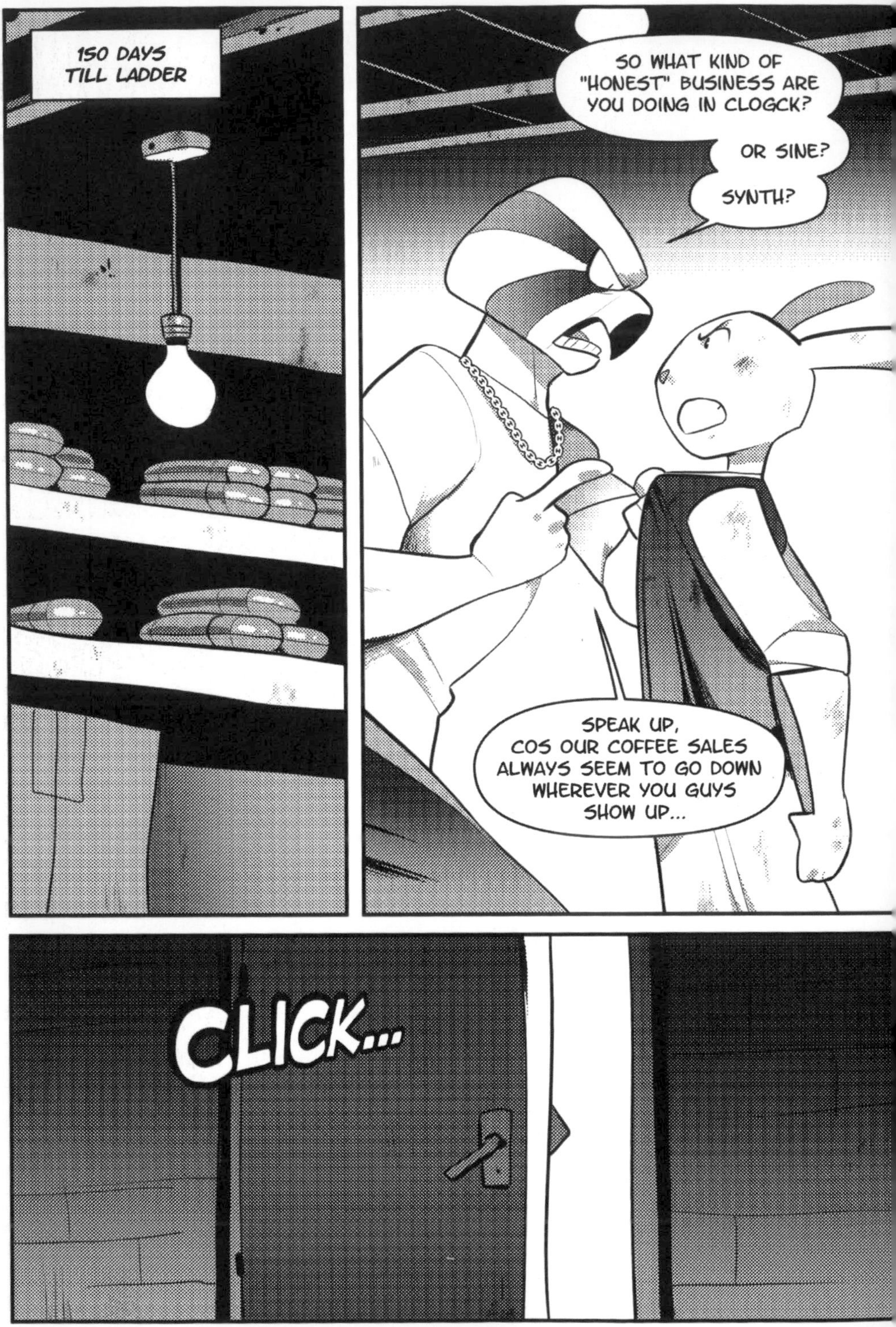
150 DAYS TILL LADDER
SO WHAT KIND OF "HONEST" BUSINESS ARE YOU DOING IN CLOGCK?
OR SINE?
SYNTH?
SPEAK UP, COS OUR COFFEE SALES ALWAYS SEEM TO GO DOWN WHEREVER YOU GUYS SHOW UP...
CLICK...

GOOD, SHUT THE DOOR.

LOOK BUNNYMAN. YOUR BUSINESS IS BAD FOR OUR BUSINESS.

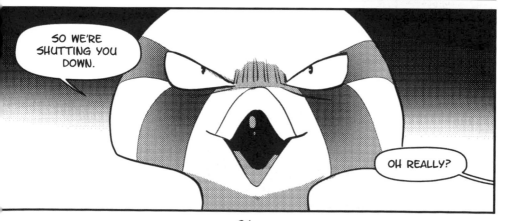

SO WE'RE SHUTTING YOU DOWN.

OH REALLY?

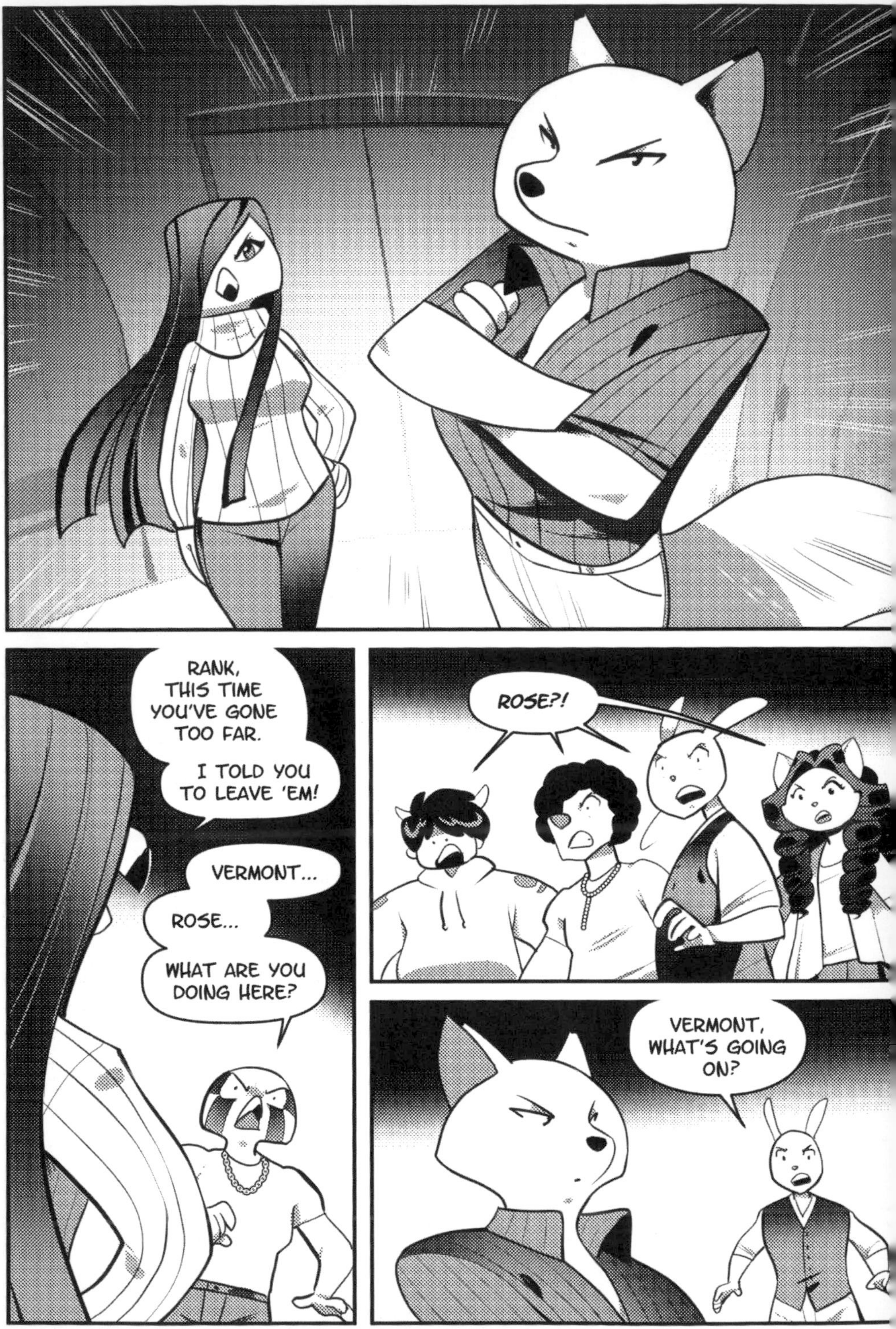
RANK, THIS TIME YOU'VE GONE TOO FAR.
I TOLD YOU TO LEAVE 'EM!
VERMONT...
ROSE...
WHAT ARE YOU DOING HERE?
ROSE?!
VERMONT, WHAT'S GOING ON?

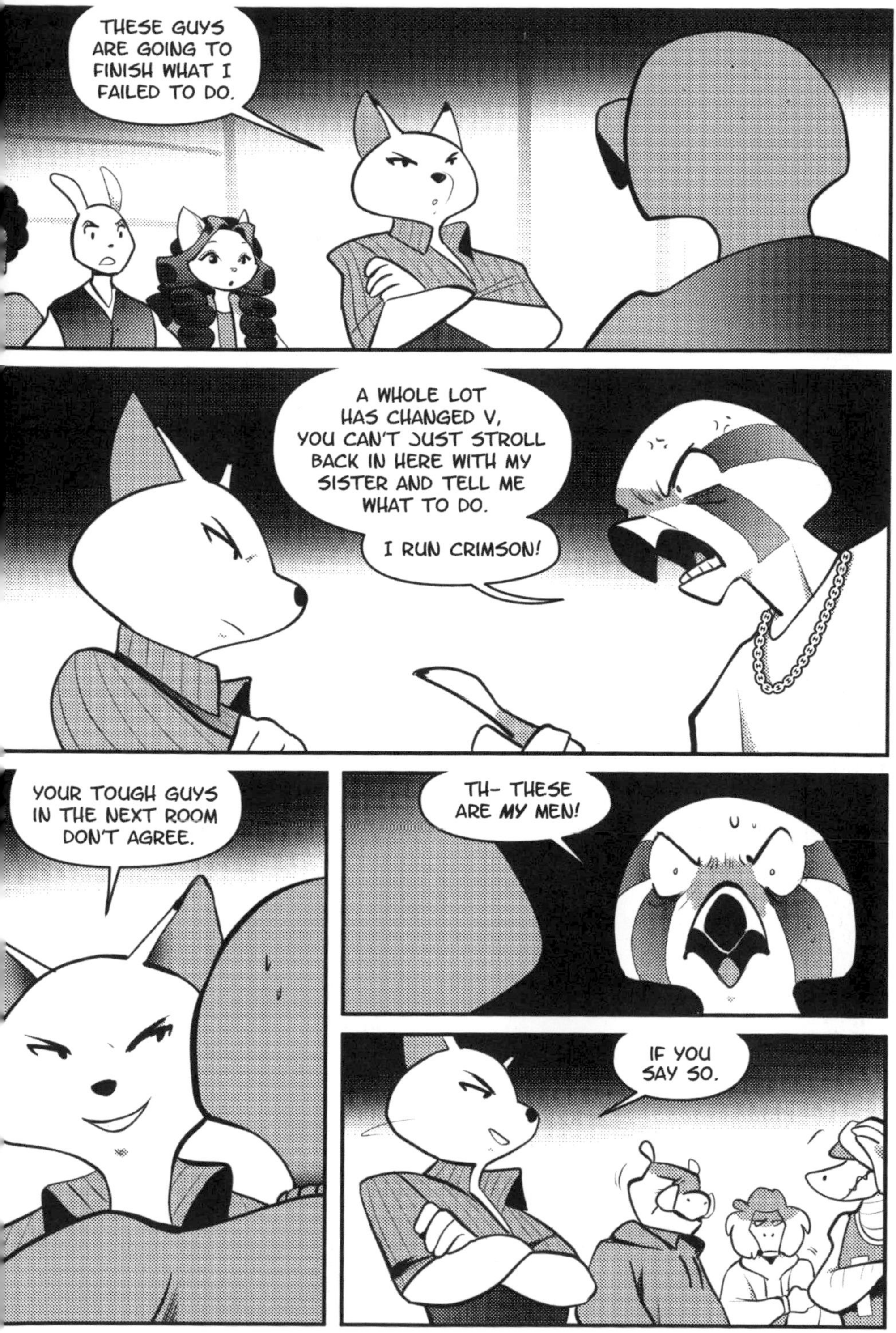
THESE GUYS ARE GOING TO FINISH WHAT I FAILED TO DO.
A WHOLE LOT HAS CHANGED V, YOU CAN'T JUST STROLL BACK IN HERE WITH MY SISTER AND TELL ME WHAT TO DO.
I RUN CRIMSON!
YOUR TOUGH GUYS IN THE NEXT ROOM DON'T AGREE.
TH- THESE ARE *MY* MEN!
IF YOU SAY SO.

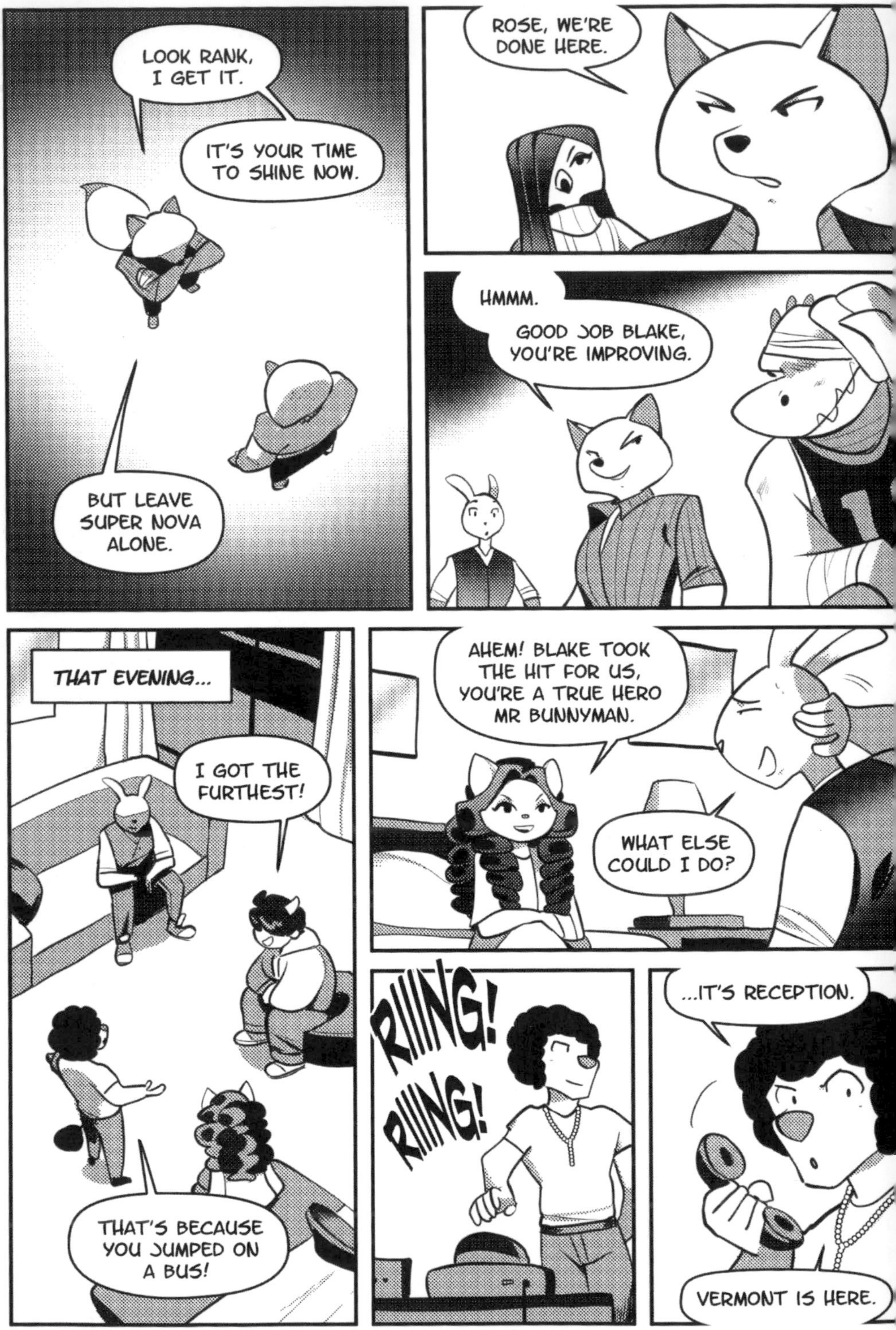
LOOK RANK, I GET IT.
IT'S YOUR TIME TO SHINE NOW.
BUT LEAVE SUPER NOVA ALONE.
ROSE, WE'RE DONE HERE.
HMMM.
GOOD JOB BLAKE, YOU'RE IMPROVING.
THAT EVENING...
I GOT THE FURTHEST!
THAT'S BECAUSE YOU JUMPED ON A BUS!
AHEM! BLAKE TOOK THE HIT FOR US, YOU'RE A TRUE HERO MR BUNNYMAN.
WHAT ELSE COULD I DO?
RIIING! RIING!
...IT'S RECEPTION.
VERMONT IS HERE.

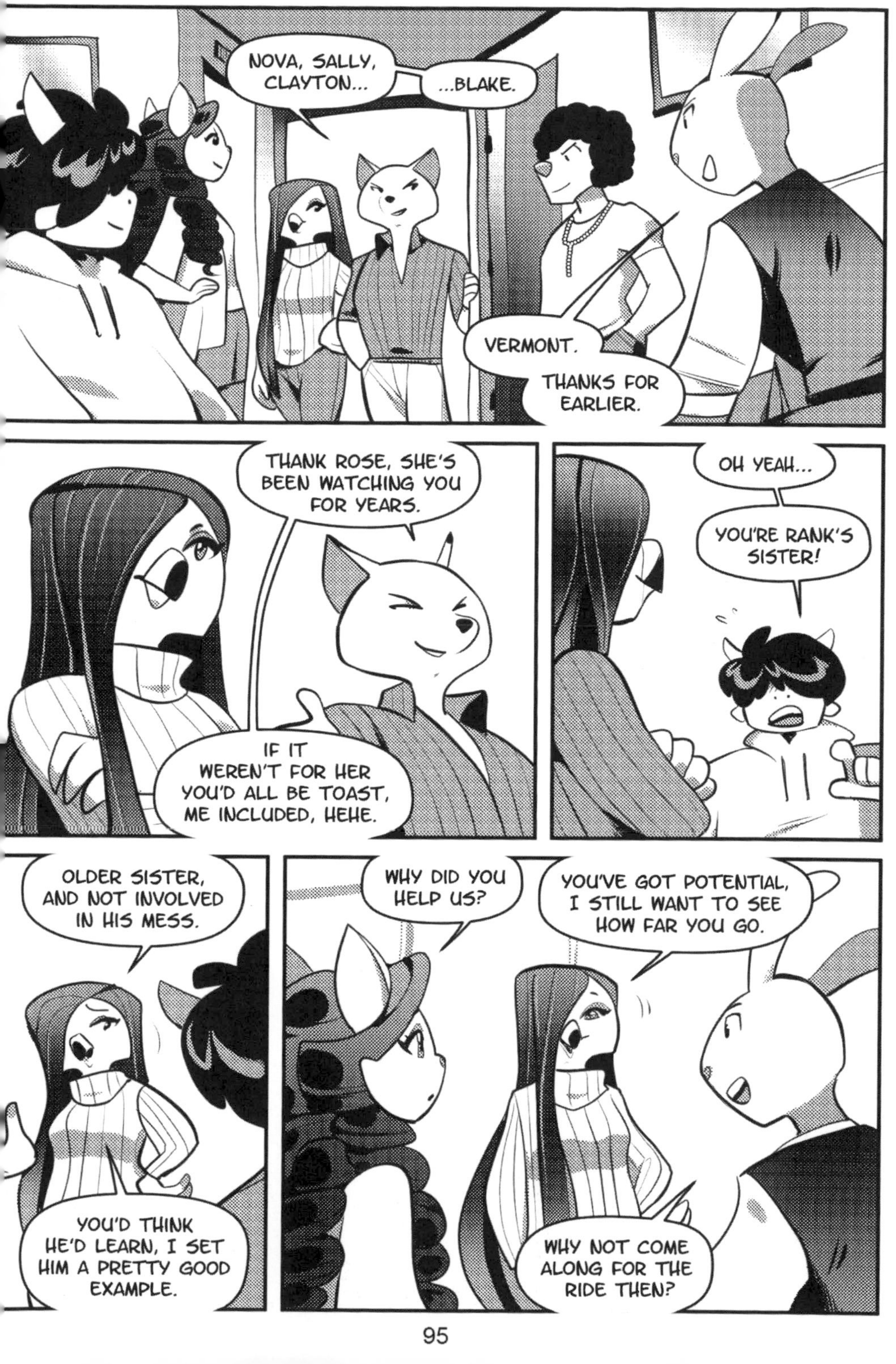
NOVA, SALLY, CLAYTON...
...BLAKE.
VERMONT.
THANKS FOR EARLIER.
THANK ROSE, SHE'S BEEN WATCHING YOU FOR YEARS.
IF IT WEREN'T FOR HER YOU'D ALL BE TOAST, ME INCLUDED, HEHE.
OH YEAH...
YOU'RE RANK'S SISTER!
OLDER SISTER, AND NOT INVOLVED IN HIS MESS.
YOU'D THINK HE'D LEARN, I SET HIM A PRETTY GOOD EXAMPLE.
WHY DID YOU HELP US?
YOU'VE GOT POTENTIAL, I STILL WANT TO SEE HOW FAR YOU GO.
WHY NOT COME ALONG FOR THE RIDE THEN?

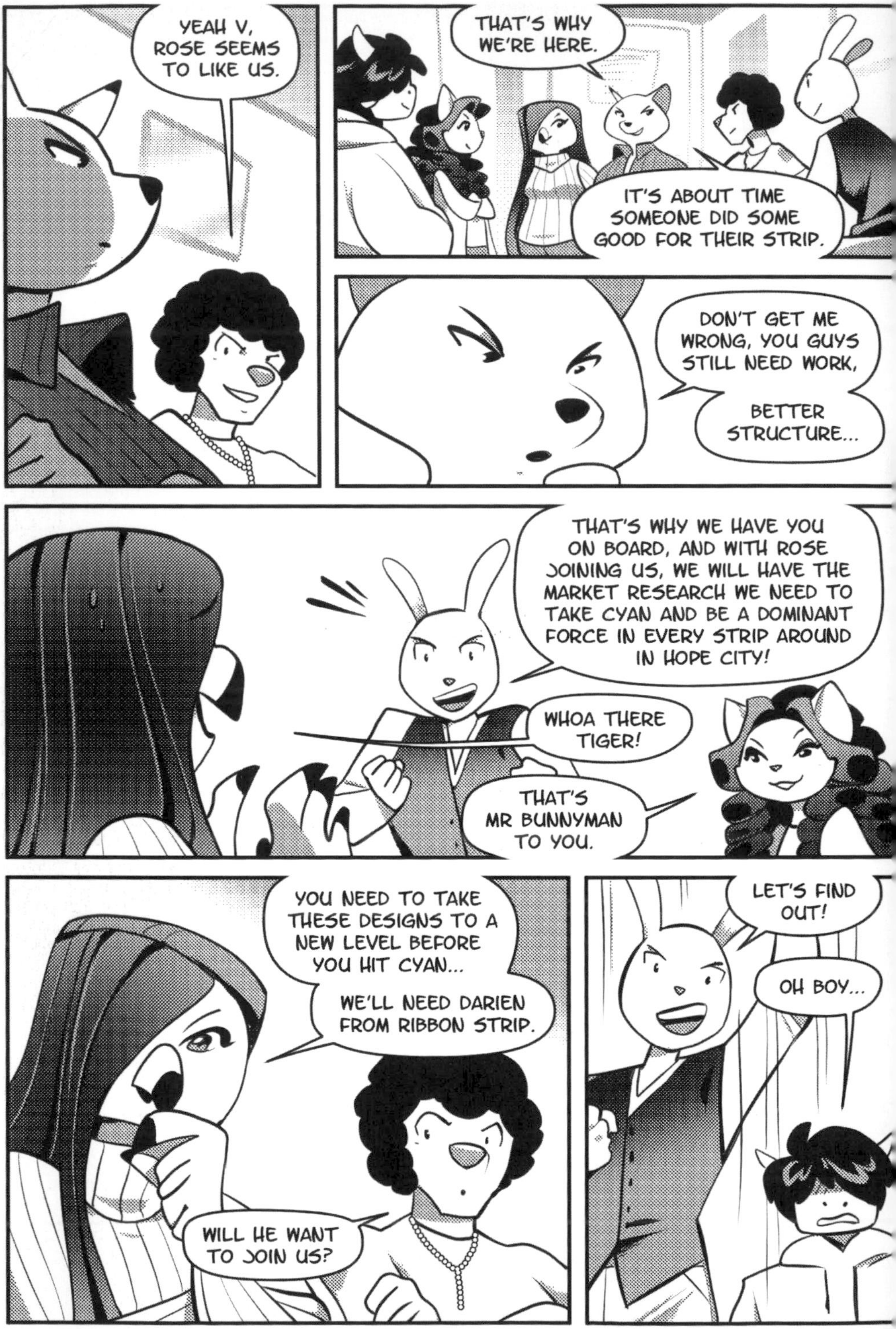
YEAH V, ROSE SEEMS TO LIKE US.
THAT'S WHY WE'RE HERE.
IT'S ABOUT TIME SOMEONE DID SOME GOOD FOR THEIR STRIP.
DON'T GET ME WRONG, YOU GUYS STILL NEED WORK,
BETTER STRUCTURE...
THAT'S WHY WE HAVE YOU ON BOARD, AND WITH ROSE JOINING US, WE WILL HAVE THE MARKET RESEARCH WE NEED TO TAKE CYAN AND BE A DOMINANT FORCE IN EVERY STRIP AROUND IN HOPE CITY!
WHOA THERE TIGER!
THAT'S MR BUNNYMAN TO YOU.
YOU NEED TO TAKE THESE DESIGNS TO A NEW LEVEL BEFORE YOU HIT CYAN...
WE'LL NEED DARIEN FROM RIBBON STRIP.
WILL HE WANT TO JOIN US?
LET'S FIND OUT!
OH BOY...

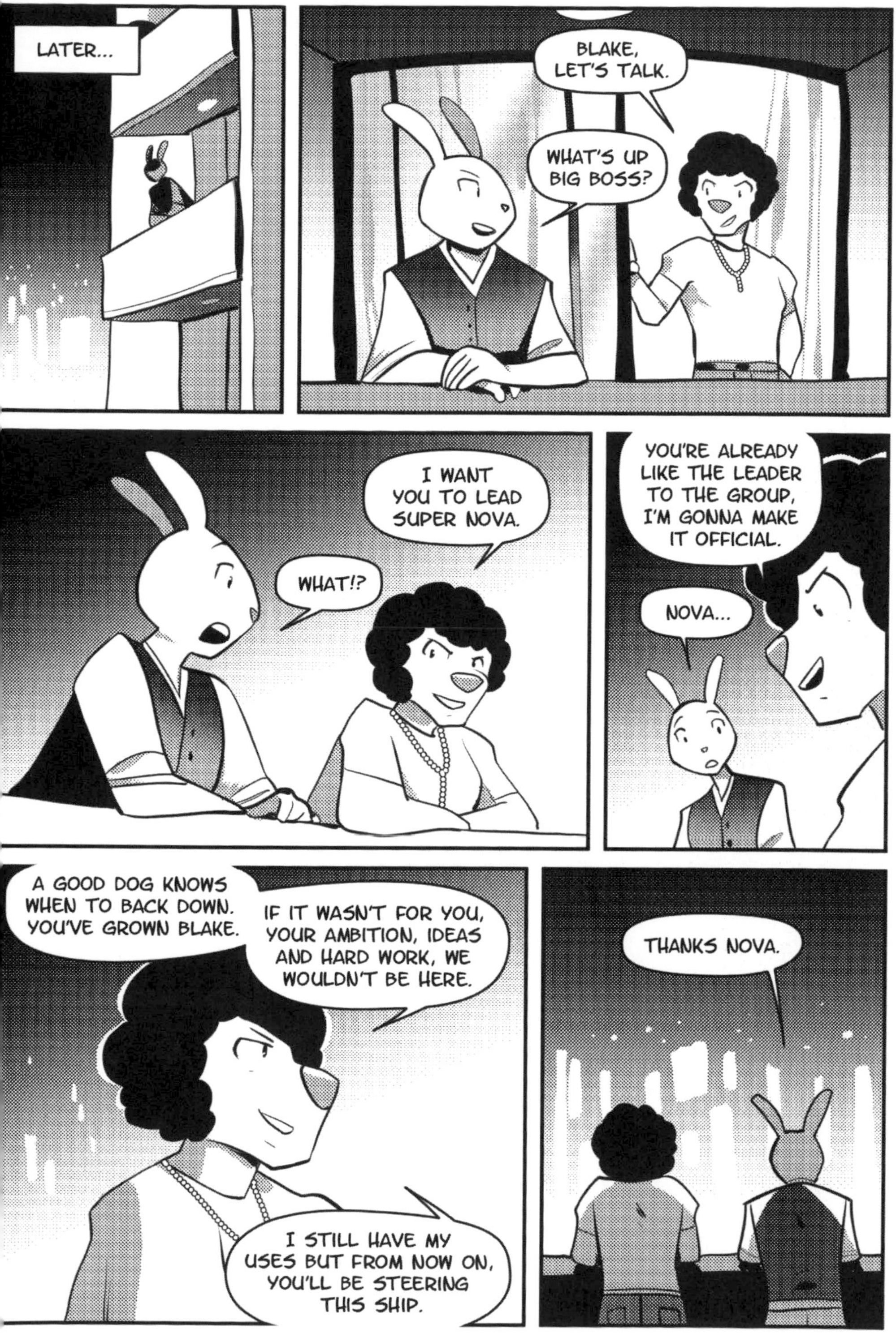
LATER...
BLAKE, LET'S TALK.
WHAT'S UP BIG BOSS?
I WANT YOU TO LEAD SUPER NOVA.
WHAT!?
YOU'RE ALREADY LIKE THE LEADER TO THE GROUP, I'M GONNA MAKE IT OFFICIAL.
NOVA...
A GOOD DOG KNOWS WHEN TO BACK DOWN. YOU'VE GROWN BLAKE.
IF IT WASN'T FOR YOU, YOUR AMBITION, IDEAS AND HARD WORK, WE WOULDN'T BE HERE.
I STILL HAVE MY USES BUT FROM NOW ON, YOU'LL BE STEERING THIS SHIP.
THANKS NOVA.

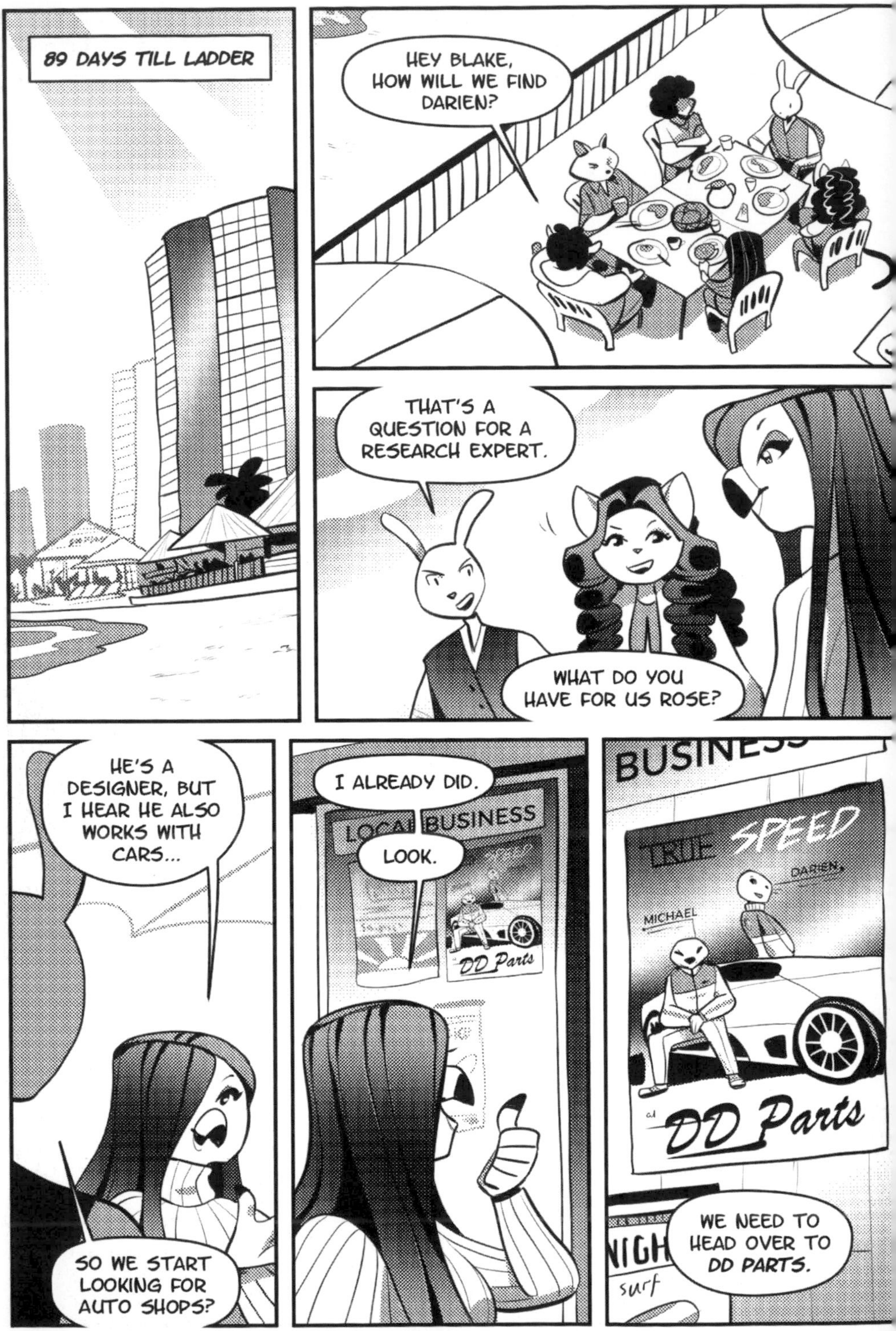
89 DAYS TILL LADDER
HEY BLAKE, HOW WILL WE FIND DARIEN?
THAT'S A QUESTION FOR A RESEARCH EXPERT.
WHAT DO YOU HAVE FOR US ROSE?
HE'S A DESIGNER, BUT I HEAR HE ALSO WORKS WITH CARS...
SO WE START LOOKING FOR AUTO SHOPS?
I ALREADY DID.
LOCAL BUSINESS
LOOK.
DD Parts
BUSINESS
TRUE SPEED
DARIEN
MICHAEL
DD Parts
NIGH
surf
WE NEED TO HEAD OVER TO DD PARTS.

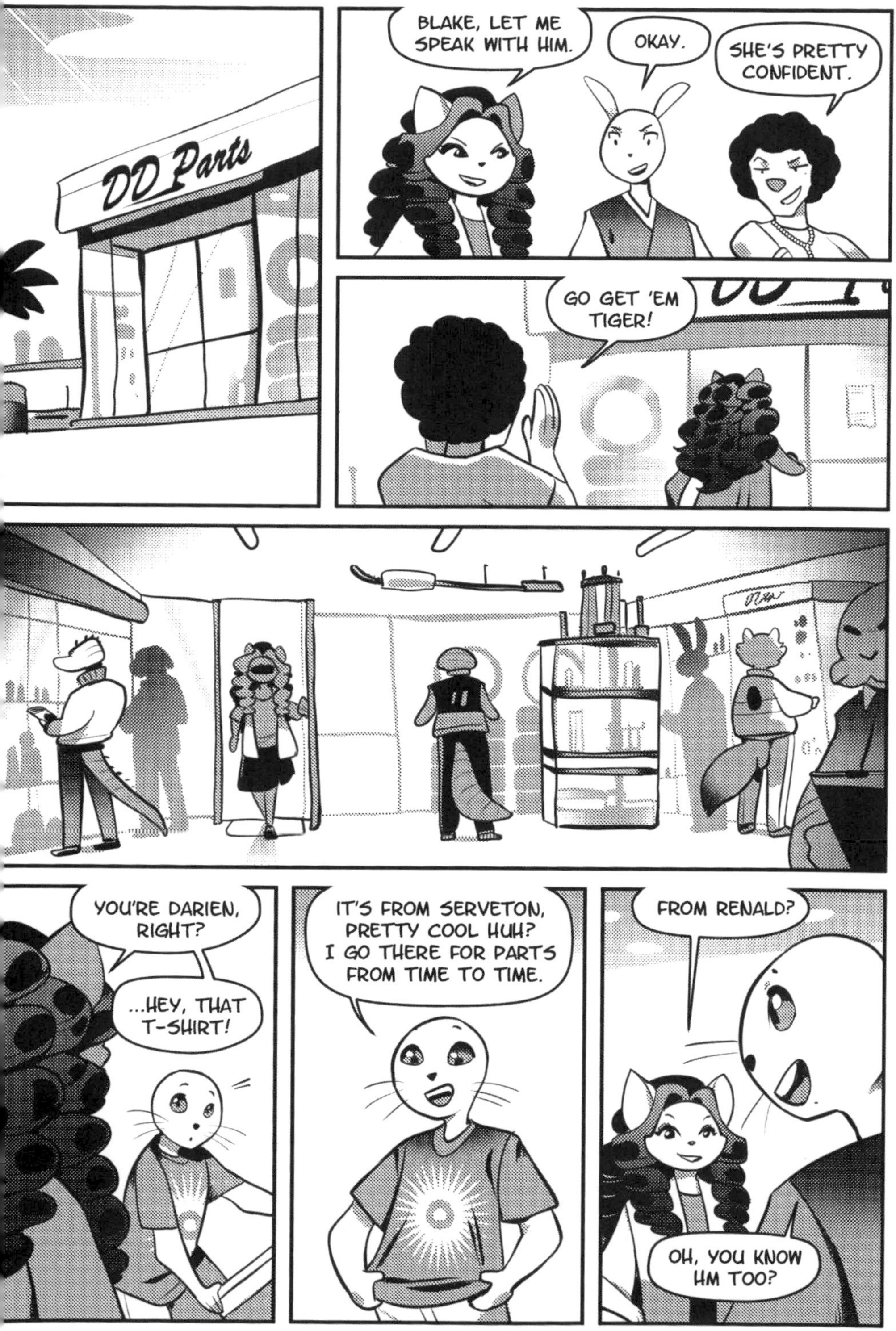
DD Parts
BLAKE, LET ME SPEAK WITH HIM.
OKAY.
SHE'S PRETTY CONFIDENT.
GO GET 'EM TIGER!
YOU'RE DARIEN, RIGHT?
...HEY, THAT T-SHIRT!
IT'S FROM SERVETON, PRETTY COOL HUH? I GO THERE FOR PARTS FROM TIME TO TIME.
FROM RENALD?
OH, YOU KNOW HM TOO?

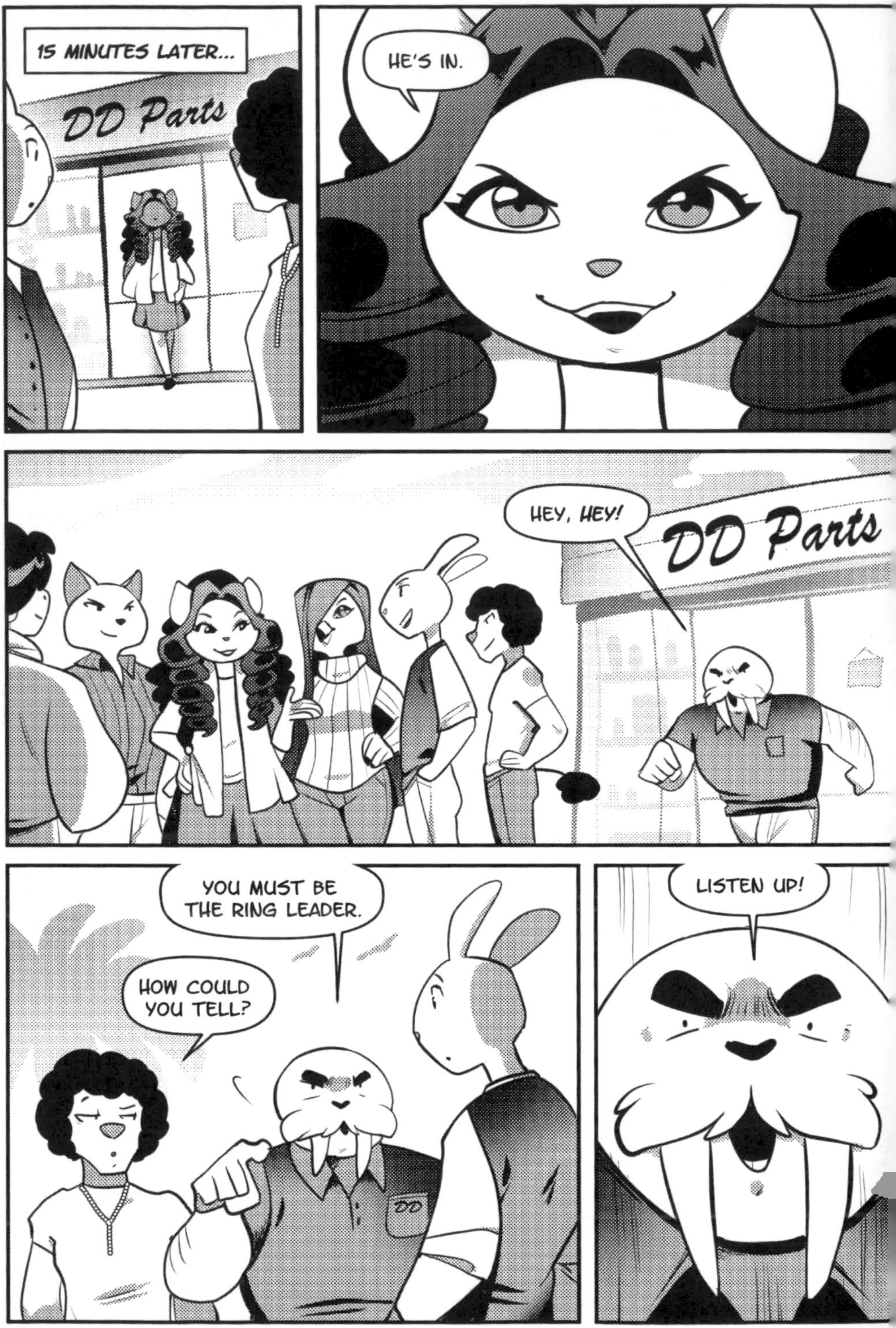
15 MINUTES LATER...
DD Parts
HE'S IN.
HEY, HEY!
DD Parts
YOU MUST BE THE RING LEADER.
HOW COULD YOU TELL?
DD
LISTEN UP!

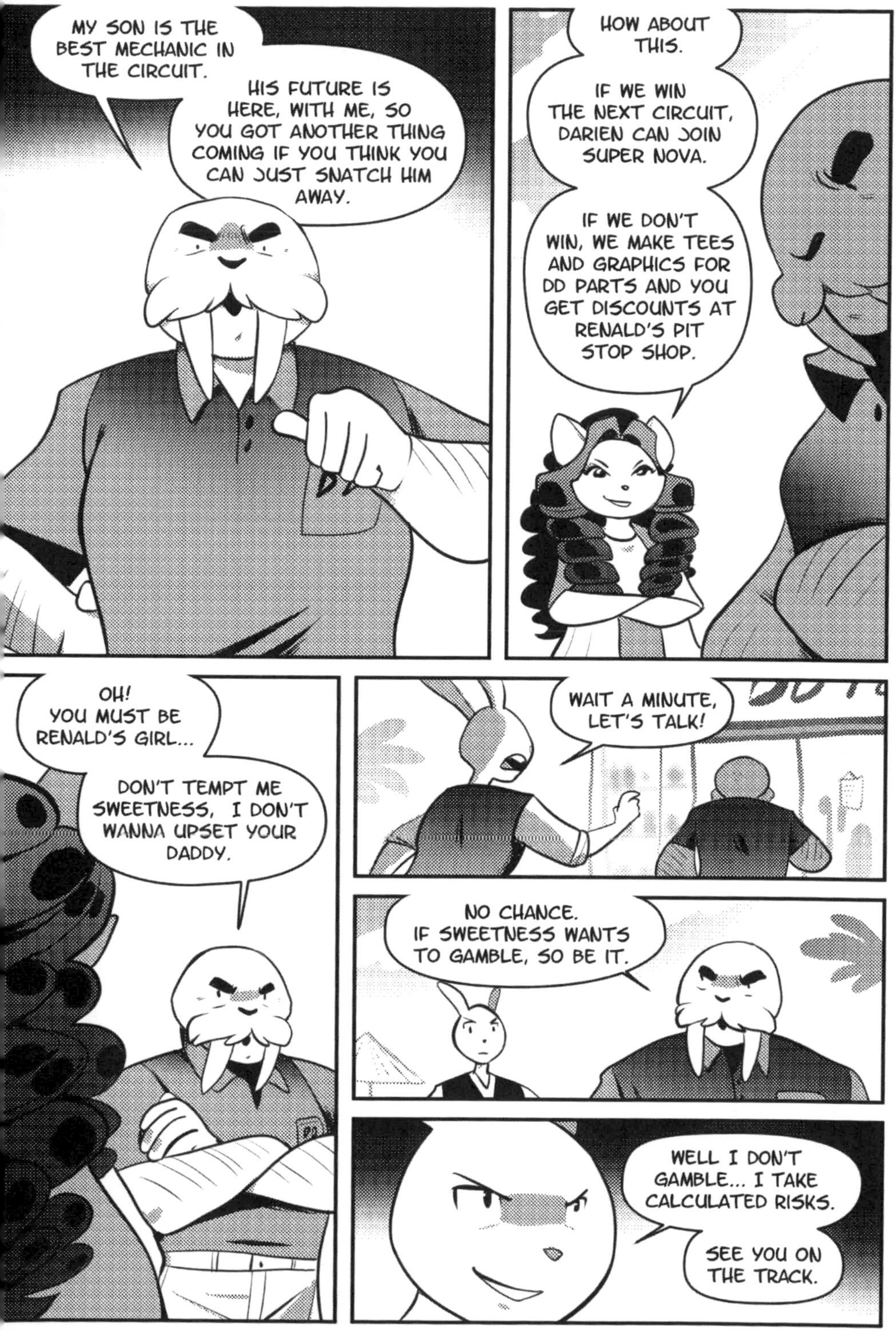
MY SON IS THE BEST MECHANIC IN THE CIRCUIT.
HIS FUTURE IS HERE, WITH ME, SO YOU GOT ANOTHER THING COMING IF YOU THINK YOU CAN JUST SNATCH HIM AWAY.
HOW ABOUT THIS.
IF WE WIN THE NEXT CIRCUIT, DARIEN CAN JOIN SUPER NOVA.
IF WE DON'T WIN, WE MAKE TEES AND GRAPHICS FOR DD PARTS AND YOU GET DISCOUNTS AT RENALD'S PIT STOP SHOP.
OH! YOU MUST BE RENALD'S GIRL...
DON'T TEMPT ME SWEETNESS, I DON'T WANNA UPSET YOUR DADDY.
WAIT A MINUTE, LET'S TALK!
NO CHANCE. IF SWEETNESS WANTS TO GAMBLE, SO BE IT.
WELL I DON'T GAMBLE... I TAKE CALCULATED RISKS.
SEE YOU ON THE TRACK.

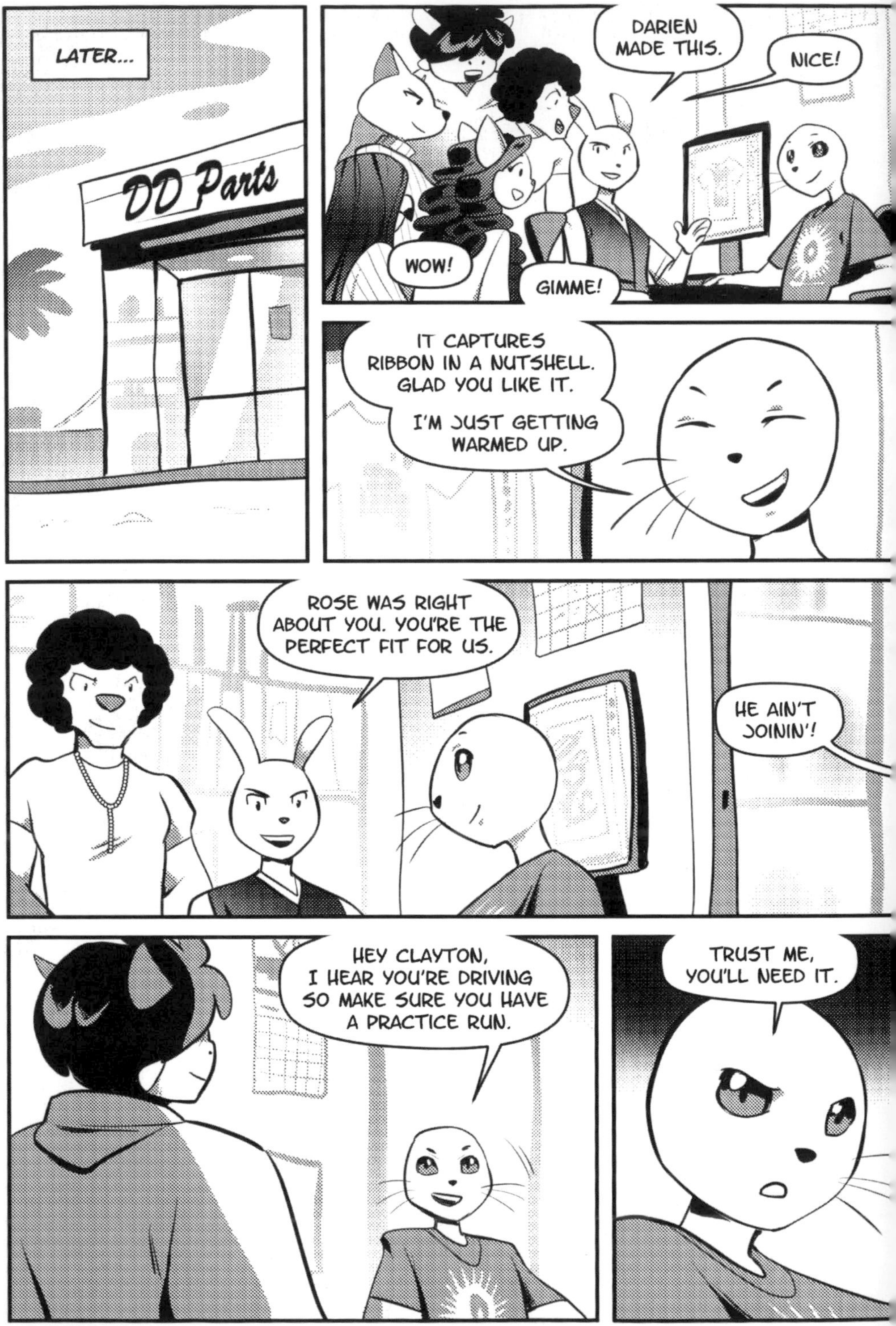
LATER...
DD Parts
DARIEN MADE THIS.
NICE!
WOW!
GIMME!
IT CAPTURES RIBBON IN A NUTSHELL. GLAD YOU LIKE IT.
I'M JUST GETTING WARMED UP.
ROSE WAS RIGHT ABOUT YOU. YOU'RE THE PERFECT FIT FOR US.
HE AIN'T JOININ'!
HEY CLAYTON, I HEAR YOU'RE DRIVING SO MAKE SURE YOU HAVE A PRACTICE RUN.
TRUST ME, YOU'LL NEED IT.

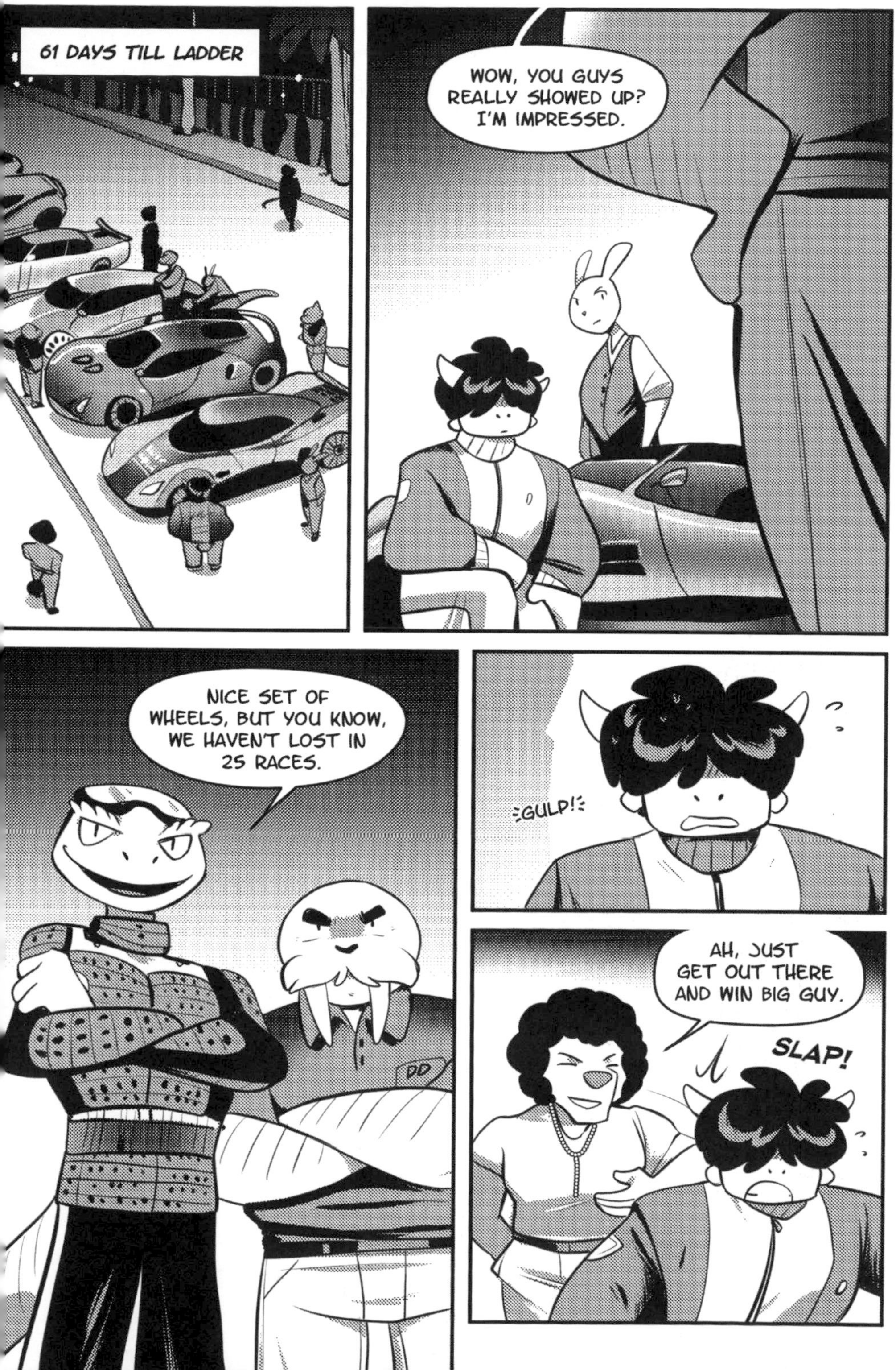
61 DAYS TILL LADDER
WOW, YOU GUYS REALLY SHOWED UP? I'M IMPRESSED.
NICE SET OF WHEELS, BUT YOU KNOW, WE HAVEN'T LOST IN 25 RACES.
DD
GULP!
AH, JUST GET OUT THERE AND WIN BIG GUY.
SLAP!

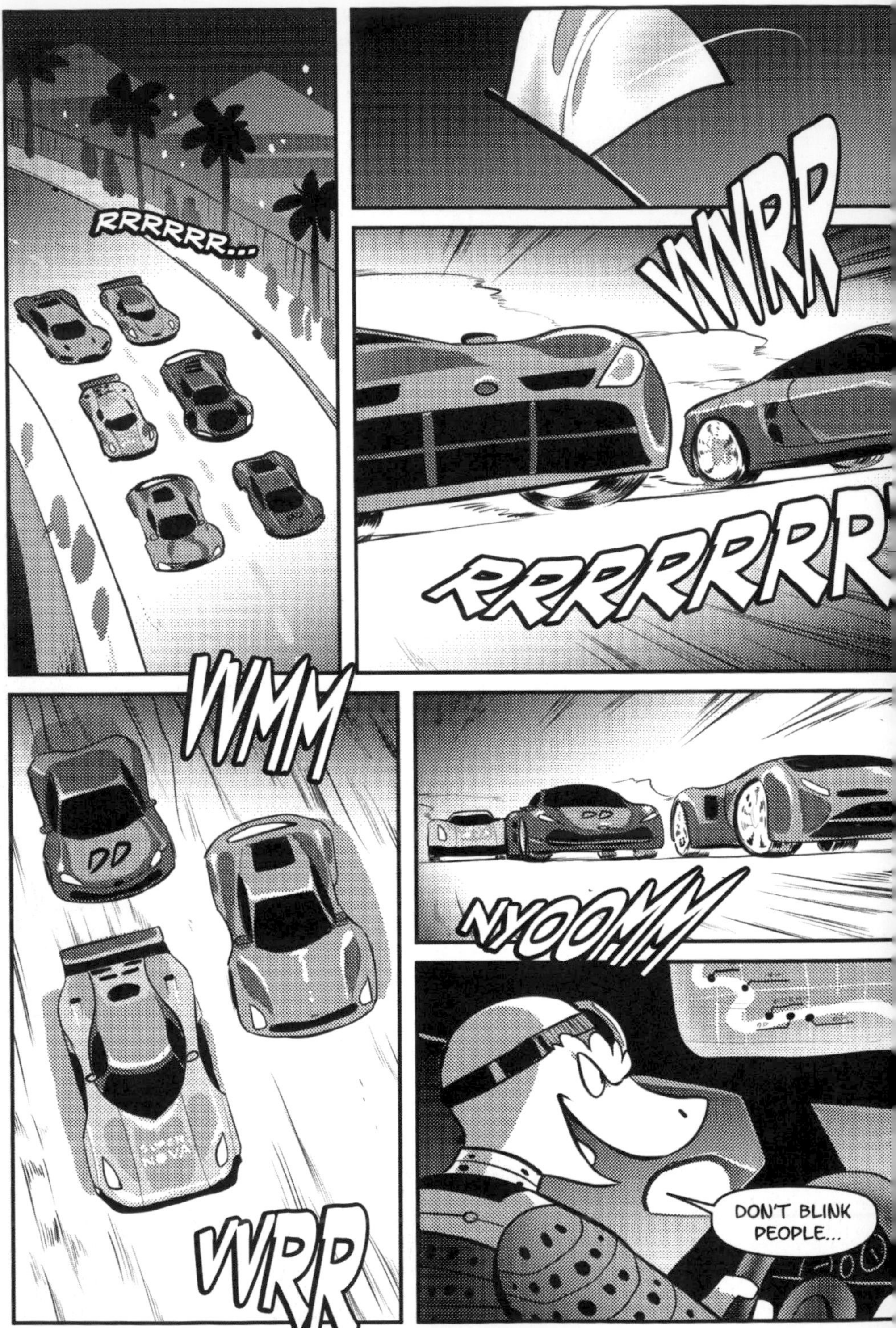

RRRRRR...
VVVRR
RRRRRRRR
VVMM
VVRR
NYOOMM
DON'T BLINK PEOPLE...

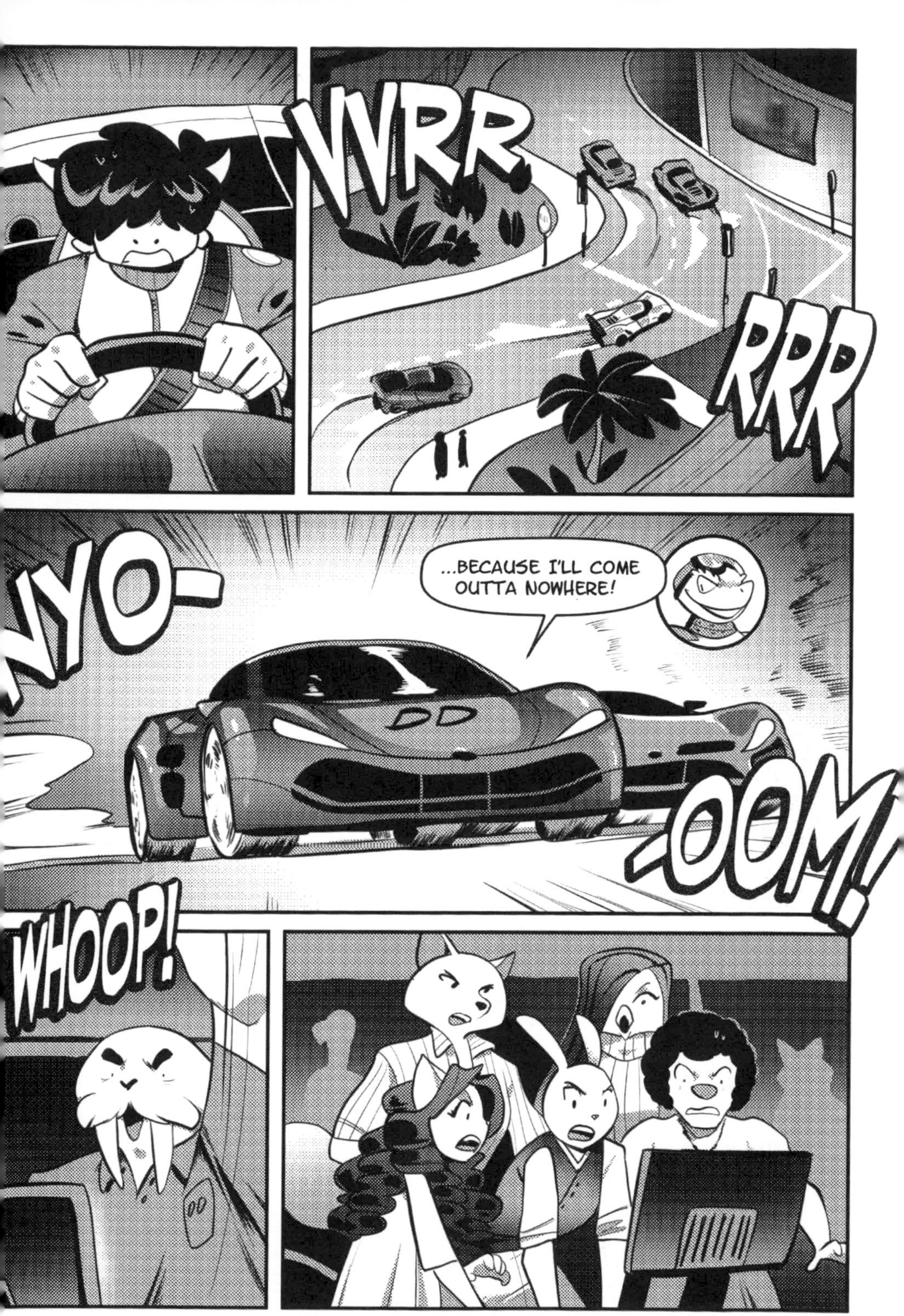
VVRR
RRR
NYO-
...BECAUSE I'LL COME OUTTA NOWHERE!
-OOM!
WHOOP!

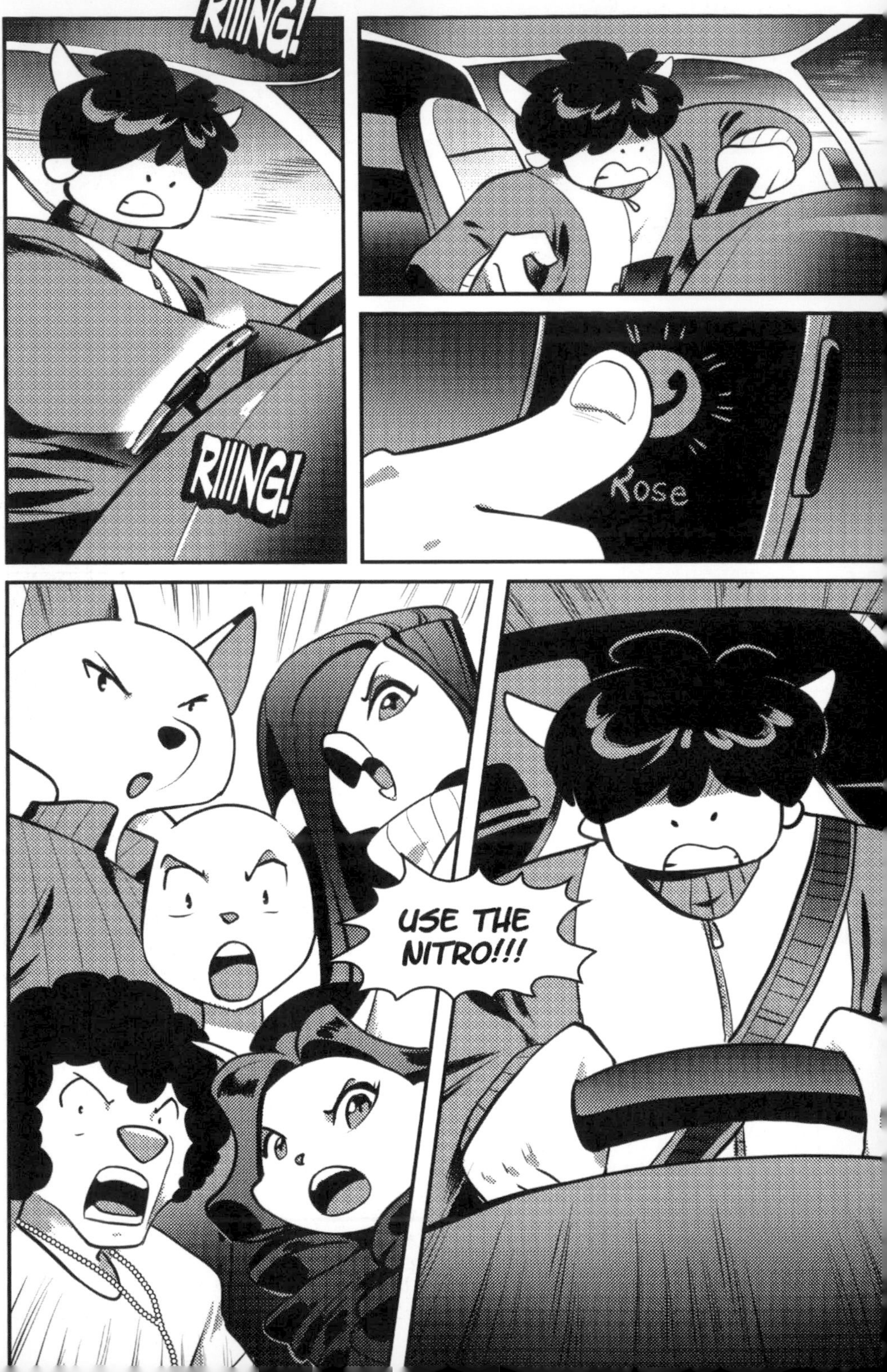
RIIING!
RIIING!
Rose
USE THE NITRO!!!

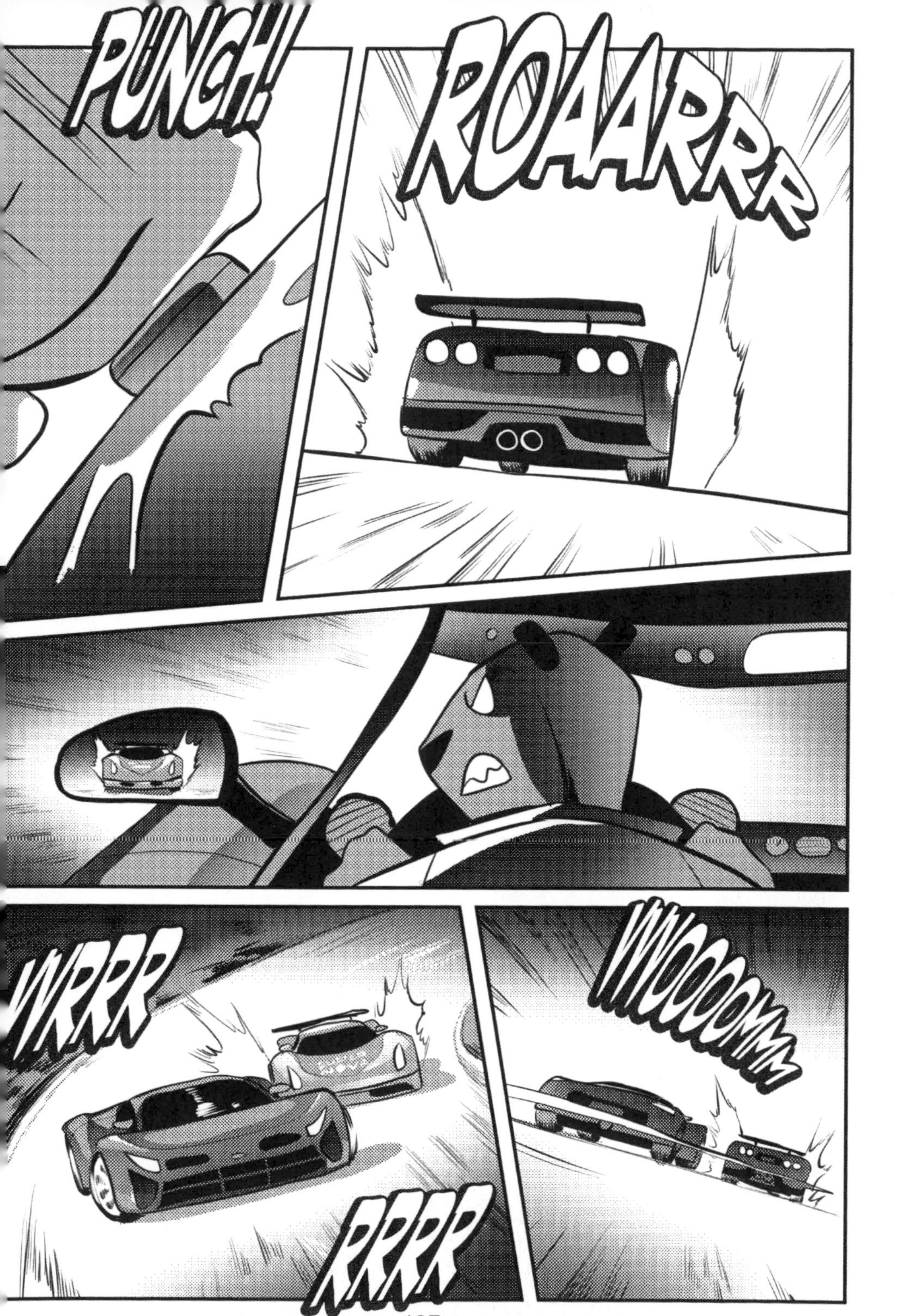
PUNCH!!
ROAARRR
WRRR
RRRR
VVOOOOMM

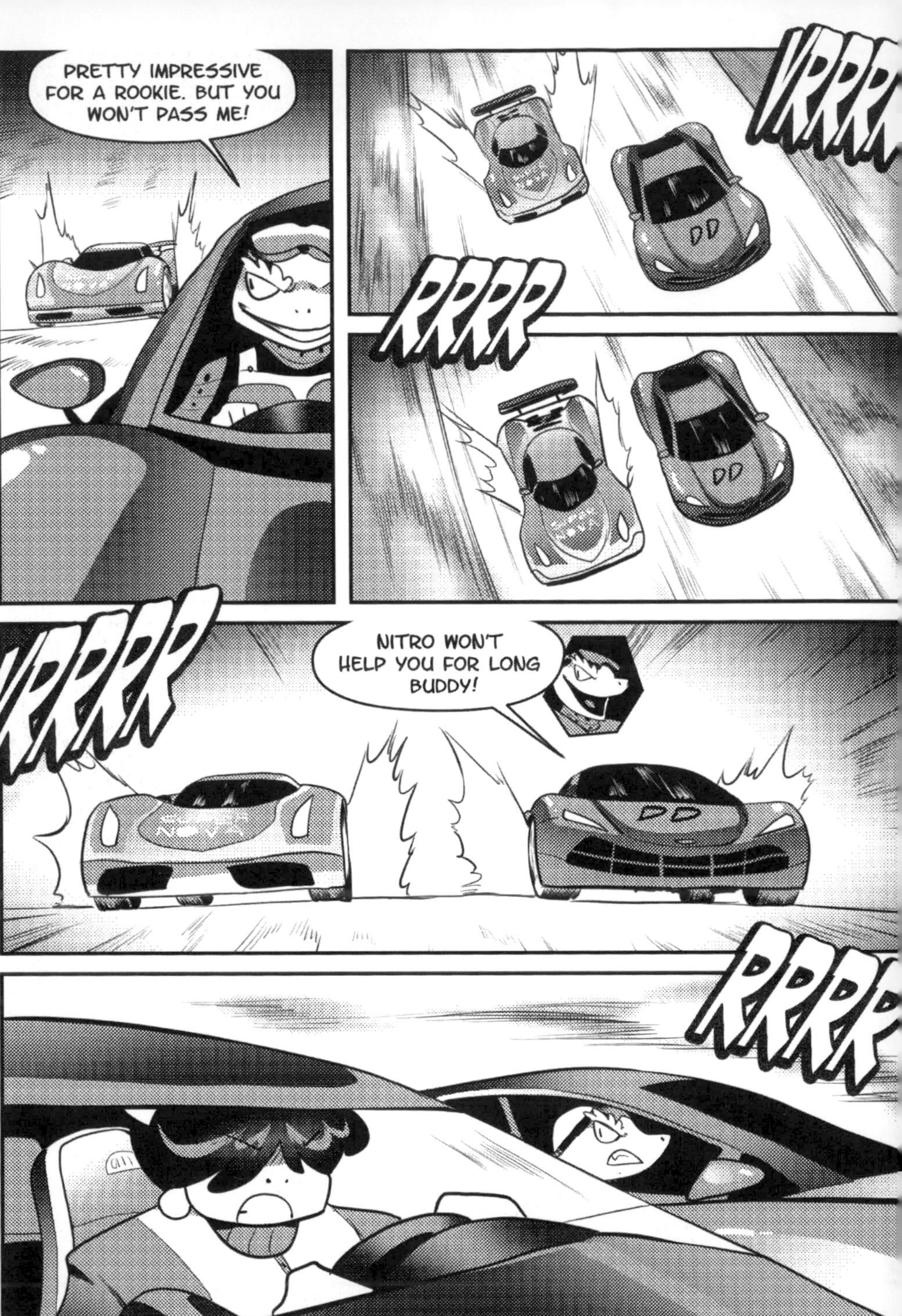
PRETTY IMPRESSIVE FOR A ROOKIE. BUT YOU WON'T PASS ME!
VRRRR
DD
RRRR
DD
VRRRR
NITRO WON'T HELP YOU FOR LONG BUDDY!
DD
RRRR

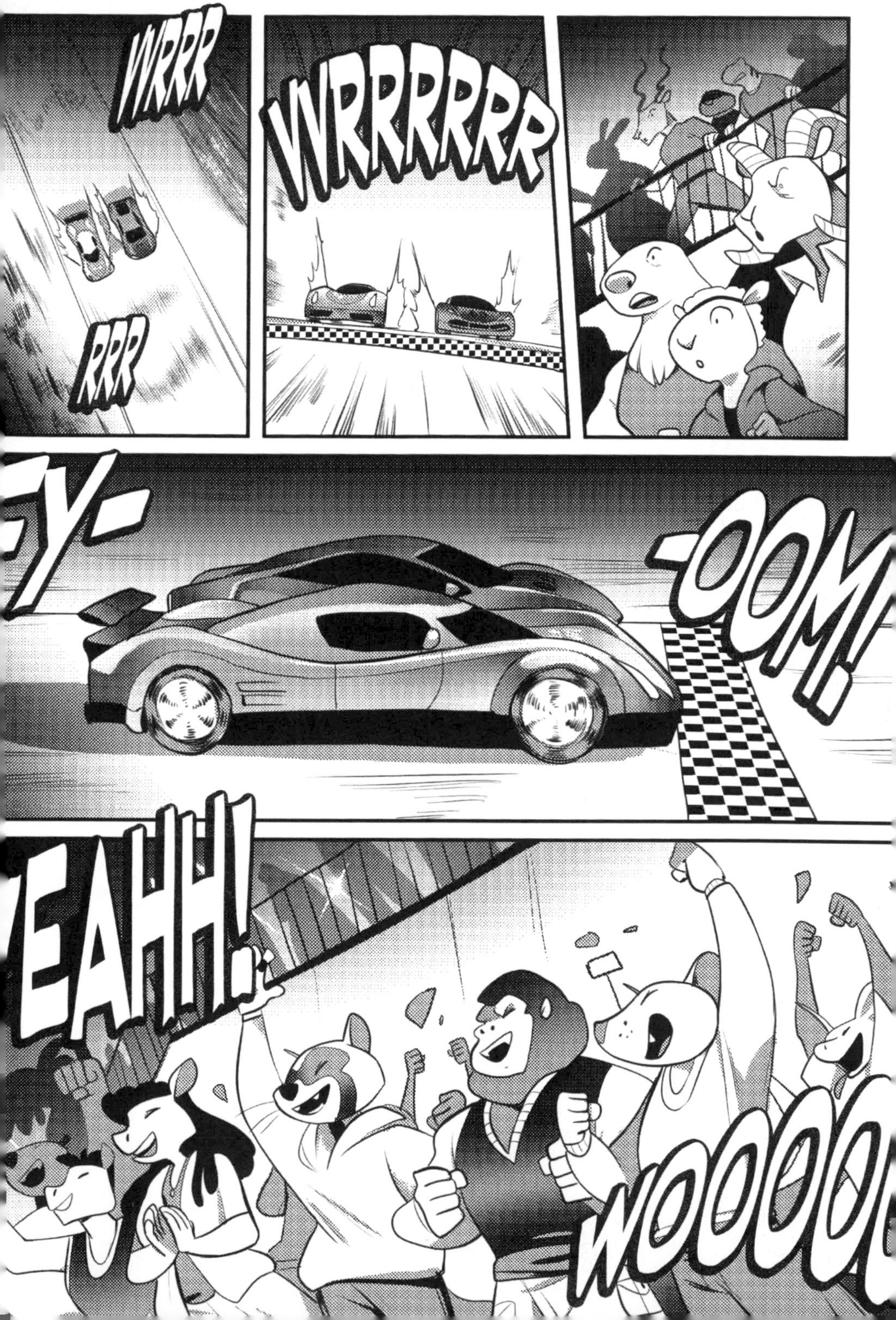

VVRRR
RRR
VVRRRRRRR
FY-
-OOM!
EAHH!!
WOOOO

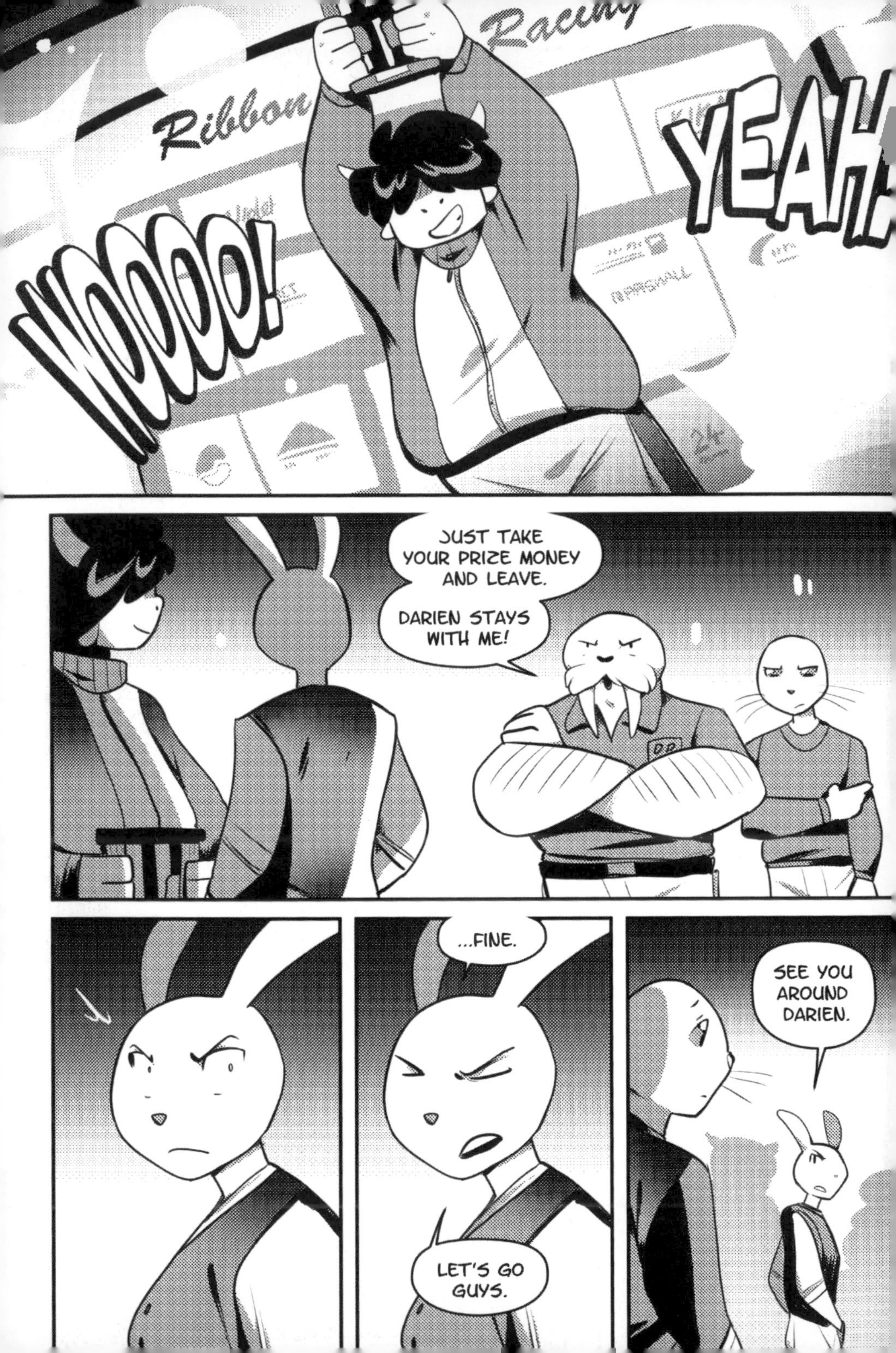
Ribbon Racing
WOOOO!
YEAH!
JUST TAKE YOUR PRIZE MONEY AND LEAVE.
DARIEN STAYS WITH ME!
...FINE.
LET'S GO GUYS.
SEE YOU AROUND DARIEN.

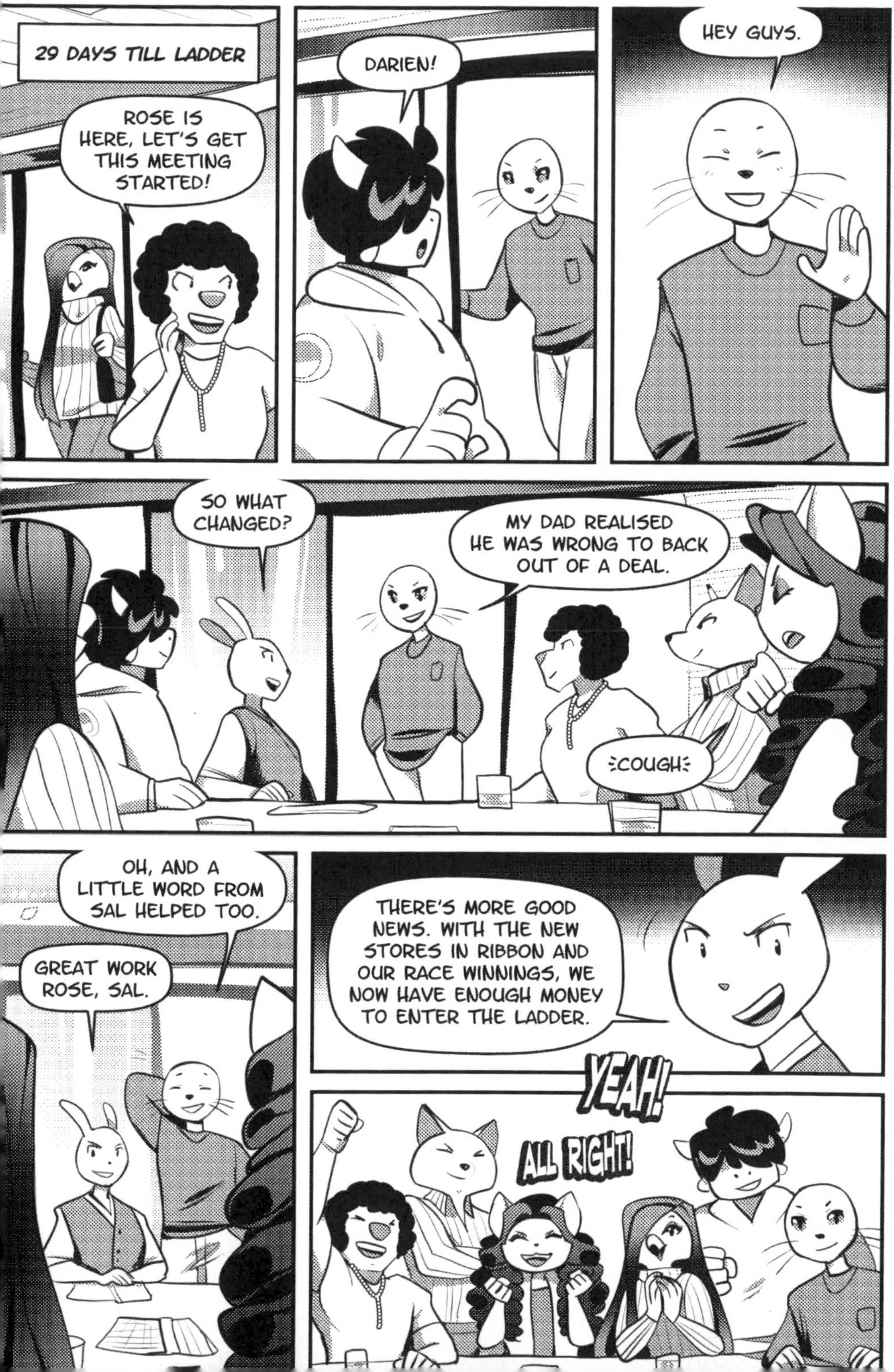
29 DAYS TILL LADDER
ROSE IS HERE, LET'S GET THIS MEETING STARTED!
DARIEN!
HEY GUYS.
SO WHAT CHANGED?
MY DAD REALISED HE WAS WRONG TO BACK OUT OF A DEAL.
COUGH
OH, AND A LITTLE WORD FROM SAL HELPED TOO.
GREAT WORK ROSE, SAL.
THERE'S MORE GOOD NEWS. WITH THE NEW STORES IN RIBBON AND OUR RACE WINNINGS, WE NOW HAVE ENOUGH MONEY TO ENTER THE LADDER.
YEAH!
ALL RIGHT!

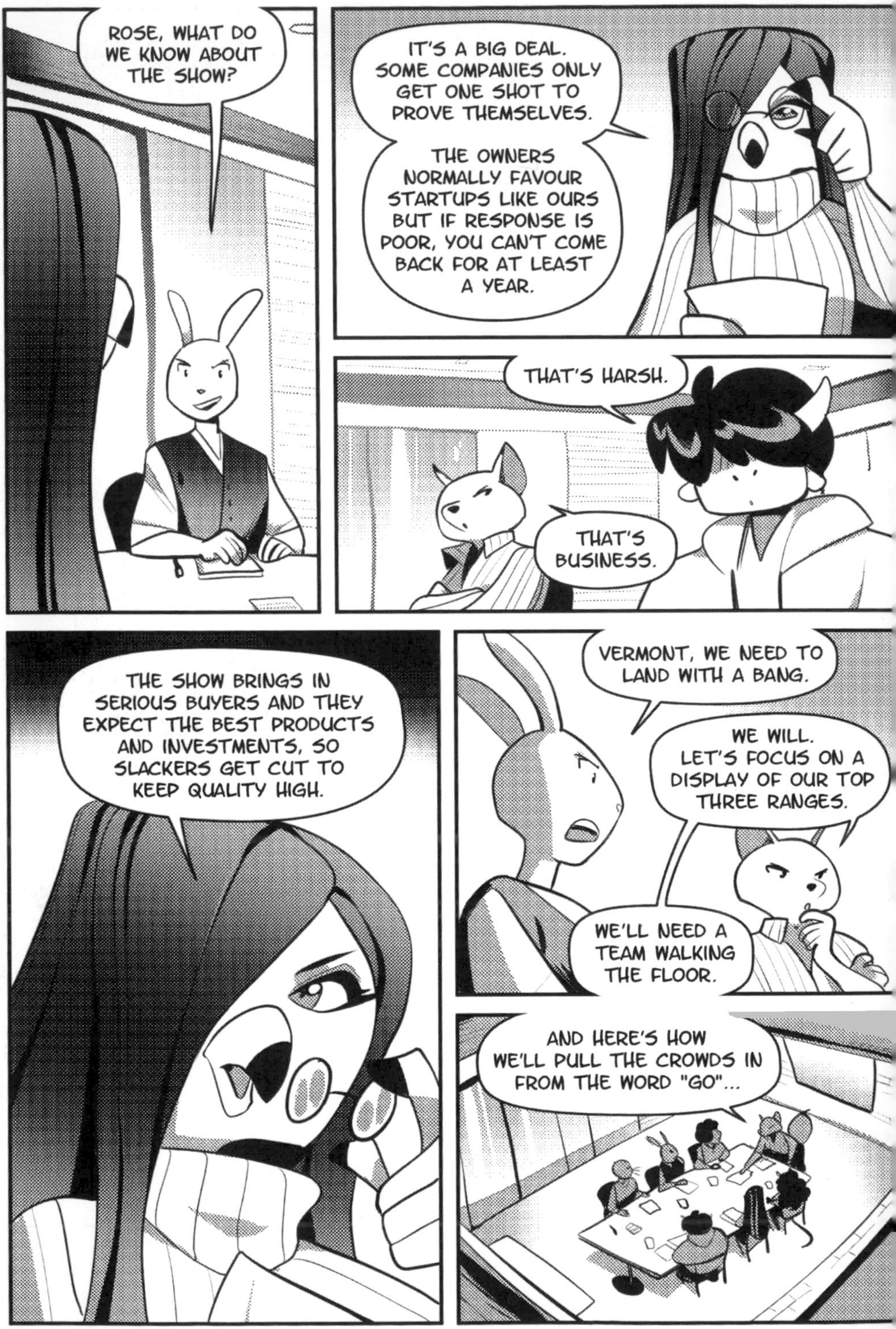
ROSE, WHAT DO WE KNOW ABOUT THE SHOW?
IT'S A BIG DEAL. SOME COMPANIES ONLY GET ONE SHOT TO PROVE THEMSELVES.
THE OWNERS NORMALLY FAVOUR STARTUPS LIKE OURS BUT IF RESPONSE IS POOR, YOU CAN'T COME BACK FOR AT LEAST A YEAR.
THAT'S HARSH.
THAT'S BUSINESS.
THE SHOW BRINGS IN SERIOUS BUYERS AND THEY EXPECT THE BEST PRODUCTS AND INVESTMENTS, SO SLACKERS GET CUT TO KEEP QUALITY HIGH.
VERMONT, WE NEED TO LAND WITH A BANG.
WE WILL. LET'S FOCUS ON A DISPLAY OF OUR TOP THREE RANGES.
WE'LL NEED A TEAM WALKING THE FLOOR.
AND HERE'S HOW WE'LL PULL THE CROWDS IN FROM THE WORD "GO"...

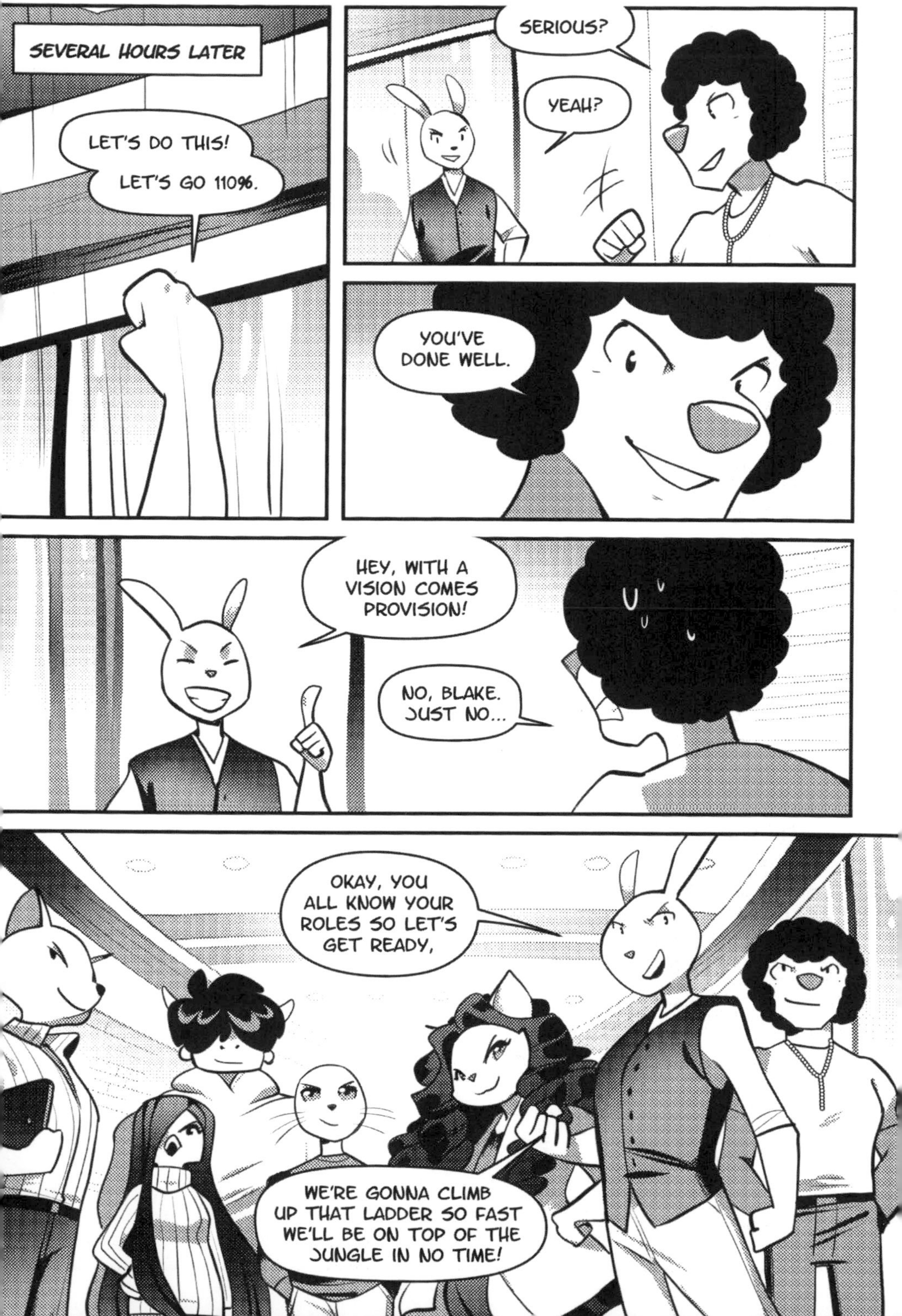
SEVERAL HOURS LATER
LET'S DO THIS! LET'S GO 110%.
SERIOUS?
YEAH?
YOU'VE DONE WELL.
HEY, WITH A VISION COMES PROVISION!
NO, BLAKE. JUST NO...
OKAY, YOU ALL KNOW YOUR ROLES SO LET'S GET READY,
WE'RE GONNA CLIMB UP THAT LADDER SO FAST WE'LL BE ON TOP OF THE JUNGLE IN NO TIME!

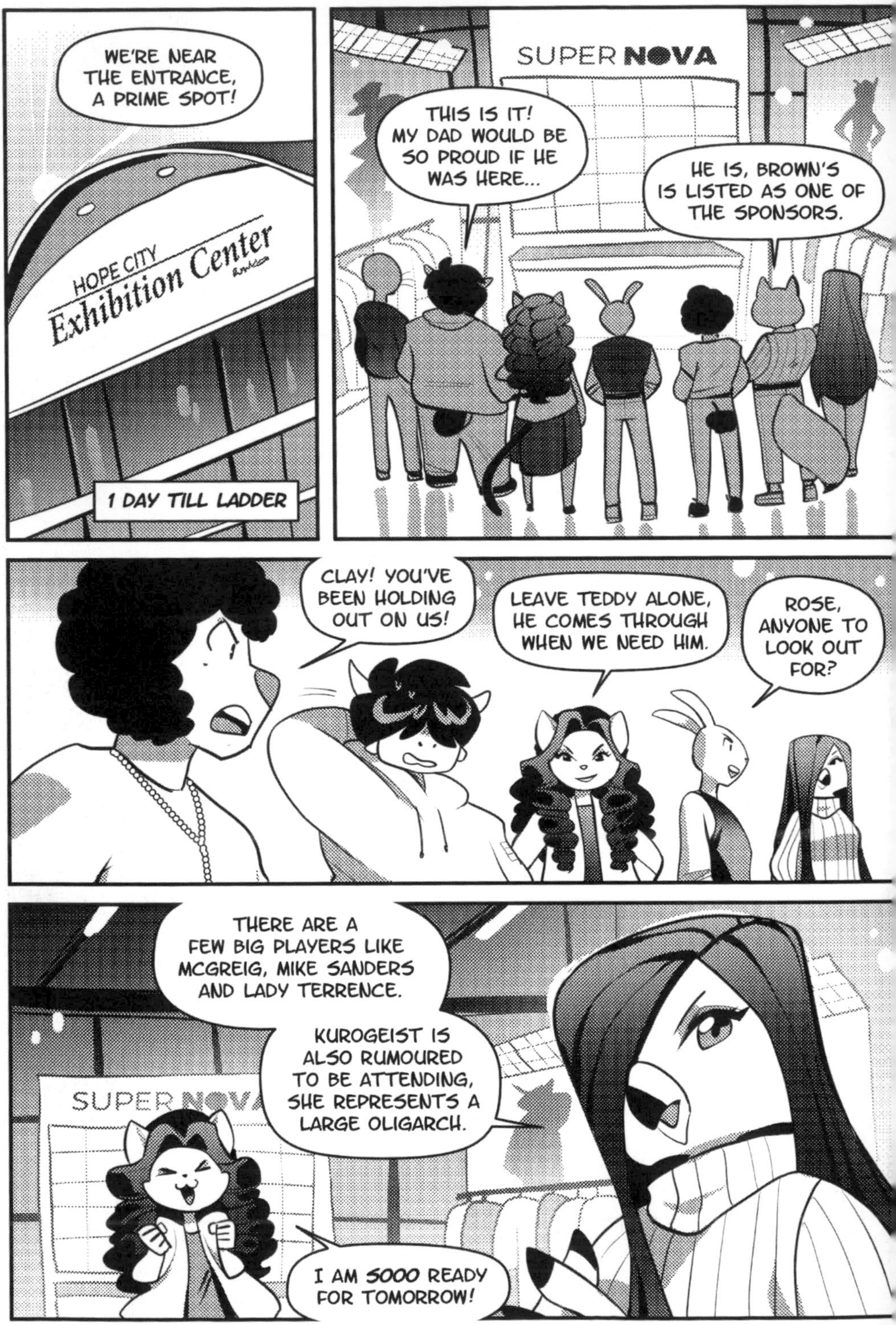
WE'RE NEAR THE ENTRANCE, A PRIME SPOT!
HOPE CITY
Exhibition Center
1 DAY TILL LADDER
SUPER NOVA
THIS IS IT! MY DAD WOULD BE SO PROUD IF HE WAS HERE...
HE IS, BROWN'S IS LISTED AS ONE OF THE SPONSORS.
CLAY! YOU'VE BEEN HOLDING OUT ON US!
LEAVE TEDDY ALONE, HE COMES THROUGH WHEN WE NEED HIM.
ROSE, ANYONE TO LOOK OUT FOR?
THERE ARE A FEW BIG PLAYERS LIKE MCGREIG, MIKE SANDERS AND LADY TERRENCE.
KUROGEIST IS ALSO RUMOURED TO BE ATTENDING, SHE REPRESENTS A LARGE OLIGARCH.
I AM *SOOO* READY FOR TOMORROW!

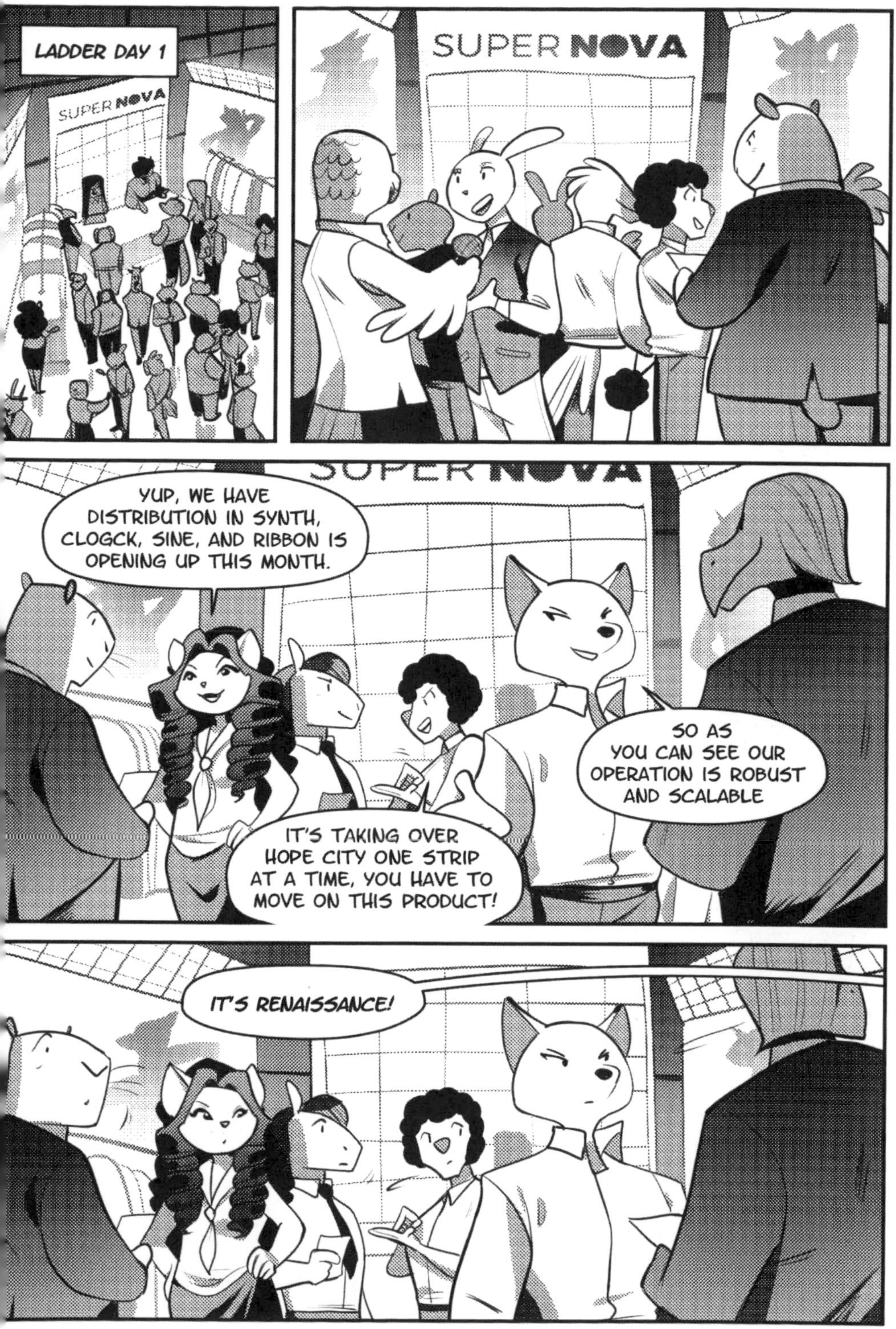

LADDER DAY 1
SUPER NOVA
YUP, WE HAVE DISTRIBUTION IN SYNTH, CLOGCK, SINE, AND RIBBON IS OPENING UP THIS MONTH.
SO AS YOU CAN SEE OUR OPERATION IS ROBUST AND SCALABLE
IT'S TAKING OVER HOPE CITY ONE STRIP AT A TIME, YOU HAVE TO MOVE ON THIS PRODUCT!
IT'S RENAISSANCE!

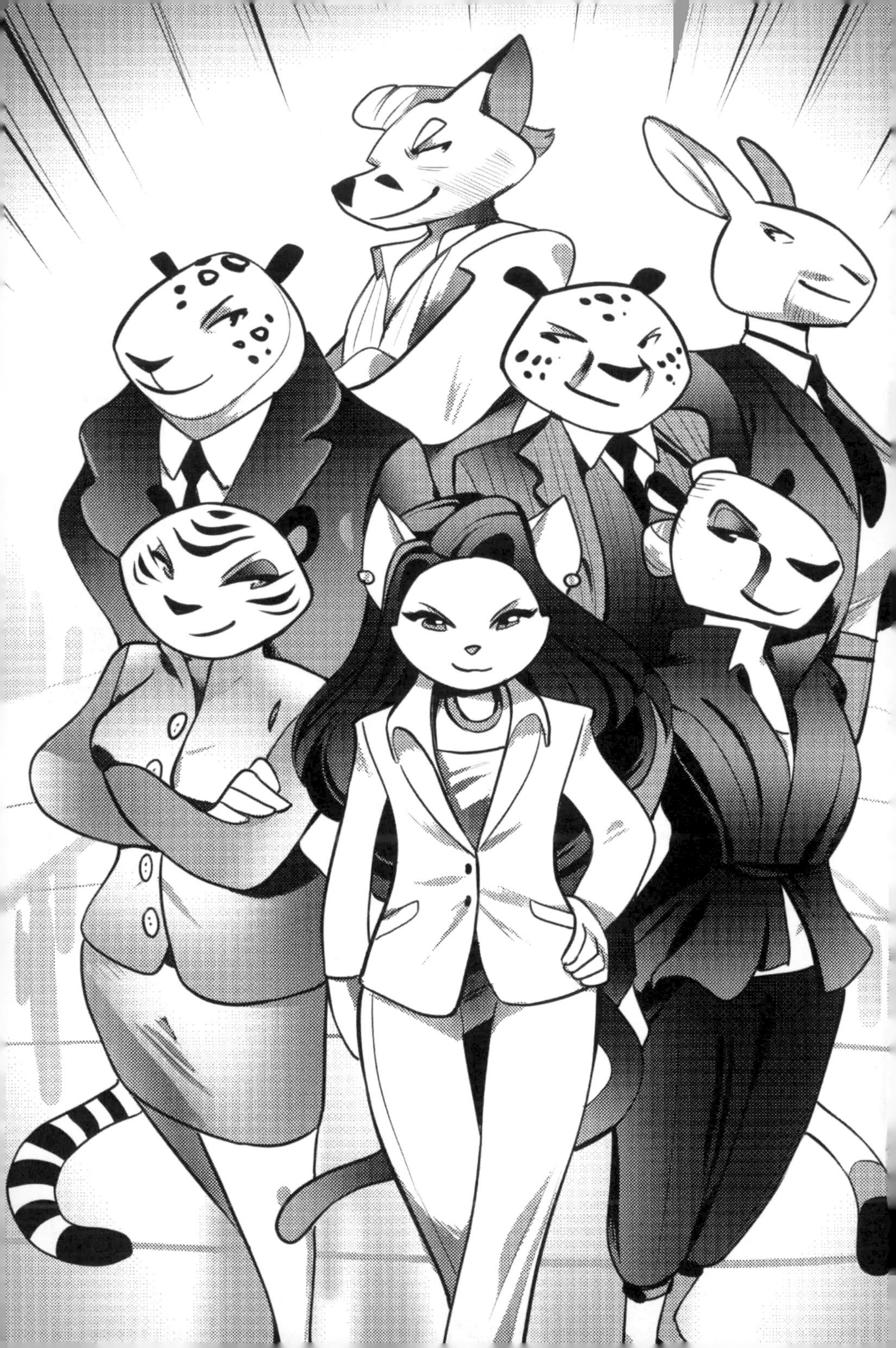

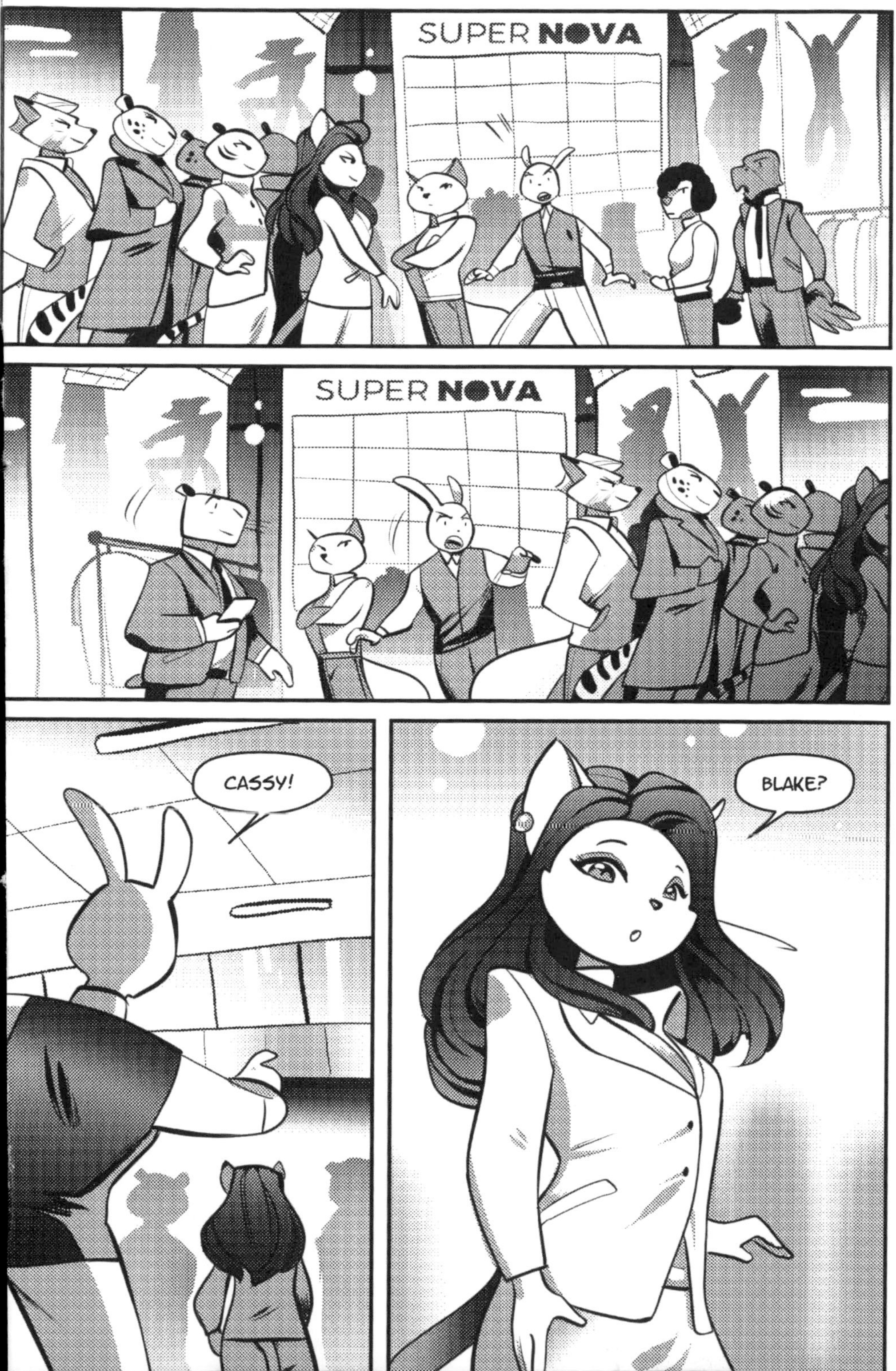
SUPER NOVA
SUPER NOVA
CASSY!
BLAKE?

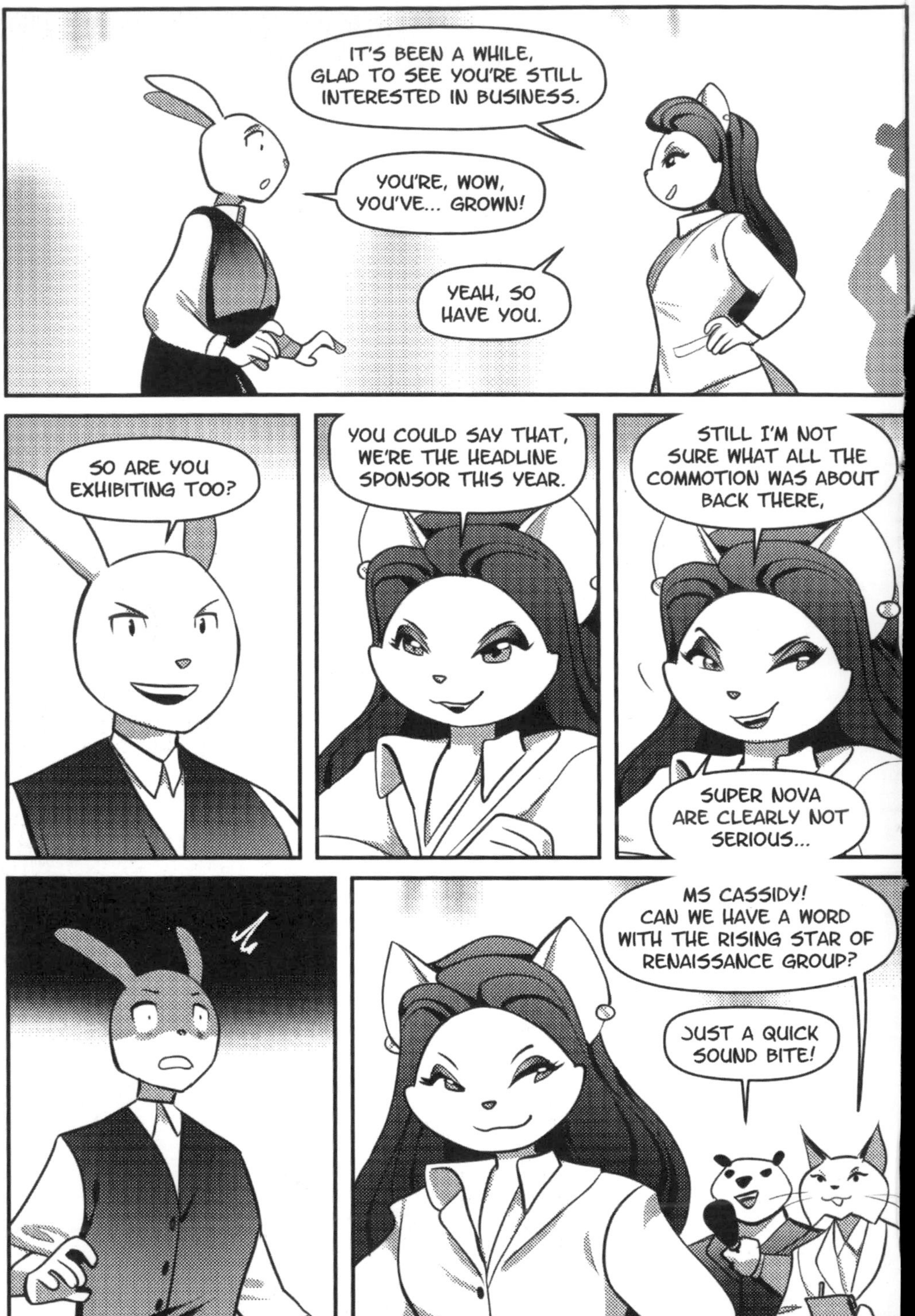
IT'S BEEN A WHILE, GLAD TO SEE YOU'RE STILL INTERESTED IN BUSINESS.
YOU'RE, WOW, YOU'VE... GROWN!
YEAH, SO HAVE YOU.
SO ARE YOU EXHIBITING TOO?
YOU COULD SAY THAT, WE'RE THE HEADLINE SPONSOR THIS YEAR.
STILL I'M NOT SURE WHAT ALL THE COMMOTION WAS ABOUT BACK THERE,
SUPER NOVA ARE CLEARLY NOT SERIOUS...
MS CASSIDY! CAN WE HAVE A WORD WITH THE RISING STAR OF RENAISSANCE GROUP?
JUST A QUICK SOUND BITE!

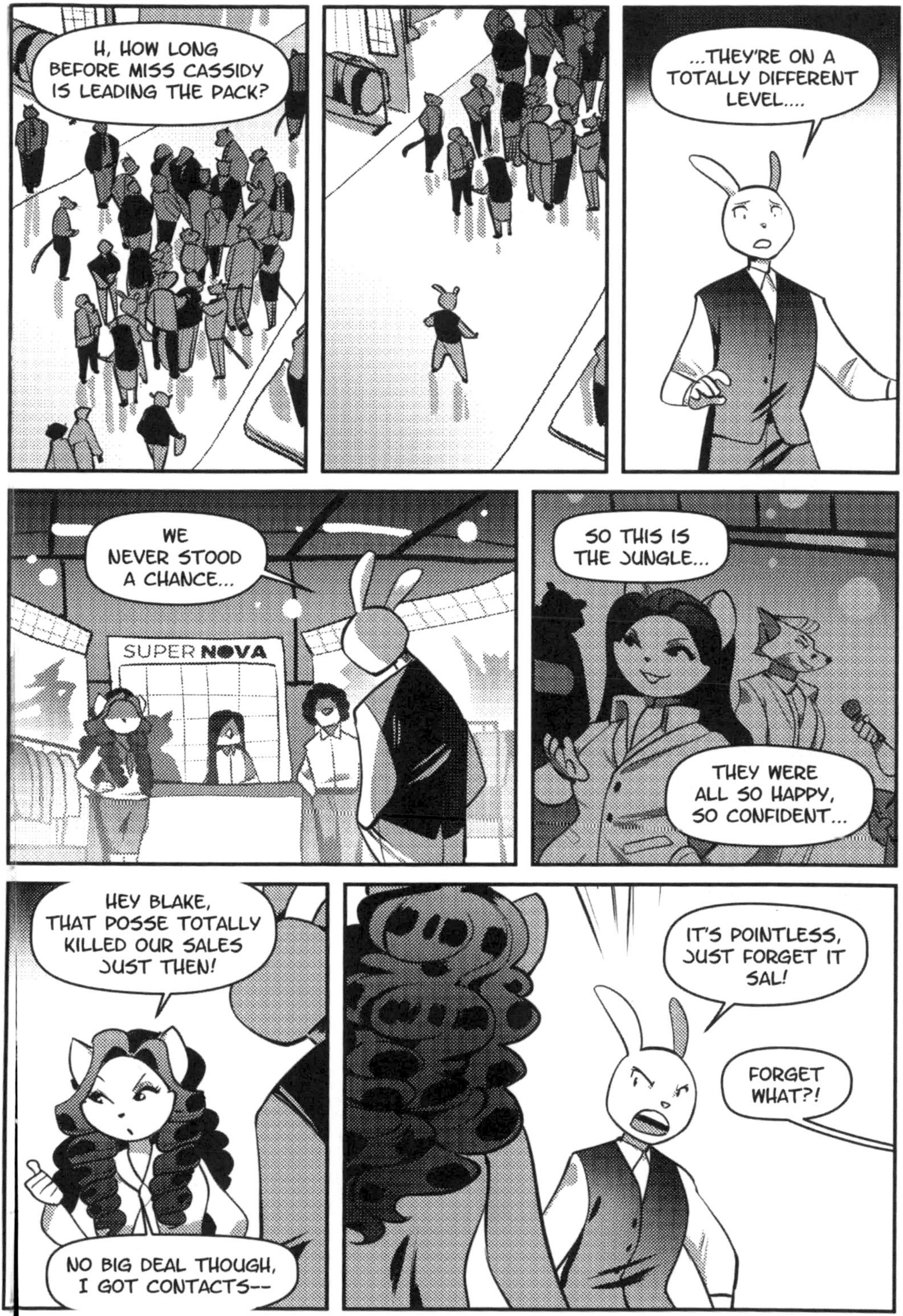
H, HOW LONG BEFORE MISS CASSIDY IS LEADING THE PACK?
...THEY'RE ON A TOTALLY DIFFERENT LEVEL....
WE NEVER STOOD A CHANCE...
SUPER NOVA
SO THIS IS THE JUNGLE...
THEY WERE ALL SO HAPPY, SO CONFIDENT...
HEY BLAKE, THAT POSSE TOTALLY KILLED OUR SALES JUST THEN!
NO BIG DEAL THOUGH, I GOT CONTACTS--
IT'S POINTLESS, JUST FORGET IT SAL!
FORGET WHAT?!

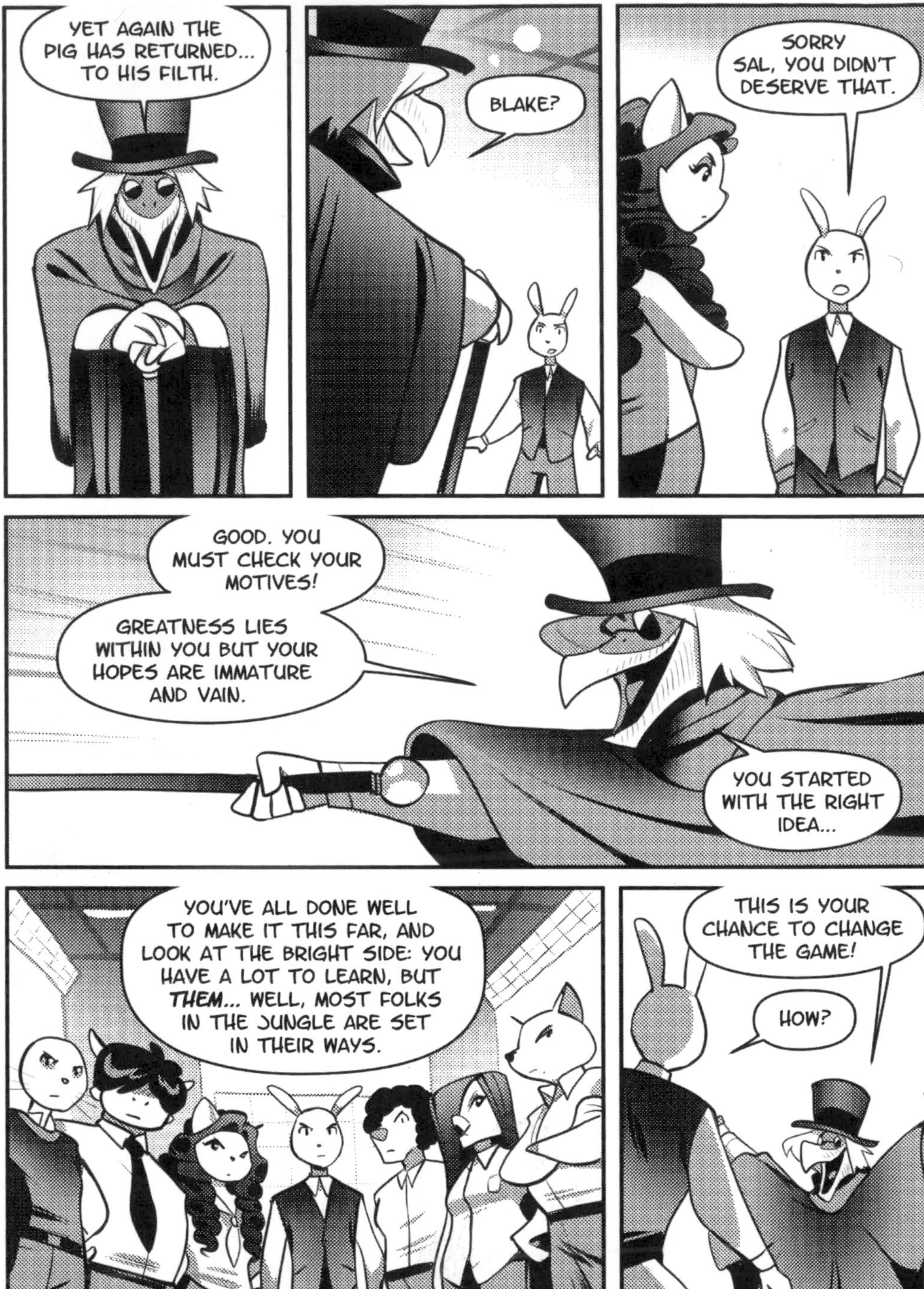
YET AGAIN THE PIG HAS RETURNED... TO HIS FILTH.
BLAKE?
SORRY SAL, YOU DIDN'T DESERVE THAT.
GOOD. YOU MUST CHECK YOUR MOTIVES!
GREATNESS LIES WITHIN YOU BUT YOUR HOPES ARE IMMATURE AND VAIN.
YOU STARTED WITH THE RIGHT IDEA...
YOU'VE ALL DONE WELL TO MAKE IT THIS FAR, AND LOOK AT THE BRIGHT SIDE: YOU HAVE A LOT TO LEARN, BUT *THEM...* WELL, MOST FOLKS IN THE JUNGLE ARE SET IN THEIR WAYS.
THIS IS YOUR CHANCE TO CHANGE THE GAME!
HOW?

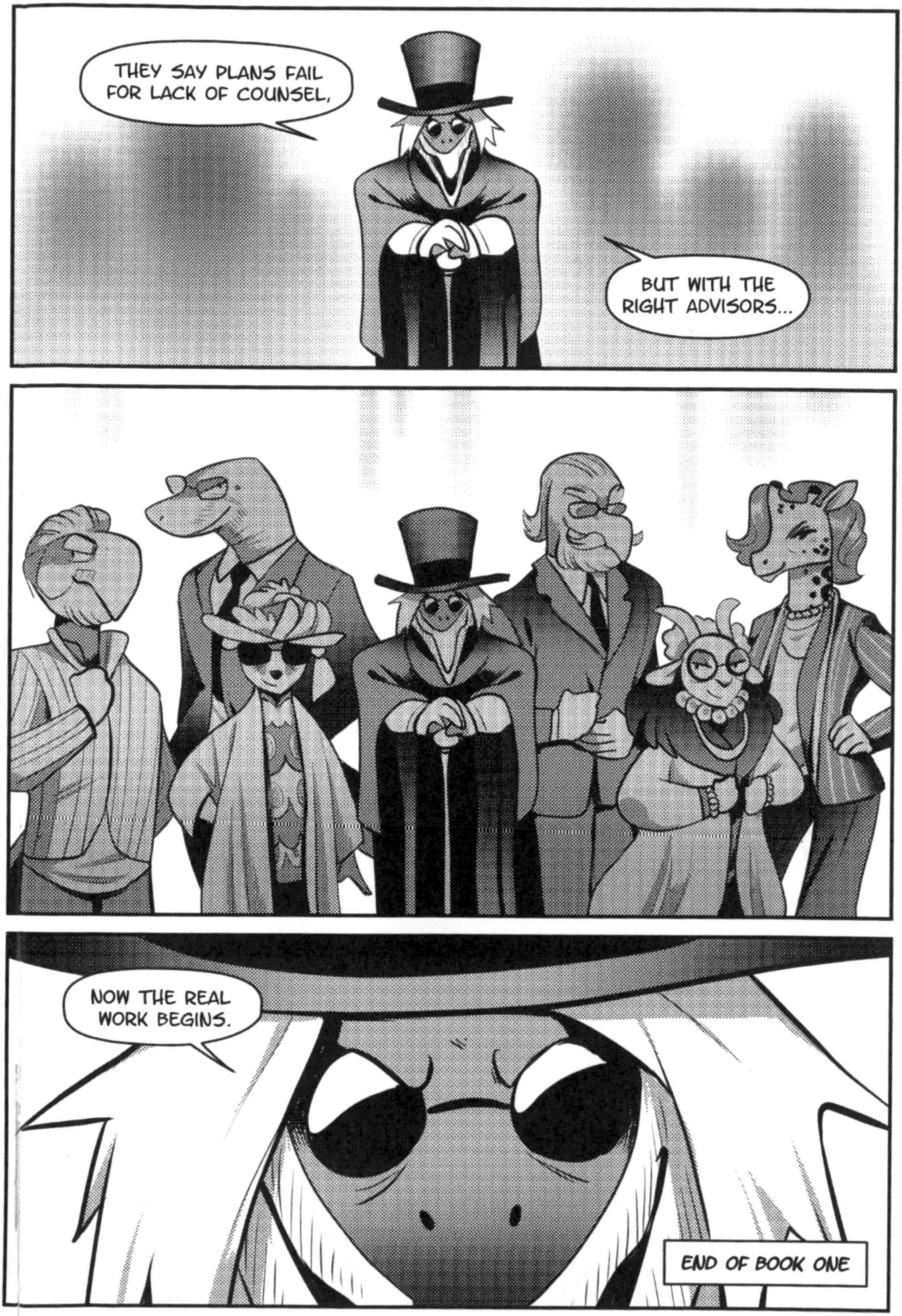
THEY SAY PLANS FAIL FOR LACK OF COUNSEL,
BUT WITH THE RIGHT ADVISORS...
NOW THE REAL WORK BEGINS.
END OF BOOK ONE

THERE'S MORE TO COME IN 2017!

STAY TUNED...

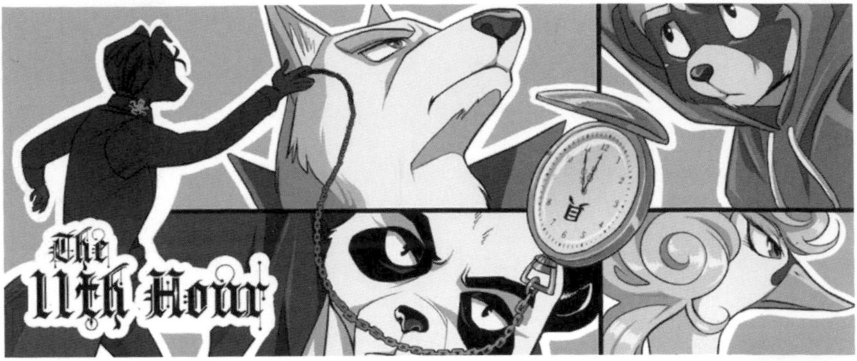
The 11th Hour

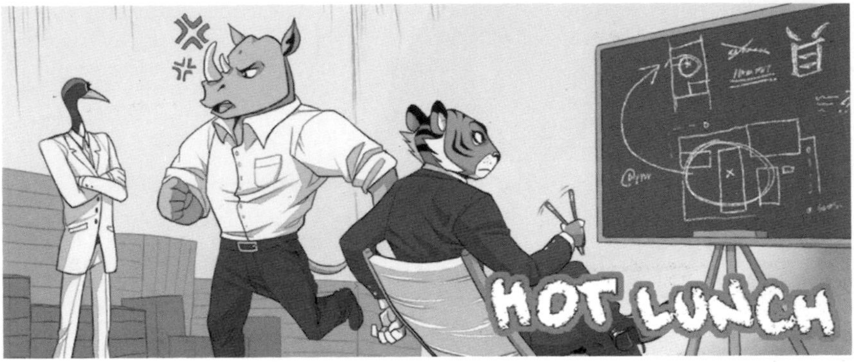
HOT LUNCH

DID YOU KNOW WE ALSO HAVE A LINE OF CLOTHING BASED ON OUR CHARACTERS?

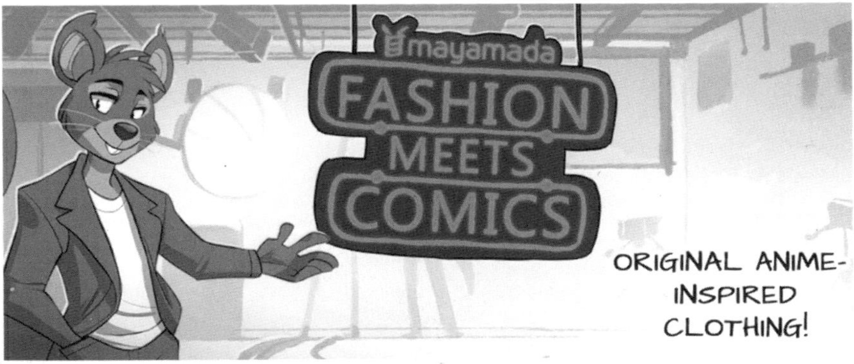
mayamada
FASHION
MEETS
COMICS
ORIGINAL ANIME-
INSPIRED
CLOTHING!

SEE IT ALL AT
WWW.MAYAMADA.COM

MAYAMADA MAYAMADATEES